Mask and Tragedy

Yeats and Nietzsche, 1902–10

Mask and Tragedy

Yeats and Nietzsche, 1902–10

Frances Nesbitt Oppel

University Press of Virginia *Charlottesville*

University Press of Virginia

First published 1987

Library of Congress Cataloging-in-Publication Data
Oppel, Frances Nesbitt, 1942-
Mask and tragedy.
Bibliography: p.
Includes index.
1. Yeats, W. B. (William Butler), 1865–1939—
Philosophy. 2. Nietzsche, Friedrich Wilhelm, 1844–1900—
Influence. 3. Philosophy in literature. 4. Masks in
literature. 5. Tragic, The, in literature. I. Title.
PR5908.P5046 1987 821'.8 86-24652
ISBN 0-8139-1104-4

Printed in the United States of America

Contents

Acknowledgments

This book began as a paper written for a graduate seminar at Rutgers University in 1974; it became a finished Ph.D. dissertation in 1983, and took its present shape in 1986. My debts to publishers, scholars, teachers, and friends on three continents who made this project possible are numerous, and I acknowledge them with gratitude.

I wish to thank those who have kindly given permission for the use of copyright material: A. P. Watt Ltd., on behalf of Michael B. Yeats and Macmillan London Limited, and Macmillan Publishing Company, Inc., New York, for permission to reprint extracts from the following published works by William Butler Yeats: *Autobiography* (copyright 1916, 1936 by Macmillan Publishing Company, renewed 1944, 1964 by Bertha Georgie Yeats); *Mythologies* (copyright Mrs. W. B. Yeats 1959); *A Vision* (copyright 1937 by W. B. Yeats, renewed 1965 by Bertha Georgie Yeats and Anne Butler Yeats); *Essays and Introductions* (copyright Mrs. W. B. Yeats 1961); *Explorations* (copyright Mrs. W. B. Yeats 1962); *The Letters,* edited by Allan Wade (copyright 1953, 1954 by Anne Butler Yeats, renewed 1982 by Anne Butler Yeats); *The Variorum Edition of the Plays of W. B. Yeats,* edited by Russell K. Alspach (copyright Russell K. Alspach and Bertha Georgie Yeats 1966; copyright Macmillan & Co. Ltd. 1965); *The Variorum Edition of the Poems of W. B. Yeats,* edited by Peter Allt and Russell K. Alspach (copyright 1912, 1916, 1924, 1928, 1933, 1934 by Macmillan Publishing Company, renewed 1940, 1944, 1952, 1956, 1961, 1962 by Bertha Georgie Yeats. Copyright 1940 by Georgie Yeats, renewed 1968 by Bertha Georgie Yeats, Michael Butler Yeats, and Anne Yeats). A. P. Watt Ltd., on behalf of Michael B. Yeats and Macmillan London Limited, for permission to reprint material from

W. B. Yeats: Memoirs; Autobiography—First Draft; Journal, edited by Denis Donoghue (1972); *A Critical Edition of Yeats's* A Vision *(1925),* edited by George Mills Harper and Walter Kelly Hood (1978); and *Letters to W. B. Yeats,* volume 1, edited by Richard J. Finneran, G. M. Harper, and W. M. Murphy (1977). Columbia University Press and A. P. Watts Ltd., on behalf of Michael B. Yeats and Macmillan London Limited, for permission to use material from *Uncollected Prose by W. B. Yeats,* edited by John P. Frayne and Colton Johnson (1975). Northern Illinois University Press, for permission to use material from *W. B. Yeats: The Writing of* The Player Queen, edited by Curtis B. Bradford (1977).

My chief scholarly debts are evident in the pages of the book, but I would single out for continuing praise the work of Richard Ellmann, whose interpretation of Yeats's masks and their connection with his life remains fundamental. David Thatcher's book on Nietzsche's reputation in England has also been invaluable.

Assistance was given by Mr. Alf MacLochlainn, Director of the National Library of Ireland; Miss Anne Yeats of Dublin sent me information about the books by and about Nietzsche in her father's library, without which my argument would have lacked conviction.

I am grateful to the staffs of the University of Queensland Library, in Brisbane, Australia, and the Hamilton College Library, in Clinton, New York, for extending me their privileges while this study was in preparation.

I thank my teachers, friends, and colleagues for their time and support, especially Carol H. Smith of Rutgers University, who from the very inception of this project has been unfailing in her advice and encouragement and has very materially assisted its progress.

Terence Diggory read the book in manuscript and made thorough, thoughtful, and useful suggestions.

Cynthia Foote at the University Press of Virginia has been a model editor—careful, considerate, and patient.

Finally, I thank my family—remembering especially my father, George L. Nesbitt, who while he lived was ceaselessly supportive of my work generally and of this project specifically; my mother, Helen W. Nesbitt; my aunt, Elizabeth A. Nesbitt; my husband, John Oppel; and my children, George, Katie, and Julia—for their encouragement, assistance, and love.

Abbreviations of Frequently Cited Works

AU	Yeats. *The Autobiography of William Butler Yeats.* New York: The Macmillan Company, 1953.
BT	Nietzsche. *The Birth of Tragedy: or Hellenism and Pessimism.* Trans. William A. Haussmann. Edinburgh and London: T. N. Foulis, 1909.
CW	Nietzsche. *The Case of Wagner, Nietzsche contra Wagner, The Twilight of the Idols, The Antichrist.* Trans. Thomas Common. London: H. Henry and Co., 1896.
Dawn	Nietzsche. *The Dawn of Day.* Trans. Johanna Voltz. London: T. Fisher Unwin, 1903.
E&I	Yeats. *Essays and Introductions.* New York: The Macmillan Company, 1961.
Ex	Yeats. *Explorations.* London: Macmillan and Company, 1962.
GM	Nietzsche. *A Genealogy of Morals.* Trans. William A. Haussmann and John Gray. London: T. Fisher Unwin, 1899.
L	Yeats. *The Letters of W. B. Yeats.* Ed. Allan Wade. London: Rupert Hart-Davis, 1954.
Mem	Yeats. *W. B. Yeats: Memoirs; Autobiography—First Draft; Journal.* Transcribed and edited by Denis Donoghue. London: Macmillan, 1972.
Myth	Yeats. *Mythologies.* London: The Macmillan Press, 1959.
PQ	Yeats. *W. B. Yeats: The Writing of* The Player Queen.

Manuscripts of W. B. Yeats transcribed, edited, and with a commentary by Curtis Baker Bradford. Dekalb: Northern Illinois University Press, 1977.

V Yeats. *A Vision*. London and Basingstoke: The Macmillan Press, 1962.

VA Yeats. *A Critical Edition of Yeats's* A Vision *(1925)*. Ed. George Mills Harper and Walter Kelly Hood. London and Basingstoke: The Macmillan Press. 1978.

VP Yeats. *The Variorum Edition of the Poems of W. B. Yeats*. Ed. Peter Allt and Russell K. Alspach. New York: The Macmillan Company, 1957.

VPl Yeats. *The Variorum Edition of the Plays of W. B. Yeats*. Ed. Russell K. Alspach. London: Macmillan and Company, 1966.

Z Nietzsche. *Thus Spake Zarathustra: A Book for All and None*. Trans. Alexander Tille. New York: The Macmillan Company, 1906.

Mask and Tragedy

Yeats and Nietzsche, 1902–10

1.

Introduction

W. B. Yeats first looked into Nietzsche's *Thus Spake Zarathustra* in the summer of 1902. He proceeded in the following year to read, in English translation, Nietzsche's *The Case of Wagner, Nietzsche contra Wagner, The Twilight of the Idols, The Antichrist, A Genealogy of Morals,* and, once more, *Thus Spake Zarathustra.* In 1904 he read and annotated an anthology of excerpts from Nietzsche's writings, compiled and translated by Thomas Common, including passages from *The Birth of Tragedy* and *Beyond Good and Evil.* This immersion in Nietzsche from 1902 to 1904 was decisive in shaping Yeats's thought and art for the rest of his life.

In *The Identity of Yeats* (1954), Richard Ellmann called attention to the Yeats-Nietzsche connection, and published a few of the comments Yeats had penciled in the margins of Thomas Common's anthology.[1] Ellmann devotes six pages of his book to a discussion of the kinship between the ideas of Nietzsche and Yeats, and remarks that "[Nietzsche's] writings were full of suggestions" for Yeats, specifically about the idea of "the mask."[2] In the pages that follow the section on Nietzsche, however, he does not again refer to the kinship he has been at some pains to establish, and in the preface to the second edition of the book (1964), he dismisses critical efforts to identify Yeats with—or as—anybody else.

Nonetheless, the efforts continue. Yeats has been paired with Blake, Shelley, Plato, Mallarmé, Michelangelo, Madame Blavatsky, Castiglione, Balzac, Pater, T. S. Eliot—for starters—and increasingly of late, with Nietzsche. Harold Bloom, in *Yeats* (1970), ranks

Nietzsche as one of five "really crucial literary influences" on Yeats,[3] but does not explore the connection. In Denis Donoghue's *Yeats* (1971), Bloom's five crucial influences are reduced to one: "I emphasize Yeats's kinship with Nietzsche: It seems to me a more telling relation than that between Yeats and Plato, Plotinus, or Blake."[4] Throughout his book, Donoghue juxtaposes Yeatsian stances with Nietzschean ones, comparing gestures, but he cannot within the scope of his general study make a systematic attempt to establish connections empirically, and he does not. Neither does Otto Bohlmann, in the first book devoted exclusively to Yeats and Nietzsche: *Yeats and Nietzsche: An Exploration of Major Nietzschean Echoes in the Writings of William Butler Yeats.* This book is an affinity study, organized thematically, suggesting shared philosophical propensities between the two writers. Although Bohlmann usefully finishes the work that Ellmann began in *The Identity of Yeats,* reproducing all of Yeats's marginalia from the Common anthology, with glosses of his own, he is more interested in philosophy and philosophical echoes than in biography, history, or poetry. In a Ph.D. dissertation, "Yeats and Nietzsche: The Antithetical Vision" (NYU, 1971), Patrick J. Keane establishes and validates the Yeats-Nietzsche connection, and discusses it broadly across the whole span of Yeats's work after 1902. He contends that Nietzsche supplied Yeats with his concept of the anti-self, and was thus instrumental in the construction of *A Vision.*[5]

Others have picked up the idea of the antithetical, or the anti-self, as a link between Nietzsche and Yeats. The connection has arisen through the translation of the German word *Gegensatz,* made famous by Hegel and usually translated as "antithesis." Early translations of Nietzsche into English adopt the adjective *antithetical,* a word Yeats appropriates to describe one of his major concepts. In translating one of Nietzsche's letters, Michael Hamburger makes the following rendering: "Even in this respect the book [*Ecce Homo*] could do some good; it may save me from being confused with my anti-self," and adds a footnote: "I render *Gegensatz* by the Yeatsian 'anti-self' because this best conveys the antithesis Nietzsche had in mind."[6] In *Christ and Nietzsche,* G. Wilson Knight makes the same association, extending it to the principle of self-dramatization: "Zarathustra often talks to his own soul, what Yeats calls his anti-self."[7]

A reversed flow of influence in the mind of the reader, from successor to precursor, appears to have occurred in the cases where Nietzsche is being interpreted in the light of Yeats. Influence is ever so, Harold Bloom assures us in his study *The Anxiety of Influence,* and further assures us that anyway "there are no interpretations but only misinterpretations, or acts of creative correction."[8] Bloom's theory of influence, he tells us, was influenced primarily by Nietzsche and Freud—Nietzsche, the "prophet of the antithetical," and Freud, father of sublimation.[9] Bloom names Yeats as Nietzsche's "disciple" in matters antithetical. Bloom's theory of influence, as I (mis)understand it, assumes that the young poet identifies himself deeply with a precursor, as, for example, Yeats identifies himself with Shelley. In order to become free from this "family romance"—to kill the poetic father and establish his own identity—the younger poet makes a deliberate swerve away from the precursor, or in Yeats's words, creates an anti-self. As Keane maintains in his dissertation, Yeats seems to have used Nietzsche as a model for his anti-self, or, as Bloom would have it, Yeats swerves away from Shelley to the antithetical Nietzsche.

Bloom says that Nietzsche himself is one of the few writers (Goethe is another) who appear singularly free of the anxiety of influence—that Nietzsche calls influence a "vitalization."[10] Bloom is inconsistent here: surely what Nietzsche says he believes about influence must be regarded in the light of what he says about other things and of what he does. Everything we know about Nietzsche and everything he writes shows that he had as great a need as Yeats to free himself from his romantic precursors (Hölderlin, Schopenhauer, Wagner, and, not inconsiderably, Shelley).

But Yeats, like Nietzsche, is full of praise for the healthy influence of "influence." His defenses are hidden from himself, subconscious; in 1901 he makes it almost a conviction that "Nobody can write well, as I think, unless his thought, or some like thought, is moving in other minds than his, for nobody can do more than speak messages from the spirit of his time."[11] The kind of passivity this position endorses would seem at first glance to reduce genius to mediumship, or individuality to collectivity. Although Yeats exaggerates the writer's dependence on a community of shared ideas, or a Zeitgeist, his displacement of originality is important. He calls into question the concept of the self as a discrete unity, preferring to think of himself as plural, and of his mind as continuous with thoughts from many minds.

In this statement, he is also speaking for poet-as-tradition-bearer—both for the anthropological tradition of poet as oracle, seer, or shaman (one who "speaks messages"), and for the classical tradition of poet as continuator and transmitter of cultural identity and values. Given his positive position on influence, it is hardly surprising that Yeats has been studied in connection with so many other writers and traditions. He set about, deliberately, to contain them all.

In this study, I shall elaborate on the position on influence stated by T. S. Eliot. It combines that of Nietzsche—influence as vitalization—and that of Yeats—influence as community or communion. In "Reflections on Contemporary Poetry," Eliot says: "We do not imitate, we are changed, and our work is the work of a changed man; we have not borrowed, we have been quickened and become bearers of a tradition."[12] In the following pages I shall be considering influence as the dynamic, transformational force described by Eliot, in an attempt both to reveal the change in Yeats, the quickening, after he reads Nietzsche, and to assess how that quickening affects his position as bearer of a tradition.

The tradition, broadly and generally speaking—the cultural history to which Yeats and Nietzsche belong before their thoughts intersect in 1902—is the subject of the chapter that follows. The first part, "Romantic Tradition," examines the currents in nineteenth-century thought that were most important to Nietzsche and then to Yeats. Part 2, "Nietzsche in France and England, 1880–1900," narrows the scope of the tradition to focus on Nietzsche's reputation in France and England as a contemporary radical thinker known to many of Yeats's friends and associates. Part 3, "Yeats at the Century's Turn," locates Yeats in relation to both the romantic and the "Nietzschean" traditions, before he reads Nietzsche, in order to gauge the difference Nietzsche makes to his thought and work after he has actually read him.

The body of the book concentrates on the years in Yeats's life from 1902 to 1910, when Nietzsche's ideas have their initial exciting impact on Yeats. Under this impact—"the shock of new material," to use a phrase Yeats liked[13]—Yeats's famous "remaking" of himself occurs. I investigate the development of his mask theory, and the related development of his ideas about the nature and purpose of tragedy, under the impetus provided by Nietzsche. I show the chronological connections, wherever possible, between Yeats's reading of Nietzsche and his aesthetic theory and practice in the first decade of the twentieth century. Because Yeats wrote comparatively little poetry in this decade, because he is himself principally concerned at this time with drama, and because my subject is the development of his concepts of mask and tragedy, I concentrate on his plays and prose essays rather than his poetry.

In chapter 7, "The Road to Zoagli," I offer a conclusion that is also an introduction to Yeats's later work. I maintain that Nietzsche's affirmation of life, even in its most difficult and paradoxical aspects, leads Yeats finally to his conception and affirmation of life as tragedy. This conception depends on a synthesis of the ideas of mask and tragedy, toward which Yeats had been steadily moving since 1902. In performing this synthesis, Yeats extends his romantic tradition into the twentieth century and, at the same time, transforms it.

2.

"The Spirit of His Time"

Yeats, Nietzsche, and the Nineteenth Century

Nobody can write well, as I think, unless his thought, or some like thought, is moving in other minds than his, for nobody can do more than speak messages from the spirit of his time.—W. B. Yeats, "John Eglington"

Romantic Tradition

Nietzsche is increasingly regarded as a primary source for understanding the first half of the twentieth century in a great many of its manifestations—philosophical, linguistic, psychological, theological, artistic, and political. A critic writing in 1922, Janko Lavrin, felt that Nietzsche exemplified major tendencies in "modern consciousness." He says:

[Nietzsche's writings] found all over Europe a soil ready prepared. Much of his philosophy existed in the air even before he gave it that provocative expression which has finally been responsible for his unheard-of vogue—a vogue owing to which, in a few years, both the real and the popularised Nietzscheanism permeated all modern culture to such an extent that in whatever direction we go: in art, philosophy, psychology, or religion, we shall almost certainly find some traces of Nietzsche.[1]

In 1966, Erich Heller claimed that Nietzsche is to twentieth-century German writers "what St. Thomas Aquinas was to Dante: the categorical interpreter of a world which they contemplate poetically or philosophically without ever radically upsetting its Nietzschean structure."[2] And in his 1979 study on Niezsche, J. P. Stern rates Nietzsche, Marx, and Freud as the most seminal thinkers of their century. He emphasizes their connection with their historical time; the nineteenth century more than any other, he says, believed in "change, reform, and revolution through the power of ideas," and continues:

The aim of their thought was to uncover a secret concealed in men's minds; these minds they wished to change, and with them the world. They saw their undertaking as the solving of a secret, and all opposition to it as a conspiracy: a conspiracy of men with vested social and religious interests, thought Marx; of men with vested moral and religious interests, thought Freud; of men who choose to be only half alive and resent the few who live generously and dangerously, thought Nietzsche.[3]

The secrets of motivation through material interest, sex, or the will to power: each is a psychological theory, fundamentally. Of the three, the will to power is the most difficult to define, the most resistant to systematic elaboration. Stern's description of the conspirators against Nietzsche's discovery reveals the comparative difficulty of summarizing Nietzsche's theory in a phrase. He calls it a conspiracy of those "who choose to be only half alive and resent the few who live generously and dangerously." This description goes part of the way toward explaining Nietzsche, but gets about as close to his essential meaning as a prose explication of a poem does to the original. Because of its intrinsic poetry—its "provocative expression," as Lavrin has it, its unsystematic, specifically antiscientific, fragmented form—Nietzsche's theory was, of the three, the most congenial to artists at the turn of the century. Of the three, furthermore, it had been the most influenced by artists.

As Lavrin also points out, Nietzsche was a kind of barometer of the times. He picked up vibrations of ideas "in the air" (or as he maintained, not yet in the air but about to be), and then put his own stamp on them by carrying them to their logical extremes, transvaluing them, or otherwise re-creating them in what he considered his own image. But the ideas grew from the soil of his time and place, a history of which Yeats was also a part. The sharing of a cultural tradition hardly explains Yeats's strong identification with Nietzsche, but a look at this tradition may be helpful in establishing a point of departure for understanding it. I intend to approach the relationship historically: first through their shared literary-philosophical tradition (and this only selectively and generally), and then through the specific European cultural climate Yeats knew in the 1890s just before his connection with Nietzsche can properly be proven to exist.

There are certain biographical similarities between the two as well. According to Daniel Halévy's *Life of Friedrich Nietzsche,* at the age of seventeen Nietzsche's reading was chiefly in the romantic poets; so was the adolescent Yeats's. Nietzsche's special loves at the time were Hölderlin and Byron. He copied in his journal for that year, 1861, these lines from *Manfred:*

> Sorrow is knowledge; they who know the most
> Must mourn the deepest o'er the fatal truth
> The tree of knowledge is not that of life.[4]

This is one of Yeats's favorite ideas as well, and it absorbs Nietzsche all his life as he plays with the concepts of knowledge and power, his bias always Byron's, toward the mutual exclusiveness of the two, though he seeks their reconciliation. Yeats is to perpetuate both bias and quest. In an 1896 essay on Blake, he separates the "Tree of Life" and the "Tree of Knowledge of Good and Evil" (*E & I,* p. 130), associating the former with passion and power, the latter with mechanical philosophies and restrictive social institutions. In this distinction he follows his romantic progenitors: Blake, Shelley, Byron, and Carlyle. Yet Nietzsche was not satisfied with the divorce of knowledge and power, nor was Yeats; for both writers, the concepts become poles of opposition whose conflict creates meaning and value.

Byron's creation of the role of artist as suffering, solitary hero must also have appealed to the seventeen-year-old Nietzsche, whose Zarathustra is to show some resemblance to Byronic heroes. The search for, and promotion of, the heroic in history and in the human psyche was very much part of "the spirit of the time." Carlyle's *On Heroes, Hero-worship, and the Heroic in History* (1840) publicized the issue. The ideas of this book derive in part from Carlyle's reading in German philosophy—an intellectual tradition that Nietzsche also knew well. As Eric Bentley points out in *A Century of Hero-Worship,* there are many parallels between Carlyle's position on the value of heroism—that courage is a moral virtue, and that "great men should rule and others revere them"—and Nietzsche's.[5] Nietzsche read Carlyle, and Yeats read them both.

Hölderlin, adolescent Nietzsche's other important poet, spins another strand of the cultural web that becomes increasingly dominant during the nineteenth century and issues in Yeats's work and in that of many others. In his poem "Bread and Wine" (1801), Hölderlin juxtaposes pagan (Greek) and Christian deities, using the sacramental bread and wine as symbols fusing the two traditions, feeling his way intuitively toward the syncretism of cultures to be demonstrated by G. B. Frazer's description of primitive rituals in *The Golden Bough* (1890).

Heinrich Heine, another German romantic poet who was read with enthusiasm, not only by Nietzsche but also by Matthew Arnold and Walter Pater in England, was also a reader of Hölderlin and carried his comparison of Greek and Christian religions into two major works. One is *The History of Religion and Philosophy in Germany* (1834), in which Heine traces the history of Jehovah through Western culture from Egypt to Palestine to Rome, where even now, says Heine, he is on his deathbed, destroyed by Kant's *Critique of Pure Reason:*

> And nothing could save him.
> Do you hear the passing bell? Kneel down.
> They are bringing the sacraments to a dying god.[6]

Nietzsche is often credited with either (most extremely) having killed God or (slightly less so) having proclaimed his death, but he is only one voice in a chorus. He makes the implications of this death the starting point of his investigations, however, which gives it more weight than others were prepared to do.

But to return: the other book by Heine in the line of Hölderlin is *The Gods in Exile* (1853), in which Heine resurrects the Greek pantheon in modern dress in modern Europe. He reverses a German tradition of admiration for Apollo by giving hero status to Dionysus, god of orgies, ecstasies, the daemonic. Again—though as E. M. Butler says in her book on the influence of ancient Greece on German writers, Dionysus was "the god who took the heart of Nietzsche by storm"[7]—Nietzsche was only one of many for whom *The Gods in Exile* was important. Pater models his "Apollo in Picardy" on Heine's book, and his *Lecture on Dionysus* (1876), included in *Greek Studies* (1895), has behind it Heine and possibly Nietzsche as well.[8] Pater also superimposes Greek and Christian mythology, most famously in the passage on the Mona Lisa that Yeats liked so much ("She is older than the rocks among which she sits"). From Hölderlin and Goethe at the beginning of the century, to David Strauss's *Das Leben Jesu* (1835), which treats the gospels as myths, to Frazer at the century's end, Christianity was seen with increasing relativity, often as a late manifestation of a ritual instinct reaching back into prehistory. Nietzsche's war cry "Dionysus vs. the Crucified!" in *The Antichrist* (1888) was another log on a fire already kindled.

Shelley, Yeats's chief precursor according to Harold Bloom, was also important to Nietzsche, who owned, in Adolf Strodtmann's translation, Shelley's *Ausgewählte Dichtungen*. In an 1877 letter to his friend Erwin Rohde, Nietzsche said: "Very recently I spent a veritable day of consecration reading *Prometheus Unbound*. If the poet is not a real genius, I do not know what a genius is; it is all wonderful, and I feel as if I have confronted in it myself, but myself made supreme and celestial."[9] Compare Yeats's terminology in his essay "The Philosophy of Shelley's Poetry" (1900): "I have re-read *Prometheus Unbound*, which I had hoped my fellow-students would have studied as a sacred book, and it seems to me to have an even more certain place than I had thought among the sacred books of the world" (*E&I*, p. 65). Bloom says that what makes Shelley so terrifying to young poets as a precursor is his "Orphic integrity, the swiftness of a spirit too impatient for the compromises without which societal existence and even natural life are just not possible."[10] Both Nietzsche and Yeats may have needed to stop their ears against Shelley's trumpet of a prophecy in order not to be overwhelmed by it, but both perpetuate his defiance of limits by pushing to extremes, with a tendency toward apocalypse; his impatience with social compromise; his essential faith (although *faith* seems inappropriate to so confirmed a skeptic as Nietzsche, I think it is the right word) in the creative power of the imagination.

Shelley's ideas in "A Defence of Poetry" (1821) on the nature of tragedy help create a context for the aesthetic of *The Birth of Tragedy* and for much of Yeats's dramatic theory as well. Shelley maintains that the Athenian drama represents tragedy at its purest: "The Athenians," he says, "employed language, action, music, painting, the dance, and religious institutions, to produce a common effect in the representation of the loftiest idealism of passion and of power." He attacks the modern stage not only for separating the arts into discrete categories but also, more specifically, for destroying the unity of tragic effect by revealing the actor's faces: "Our system of divesting the actor's face of a mask, on which the many expressions appropriate to his dramatic character might be moulded into one permanent and unchanging expression, is favorable only to a partial and inharmonious effect." Shelley realizes the importance of the religious impulse to the creation of the effects of unity and permanence in Greek tragedy. He realizes too that the effect of tragedy is based on a psychological paradox of human nature. "Sorrow, terror, anguish, despair itself," he says, "are often the chosen expression of an approximation to the highest goods; . . . tragedy delights by affording a shadow of that pleasure which exists in pain."[11] This thought, not explicitly enlarged on by Shelley, brings us close to Nietzsche's principle of heroic joy and Yeats's of tragic ecstasy.

A Defence of Poetry represents major romantic temperamental biases, of which the dialectical pull toward synthesis, the integrative impulse, is strongest. The human agent of integration, Shelley says, is the imagination; poetry is its expression; and in a sentence implicitly developing his earlier one about tragedy's capacity to unite pleasure and pain, Shelley says that poetry "marries exultation and horror, grief and pleasure, eternity and change; it subdues to union under its light yoke, all irreconcilable things."[12] Blake demonstrates the same dialectical tendency in *The Marriage of Heaven and Hell,* and the biblical allusiveness of Shelley's language ("its light yoke" being, as G. W. Knight says, a New Testament reminiscence[13]) shows that Shelley, like Blake, found in the synthesizing power of the imagination a redemption similar to the one traditionally provided by religion. Indeed, Shelley implies the substitution of poetry for religion throughout his essay. By describing the offices of poetry as holy and moral, and the power of the poetic imagination as transformational and redemptive, he foreshadows similar claims for the function of poetry by Arnold and then by Yeats, by Wagner, and by others who saw that the loss of religion as a binding or integrating personal and social force was serious, but hoped that the language of poetry (and of music), metaphoric and archetypal, could provide the same psychological, if not social, integration.

This integrative impulse, this bias toward continuity, takes its philosophical impetus from Hegel. In his *Logic* (1812), Hegel decribes the elements of his three major categories (generally known as thesis, antithesis, and synthesis), his object being to set abstract oppositions to interaction in the mind and thus to create a dynamic unity. Following Heraclitus, whose "flux is all" he quotes, Hegel proposes the following "truth," which stands as a locus classicus for ideas on which theories of Nietzsche and Yeats are based: "Parmenides, to whom the absolute was known as Being, says that 'Being alone is and Nothing is not.' . . . The Buddhists [make] Nothing the principle of all things, the final aim and end of everything. . . . Nothing, which is thus immediate and identical with itself, is also conversely the same as Being is. The truth of Being and of Nothing is accordingly the unity of the two: and this unity is Becoming."[14] Nietzsche's idea of the birth of tragedy at the moment when Apollonian form (being) meets Dionysian formlessness, producing tragic affirmation (becoming), has its roots in Hegel's theory; Yeats's poles of objectivity and subjectivity in *A Vision* share the same philosophical heritage. Nietzsche grudgingly acknowledges his debt to Hegel in his late autobiographical piece, *Ecce Homo*. Describing his own disenchantment with the structure of *The Birth of Tragedy,* he says that it "smells offensively Hegelian."[15]

Yeats follows Nietzsche's line on Hegel, denouncing him for oversystematization and abstraction. But he seems in one instance to have badly misread Hegel himself. In his Preface to *A Phenomenology of the Mind,* Hegel discusses the concept of contradiction, and the nature of the kind of mind that holds to the static concept of fixed opposites. This kind of mind, he says, "does not conceive the diversity of philosophical systems as the progressive evolution of truth; rather, it sees only contradiction in that variety. The bud disappears when the blossom breaks through, and we might say that the former is refuted by the latter." He continues, maintaining the fallacy of such thinking: "But the ceaseless activity of their [opposites'] own inherent nature makes them at the same time moments of an organic unity, where they do not merely not contradict one another, but where one is as necessary as the other; and this equal necessity of all moments constitutes from the outset the life of the whole."[16] Hegel's dialectic fundamentally explains the symbolism of Yeats's gyres, it seems to me, yet in *A Vision* Yeats says "I had never . . . thought with Hegel that the two ends of the see-saw are one anothers' negation, nor that the spring vegetables were refuted when over" (*V*, pp. 72–73). Neither had Hegel. Yeats quite simply reverses Hegel's meaning, in what may be understood as a case of defensive misinterpretation, for, in fact, they are in agreement.

The other important philosopher father figure for Nietzsche and the nineteenth century is Schopenhauer. Nietzsche's relationship with Schopenhauer was, at least initially, passionate. When as a university student at Leipzig in 1862, he picked up from a bookstall a volume of *The World as Will and Idea,* and read it, it swept him off his feet, as he put it himself.[17] Yeats also describes his response to Schopenhauer in dynamic terms; in a letter to Sturge Moore he says: "Schopenhauer can do no wrong in my eyes—I no more quarrel with his errors than I do with a mountain cataract."[18]

Schopenhauer has strong affinities with that philosophy of the Orient described by Hegel as placing ultimate truth in the void. The Oriental void, however, is pure nothingness, vacuum, and Schopenhauer's contains energy, which he calls will and describes as dynamic, chaotic, and meaningless or "blind." He also calls this force "nature," in relation to which the individual human life—and within that life the capacity termed intellect or reason—is a mere puppet or slave, doing nature's bidding. Schopenhauer's descriptions of the will set the tone for much late nineteenth-century literary pessimism. For example, in *The World as Will and Idea:* "Every individual, every human being and his course of life, is but another short dream of the endless spirit of nature, of the persistent will to live; is only another fleeting form which it carelessly sketches on its infinite page space and time . . . and then obliterates to make new room."[19] Pater's famous Conclusion to *The Renaissance: Studies in Art and Poetry,* for example, emphasizes the flux of which human "impressions" are composed. Pater identifies the flux, however, not as an external "spirit of nature," but as a property inherent in the mind, whose nature is, as Schopenhauer says, "fleeting": "Every one of those impressions is the impression of the individual in his isolation, each mind keeping as a solitary prisoner its own dream of a world. Analysis goes a step further still, and assures us that those impressions of the individual mind to which, for each one of us, experience dwindles down, are in perpetual flight; that each of them is limited by time, and that time is infinitely divisible."[20] Yeats, as we know, was both attracted and disturbed by Pater's "philosophy." He himself escapes being engulfed in Paterian flux by leaning on Nietzsche, who offers a support because he in his turn has resisted being engulfed by Schopenhauer's will.

He remains one of Schopenhauer's followers, however, in many respects, the principal one perhaps being the elevation of will above reason, and the integration of body and mind through the will, which is represented in a human's bodily organs and functions. "The whole body," says Schopenhauer, "must be nothing but my will become visible"[21]—an idea that supposes a physiological basis of knowledge. Nietzsche also insists on the value of physical, instinctive modes of cognition; "I have at all times," he declares, "written my work with my whole body and my whole life," and Yeats agrees in principle:

> God guard me from those thoughts men think
> In the mind alone;
> He that sings a lasting song
> Thinks in a marrow-bone.

Even his late summation of his own philosophy reduced to a sentence—"Man can embody truth but he cannot know it"[22]—comes out of this general tradition, irrationalist and voluntarist.

Another nineteenth-century writer whose work shows some affinities with this tradition should be mentioned here. He is Balzac; and he should be mentioned here because Yeats associates him with Nietzsche in two of the comparatively few explicit references to Nietzsche that exist in all his writing. The first appears to be a more or less unconscious association; it occurs in Yeats's 1909 Journal, where Yeats is thinking about Blake's preference for "a happy thoughtless person" to any man of intellect. Balzac, he says, sometimes makes one think he has the same preference, but he is "too much taken up with his worship of the will, which cannot be thoughtless even if it can be happy, to be aware of the preference if he has it. Nietzsche had it doubtless at the moment when he imagined 'the superman' as a child" (*Mem,* p. 158). Ten years later, in his more coherently unified set of jottings called *If I Were Four and Twenty,* Yeats discusses the synthetic powers of Balzac, whose purpose he says is to "expound the doctrine of his Church as it is displayed . . . in the institutions of

Christendom. Yet Nietzsche might have taken, and perhaps did take, his conception of the superman in history from his *Catherine de Medici*" (*Ex*, p. 269).

Yeats seems to be associating the writers specifically through their advocacy of the will, which is to identify the voluntarism both share with Schopenhauer. Voluntarism holds that the will is more fundamental than the intellect and that moreover the intellect is under the will's control. Balzac has a good deal to add to this definition; in two stories Yeats talks about, "La peau de chagrin" and "Louis Lambert," he creates characters who have elaborate theories of the will. In "La peau de chagrin," Raphael's theory is "that the human will was a material force like steam; that in the moral world nothing could resist its power if a man taught himself to concentrate it, to economize it, and to project continually its fluid mass in given directions upon other souls." And in "Louis Lambert," the precocious hero writes a treatise on the will that is confiscated by a schoolmaster and given to us through the recollection of the narrator:

> The word Will [Lambert] used to connote the medium in which the mind moves, or to use a less abstract expression, the mass of power by which a man can reproduce, outside himself, the actions constituting his external life. . . . The word Mind, or Thought, which he regarded as the quintessential product of the Will, also represented the medium in which the ideas originate to which thought gives substance. . . . He gave the Will precedence over the Mind.[23]

It is hard to read this passage as other than a brilliant parody of Schopenhauer. Schopenhauer's will, the blind but potent life force, has a distinguished line of progeny—as Nietzsche's Dionysus, Freud's id, Conrad's destructive element, Lawrence's religion of the blood, Woolf's waves, and Yeats's own Will (in *A Vision*) all bear some family resemblance to this archromantic ancestor.

As Schopenhauer and Balzac (among others) are elevating the will, and Byron and Carlyle (among others) are promoting the artist as hero, and Hölderlin and Heine (among others) are investigating religious relativity, something (among other things) is happening in the realm of cultural sensibility in the first half of the nineteenth century that is relevant to the direction of thought taken by Nietzsche and then by Yeats. It is a phenomenon, or a climate of feeling, that George Steiner calls the "nostalgia for disaster." In *In Bluebeard's Cas-*

tle, Steiner says, "To me the most haunting, prophetic outcry of the nineteenth century is Theophile Gautier's 'plutot la barbarie que l'ennui!' "[24] Boredom has become an enemy; but the means to its defeat are also ready to hand, in the irrational forces embodied by Schopenhauer's Will and developed by its progeny. Nietzsche justifies *la barbarie*—the forces of cruelty and violence in human nature—on the grounds that to deny their existence through their continued repression is to sap, progressively, the human will to live.

L'ennui—boredom, world-weariness—becomes an artistic motif, especially in France, in the latter part of the century. In 1884, Huysmans's *A rebours* brought decadence to the attention of the general public. Its hero, Des Esseintes, the last scion of a noble line, is weary, jaded, misanthropic, and seeks "refuge from the incessant deluge of human stupidity." He indulges his taste for artifice; "Nature, he used to say, has had her day. . . . What platitudinous limitations she imposes." Despite his attempts to create his own values, however, in a fragmented world where Schopenhauer offers the chief philosophical consolation ("[Schopenhauer] claimed no cures, offered the sick no compensation, no hope; but when all was said and done, his theory of Pessimism was the great comforter of superior minds and lofty souls"), his final words, which are also the novel's, make a plaintive cry: "Ah, but my courage fails me, and my heart is sick within me!—Lord, take pity on the Christian who doubts, on the unbeliever who would fain believe, on the galley-slave of life who puts out to sea alone, in the night, beneath a firmament no longer lit by the consoling beacon-fires of the ancient hope!"[25] This failure of courage becomes, like decadence itself, a characteristic of age—the other side of heroism. In *Nouveaux Essais* (1885), Paul Bourget calls it "mal du siècle," a kind of romantic melancholy, which he describes as "une mortelle fatigue de vivre, une morne perception de la vanité de tout effort."[26] According to Nietzsche, romantic melancholy defines the spirit of Wagner's music, and Wagner's music, according to Nietzsche, epitomizes the decadence of the time.

In transferring thoughts from their own particular contexts to the general one of intellectual atmosphere, Yeats's "spirit of the time," one inevitably abstracts them and reduces their complexity. Intellectual atmosphere as a force seems to behave like Schopenhauer's will. When ideas become fashionable, they lose their authorial identity and individuality. Thus intellectual atmosphere is chaotic; it is protean, for ideas change their form; and it is powerful. Following the movement of an idea or set of ideas from mind to mind during any given period of time becomes an experiment where absolute proofs are impossible. Yet the relationships among writers, readers, and texts that the experiment discovers provides a basis for cultural history. My experiment proposes to move now from a very generally sketched set of ideas inherited by and important to both Nietzsche and Yeats to a more specific set of ideas about Nietzsche "in the air" in the 1880s and 1890s.

Nietzsche in France and England, 1880–1900

Although only three volumes of Nietzsche's work existed in English translation before 1903, his name and ideas had been part of the spirit of the time in England for at least a decade. Nietzsche died (after eleven years of madness) in 1900. At the time, English artist Charles Ricketts, later Yeats's friend and designer, noted in his diary: "Aug 27, 1900: Death of Nietzsche. Years ago when I first read him I was half-frightened to find in print so many things which I felt personally, and to hear them from a mouth I loved so little. . . . His end is even more tragic than Heine's—what a temptation for the righteous to rejoice!"[27] Ricketts's words *years ago* indicate that Nietzsche was not news, to Ricketts anyway, in 1900. Given the growth of Nietzsche's reputation among artists and writers, and of these among Yeats's friends and associates, it seems certain that Yeats would have seen Nietzsche's ideas in print in digests and reviews and heard them discussed—either with or without attribution to their author—before he ever read a book by Nietzsche.

Books by Nietzsche, in fact, began to appear in Germany in 1872 with *The Birth of Tragedy;* by the end of the 1880s everything was published but his late tracts (*Nietzsche contra Wagner, The Antichrist,* and *Ecce Homo*) and *The Will to Power.* With the exception of a French translation of *Richard Wagner in Bayreuth* in 1877, however, there were no translations at all until the 1890s. But as early as 1892, Max Nordau, author of *Degeneration,* talks about Nietzsche's "disciples" and is genuinely worried that Nietzsche has already gained a following. He cites German, French, Danish, and Swedish "Nietzscheans";

and he quotes from one of the disciples, Hugo Kaatz, who in *Die Weltanschauung Friedrich Nietzsches* (Dresden and Leipzig, 1892) says that Nietzsche's " 'intellectual seed' " is everywhere "beginning to germinate. Now it is one of Nietzsche's most incisive points which is chosen as the epigraph of a modern tragedy, now one of his pregnant turns of expression incorporated in the established usage of the language. . . . At the present time one can . . . read hardly any essay touching even lightly on the province of philosophy, without meeting with the name of Nietzsche." Nordau comments that "this is certainly a calumnious exaggeration. Things are not quite so bad as that."[28]

However, the publication of *Degeneration* ensured that things, from Nordau's point of view, became worse; if it did not add numbers to the discipleship of Nietzsche, it increased the numbers of those aware of his name and misinformed of his ideas. The book appeared in English translation in 1895 (before Nietzsche was available in English translation) and ran through seven impressions in that year alone. Reviews linked Nordau and Nietzsche: "Both excel in vituperation and constantly substitute abuse for argument," said *The Nation*.[29] The popularity of *Degeneration* made sure that Nietzsche's "pregnant turns of expression" became "incorporated in the established usage of the language," ignorantly and mistakenly. The sneer with which Nordau quotes—out of context and without understanding—such "Nietzscheanisms" as "over-man," "slave morality," "master morality," "nothing is true, all is permissible," "the great blonde beast," "the laughing lion," "the transvaluation of all values," and "God is dead" promoted a horrified popular response to Nietzsche, which lasted well into the twentieth century.

Nordau provides a chapter on Nietzsche in the section of his book entitled "Ego-mania." His polemic begins: "As in Ibsen ego-mania has found its poet, so in Nietzsche it has found its philosopher. The deification of filth by the Parnassians with ink, paint, and clay; the censing [*sic*] among the Diabolists and Decadents of licentiousness, disease, and corruption; the glorification, by Ibsen, of the person who 'wills,' is 'free,' and 'wholly himself'—of all this Nietzsche supplies the theory, or something which proclaims itself as such."[30] Nordau's main purpose in the chapter is to discredit Nietzsche's writings by attempting to prove them the ravings of a "maniac." But

Nordau also makes Nietzsche an example of a diseased age, a civilization itself "degenerate." He undermines Nietzsche's claims to originality by comparing his ideas to similar ones in Ibsen, Huysmans, Barrès, and Wilde. He pays special attention to the resemblance to Wilde, and exhibits parallels he finds in the writings of the two "degenerates":

> The passage in *Zur Genealogie der Moral* in which [Nietzsche] glorifies art, because in it "the lie sanctifies itself, and the will to deceive has a quiet conscience on its side," might be in Wilde's *Intentions* on "The Decay of Lying," as, conversely, Wilde's aphorisms: "There is no sin except stupidity." "An idea that is not dangerous is unworthy of being called an idea at all." And his praise of Wainwright the poisoner, are in exact agreement with Nietzsche's "morality of assassins," and the latter's remarks that crime is calumniated, and that the defender of the criminal is "oftenest not artist enough to turn the beautiful terribleness of the crime to the advantage of the doer." Again, by way of a joke, compare these passages: "It is necessary to get rid of the bad taste of wishing to agree with many. Good is no longer good when a neighbour says it is 'good' " (Nietzsche, *Jenseits von Gut und Bose*), and "Ah! don't say that you agree with me. When people agree with me, I always feel that I must be wrong" (Oscar Wilde, *Intentions*). This is more than a resemblance, is it not? . . . The similarity, or rather identity, is not explained by plagiarism; it is explained by the identity of mental qualities in Nietzsche and other egomaniacal degenerates.[31]

As always in this instructive book, Nordau's real perceptions are marred by his narrow-minded and polemical spirit. For instance, his confident assertion that the identity between Nietzsche's and Wilde's aphorisms "is not explained by plagiarism" is based on his own thesis about the moral and psychological degeneracy of the age. The fact is, of course, that Wilde was a notorious plagiarist. Whistler's remark on the subject is well known: "Oscar . . . has the courage of the opinions of others"; and Wilde himself declares: "The true artist is known by the use he makes of what he annexes, and he annexes everything."[32] It is probable that on his trips to Paris in the 1880s Wilde heard Nietzsche's ideas being discussed in literary salons and cafés, perhaps without even being identified, and "annexed" the ones he liked. At the time, the Parisian artists' milieu was a small world where, according to one study of the period, "there is a constant overlapping of names among the various patrons of the cafés and the contributors to the periodicals."[33]

By the mid-eighties in Paris, the café circuit would have begun to hear of Nietzsche. Writers whose articles on Nietzsche begin to appear in the literary journals in 1890—Teodor de Wyzewa, Dujardin, Halévy, Henri Mazel—were on the scene in the 80s, contributing to the intellectual climate at the cafés as well as in *Le Decadent, La Revue Indépendent, La Revue Wagnerienne,* and others. We have been told by Roger Shattuck in *The Banquet Years* that in 1891 Alfred Jarry, the author of *Ubu Roi,* attended lectures at the Lycée Henri IV, where "from Professor Bourdon [he] heard the revolutionary doctrines of Nietzsche before his works were translated into French," which could account for the "Nietzschean and prophetic strain" in Jarry; and that "Jarry came to the theatre several times in the company of Oscar Wilde and Lord Douglas."[34] A case could be made, given the evidence, for the probable transmission of Nietzsche's ideas to Wilde, via the Parisian artists' grapevine.

Yeats knew Wilde in London in the late 1880s and early 1890s; Wilde read him the proofs of *The Decay of Lying* on Christmas Day, 1888. Richard Ellmann states that the reading "had an immediate and lasting effect on this first auditor," Yeats.[35] I suggest that this occasion provided Yeats not only with a direct and impressive introduction to the ideas and personality of Oscar Wilde, but also with an indirect introduction to ideas of Nietzsche that Wilde acquired in Paris and adapted to his own purposes. The Nietzsche-Wilde resemblance could be profitably analyzed, with a view to bringing the problem of the transmission of ideas "in the air" down to earth.

A comparative spate of articles on Nietzsche began appearing in the 1890s, in German, French, Danish, and English. Among Nietzsche's first British publicists was the poet John Davidson (one of Yeats's poet friends of the nineties), who in a *Speaker* article entitled "The New Sophist" in 1891 hailed Nietzsche as "the Nihilist of philosophy" and translated parts of an article about Nietzsche from a French journal.[36] His 1893 book of aphorisms, *Sentences and Paragraphs,* develops his commendation of the new sophist: "Nietzsche is the most unphilosophic mind that ever attempted philosophy. He is a great poet seeking a system, instead of taking things on trust. He starts from nothing, and ends in nothing. He proves and disproves, believes and disbelieves everything." An article in the French journal *l'Ermitage* by Henri Mazel, "Nietzsche et le présent" (1893), calls

Nietzsche a "valuable stimulant for our times"—emphasizing the antidecadent Nietzsche, seeing him as an answer to the weariness and *mal du siècle* of the *tradition à rebours*. Davidson says much the same thing in another *Speaker* article late in the decade (1899): "Such a tonic the world of letters has not had for a thousand years. Nietzsche set himself, smiling, to dislodge the old world from its orbit."[37] His phraseology is echoed by Yeats when he explains dropping his play *Where There Is Nothing* from his collected works. He says of its hero, Paul Ruttledge: "I came to dislike a central character so arid and so dominating. We cannot sympathize with a man who sets his anger at once lightly and confidently to overthrow the order of the world" (*VPl*, p. 712).

The echo may not be coincidental; Yeats could have seen Davidson's article and hoarded the thought—that Nietzsche set himself, smiling, to dislodge the old world from its orbit—in his memory, until the need to deal with his "Nietzschean" hero, Paul, called it up to the surface. It is moreover highly probable that Yeats heard Nietzsche discussed by other friends—Arthur Symons, Havelock Ellis, and George Moore. Of the three, Ellis was the best read in Nietzsche; he shared rooms with Symons at Fountain Court in the Temple from 1891, until Yeats moved in in 1895, and he must have talked about Nietzsche with Symons. Furthermore, Symons edited *The Savoy*, which printed in the April, July, and August 1896 numbers Ellis's three-part retrospective, "Friedrich Nietzsche."

This series of articles was timed to coincide with the first English translations of Nietzsche: Thomas Common's *The Case of Wagner, The Twilight of the Idols, Nietzsche contra Wagner,* and *The Antichrist* (in one volume), and Alexander Tille's *Thus Spake Zarathustra*. In the July number of *The Savoy*, Ellis's "Friedrich Nietzsche" directly follows Yeats's mystical story "Rosa Alchemica." It is a wonderful juxtaposition, as though the Rosa-Alchemica Yeats were being introduced to Nietzsche at a large party where they have, on the surface, little in common. Yeats's emphasis is on the occult, his bias predominantly toward self-dissolution in a mystic Oneness. The Nietzsche Ellis introduces, on the other hand, is the very type of self-affirmation. Although Ellis proclaims his own impartiality in what he reports as a passionate partisan struggle in the German press between Nietzsche's admirers and detractors, his treatment is transparently sympathetic.

In opening (the April number), he says that Nietzsche is the "modern incarnation of that image of intellectual pride which Marlowe created in Faustus; . . . he represents, perhaps, the greatest spiritual force which has appeared since Goethe."[38] He gives a brief biography, based on the first volume of Nietzsche's sister Elisabeth Forster-Nietzsche's *Leben Friedrich Nietzsches* (1895) and on "more fragmentary data" to cover the more recent years. Forster-Nietzsche's main intentional inaccuracy, repeated by Ellis unintentionally, is her insistence on the family's healthiness, to quash suspicions of congenital madness.[39] She also insists on the moral soundness of the line, which Ellis turns: "Nietzsche came of a race of Christian ministers, . . . and from first to last the preacher's fervour was in his blood." Ellis then offers synopses of Nietzsche's major works, which he has read in German. His article would have provided the English-reading world with its first exposure to *The Birth of Tragedy* (not translated in full until 1909), containing ideas that were substantially to revise the long-accepted view of classical Greece as embodying ideals of noble simplicity and serene greatness. Aware of the radical nature of the shift (adumbrated by Heine) from a critical view essentially Apollonian to one more Dionysian, Ellis take some pleasure in the anti-Victorian revolt: "For Nietzsche the Greek world was not the model of beautiful mediocrity imagined by Winckelmann and Goethe, nor did it date from the era of rhetorical idealism inaugurated by Plato. The real Hellenic world came earlier, and the true Hellenes were sturdy realists enamoured of life, revering all its manifestations and returns, and holding in highest honour that sexual symbol of life which Christianity, with its denial of life, despises."[40] Ellis emphasizes Nietzsche's interest in sources or beginnings—*The Birth of Tragedy from the Spirit of Music* was the original title; *music* meant ritual dithyramb and dance. Nietzsche thus suggests what Frazer in *The Golden Bough* (1890), Jane Harrison in *Prolegomana to the Study of Greek Religion* (1903), and Gilbert Murray in *Classical Tradition in Poetry* (1927) were to establish explicitly and definitively: that tragedy as a *genre* has its roots in primitive ritual.

The next number of *The Savoy* (July 1896) contains the second installment of the Nietzsche article and Yeats's essay "William Blake and His Illustrations to the Divine Comedy, I." Yeats's piece begins with a description of the *symboliste* spirit of the 1890s as "the recoil from scientific naturalism," "the desires of our hearts grown weary with material circumstances."[41] If "Hearts Grown Weary" is the time's theme song, according to Yeats, it is countered by another called "Life's an Adventure," according to Ellis on Nietzsche. In the July installment, Ellis discusses what he takes to be Nietzsche's main ideas. The body of the article defines Nietzsche's attitude toward "modern religion" and "modern morals," with an important qualifier:

> He is not bent on destroying religion from any anaesthesia of the religious sense, or even in order to set up some religion of science which is practically no religion at all. . . . When he writes of the founder of Christianity and the great Christian types, it is often with a poignant sympathy which the secularist can never know. . . . When he analyzes the souls of these men and the impulses which have moved them, he knows with what he is dealing: he is analyzing his own soul.[42]

Later biographers and critics of Nietzsche have also stressed this point, and it is a good service done by Ellis that he points out that it was not the times alone Nietzsche was fighting, it was himself in the times, a struggle with his own conditioning. (Nietzsche puts it succinctly in *Ecce Homo,* a work Ellis didn't know: "My humanity is a constant self-overcoming."[43]) Ellis describes Nietzsche's attitude toward Christianity as one of "repulsion and antagonism" and quotes (from *The Antichrist*): " 'With its contempt for the body Christianity was the greatest misfortune that ever befell humanity.' " Nor is Nietzsche in favor of shoring up Christian morality, says Ellis; he opposes the approach of George Eliot, J. S. Mill, Herbert Spencer, "and so many more of our favourite intellectual heroes who have striven to preserve Christian morality while denying Christian theology." To explain Nietzsche's revolutionary position, Ellis summarizes his main arguments (from *A Genealogy of Morals,* though he doesn't identify the source) about bad conscience or guilt, altruism, and "negative virtues" or "Thou-shalt-not's." Ellis reports the following ideas, among others: "Morality is the mob instinct working in the individual; . . . faith in authority is thus the source of conscience. . . . The sphere of the moral is the sphere of tradition, and a man is moral because he is dependent on a tradition and not on himself. . . . Every kind of originality involves a bad conscience. . . . Every good thing was once new, unaccustomed, *immoral,* and gnawed at the vitals of the finder like a worm." He closes this section with the injunctions of

Zarathustra: "Men must become both better and *wickeder*"; and " 'Do what you will,' said Zarathustra, 'but first be one of those who are *able to will*. Love your neighbour as yourself—but first be one of those who *are able to love themselves*.' "

Ellis does not give much time to Nietzsche's considerable relationship with art in general, Wagner in particular, but he includes a passage on moraliity in literature from *The Dawn of Day* that Yeats was to find especially congenial:

> And if we turn to literature, Nietzsche maintains, it is a vast mistake to suppose that, for instance, great tragedies have, or were intended to have, any moral effect. Look at "Macbeth," at "Tristan and Isolde," at "Oedipus." In all these cases it would be easy to make guilt the pivot of the drama. But the great poet is in love with passion. "He calls to us: 'It is the charm of charms, this exciting, changing, dangerous, gloomy, yet often sun-filled existence! It is an adventure to live!' "

Although Nietzsche suffers from being read out of context more than most writers—and even to read one whole work, apart from the others, is to receive a partial and incomplete impression—he fared reasonably well at the hands of Ellis, who says in his final section that "Nietzsche had no system" and that he "desires to prove nothing, and is reckless of consistency."[44] However true this may be of Nietzsche, it is much less true of his commentators. To fix or formulate Nietzsche in one position is to falsify his commitment to "becoming," yet the temptation to do so has proved almost irresistible. As an example of the kind of falsification done by well-intentioned, sober-minded exegetes who follow onc of Nietzsche's lines of thought without picking up the counterthought, or without explaining the symbolic value of the concepts used, here is the closing paragraph of Ellis's second article. Just because Ellis is not a Nordau, not one of the passionate partisans he mentions in opening, his distortions are disturbing. He is explaining what he understands as Nietzsche's "three stages of moral evolution." The first stage Ellis labels "pre-moral" or animal, unselfconscious, guiltless. The second is the "moral," which Ellis has already outlined as guilt-ridden herd behavior or "slave morality," or where we are now. Then Ellis says:

> Nietzsche ingeniously connected his slave-morality with the undoubted fact that for many centuries, the large, fair-haired aristocratic race has been dy-

ing out in Europe, and the older down-trodden race—short, dark, and broad-headed—has been slowly gaining predominance. But now we stand at the threshold of the *extra-moral* period. Slave-morality, Nietzsche asserted, is about to give way to master-morality; the lion will take the place of the camel. The instincts of life, refusing to allow that anything is forbidden, will again assert themselves, sweeping away the feeble negative democratic morality of our time. The day has now come for the man who is able to rule himself, and who will be tolerant to others not out of his weakness, but out of his strength; to him nothing is forbidden, for he has passed beyond goodness and beyond wickedness.[45]

It is hard to know where to start unraveling this sort of commentary. Perhaps with Ellis himself, who, although he knows—or anyway says—that "Nietzsche desires to prove nothing," is still determined to force him into a position that Ellis approves (eugenics being one of Ellis's interests). The problem is that while Nietzsche does say most of the things Ellis says he says, he has no interest in applying them practically, does not put them in chronological order, does not write a program—much less a pogram. He is, above all, descriptive.

Nietzsche was himself aware, in the end, of the possible political repercussions of his ideas, and, as Walter Kaufmann tells us in his *Nietzsche,* he sketched a preface in the fall in 1888 for his planned magnum opus, in which he wrote:

The Will to Power. A book for *thinking,* nothing else: it belongs to those to whom thinking is a *delight,* nothing else. That it is written in German is at least untimely: I wish I had written it in French in order that it might not appear as a confirmation of any reichdeutschen aspirations.[46]

Ellis, in 1896, would have been far from imagining the lengths to which future publicists and propagandists might carry some of Nietzsche's ideas. He saw Nietzsche as a liberator, beyond conventional goodness and wickedness, and thus, in the pages of *The Savoy,* he interpreted and mythologized him.[47]

Another mythologizer, George Moore, must come into the story at this point. He will reenter in connection with Yeats's 1902 play *Where There Is Nothing,* but he appears here because he knew Yeats in the 1890s, and he also knew and visited both Dujardin and Halévy, confirmed Nietzscheans, in Paris. Moore's biographer, Joseph Hone (who was Yeats's biographer as well, and also a translator of Halévy's *Life of Nietzsche* into English), says that Moore "caught a good deal from the German 'impressionist' philosopher of whom he had heard much earlier from Dujardin. I myself remember his admiration for his friend, Daniel Halévy's, *Vie de Nietzsche*."[48] Moore admired his book so much, apparently, that he plagiarized wholesale from it. According to Patrick Bridgwater in *Nietzsche in Anglosaxony,* there is a passage in *Evelyn Innes* (1898; the novel in which Yeats is the model for the artist Ulick Dean) taken from Nietzsche's *The Joyful Wisdom* via Halévy's *Life,* where the passage is quoted.[49] But Moore's plagiarisms (which were about as notorious as Wilde's) aside, it is interesting to know that another of Yeats's friends and future collaborators was using Nietzschean ideas in the 1890s. In *Hail and Farewell,* Moore writes a paragraph in which he revealingly juxtaposes Dujardin-Nietzsche and Yeats-Boehm. He is speaking of his friends of the 1890s and of their absorbing intellectual interests. Dujardin, he says, would be happy to explain German philosophy at any hour of the night, as would Yeats to explain Blake: "And if one were to go to Yeats's bedside at three o'clock in the morning and beg him to explain a certain difficult passage, let us say, in the *Jerusalem,* he would raise himself up in bed like Dujardin, and, stroking his pale Buddhistic hands, begin to spin glittering threads of argument and explanation; instead of Schopenhauer and Nietzsche, we should hear of the Rosicrucians and Jacob Boehm."[50] The juxtaposition is interesting because the philosophers represent the two poles, self-assertion and self-surrender, that Yeats himself describes in several works of the time. As Yeats thought, the poles are parts of the same whole and need each other, as day needs night. But as Moore suggests, Yeats in the 1890s concentrated more intellectual energy at the Rosicrucian pole of self-surrender than at the Nietzschean one of self-assertion. Yeats almost says as much in a letter to Robert Bridges (December, 1896): "Your praise of my work gave me great pleasure as your work is to me the most convincing poetry done by any man among us just now. I said this to Brandes, the Norwegian, the other day when he was praising all manner of noisy persons. Your work alone has the quietude of wisdom and I do most firmly believe that all art is dedicated to wisdom and not because it teaches anything but because it reveals divine substances" (*L,* p. 268). George Brandes, actually a Dane, was one of the very first, and very few, of his admiring readers of whom Nietzsche was aware. Brandes lectured on Nietzsche at the

University of Copenhagen in 1888 and published a book on aristocratic radicalism that included Nietzsche in 1899. In 1896 when Yeats met him, he was in London on a lecture tour, speaking on Ibsen and Nietzsche, "all manner of noisy persons." It is certain that if Yeats had heard about Nietzsche in the 1890s—as this letter to Bridges suggests he had—he resisted Nietzsche's "noise" in favor of the quietude of wisdom. In order to gauge the effect on Yeats of his reading of Nietzsche in 1902, I turn now, continuing my progress from the general to the particular, to consider some of Yeats's activities and thoughts around the turn of the century.

Yeats at the Century's Turn

Although Yeats's affinity in the 1890s was with the symbolist and occultist emphasis on transcendence of material reality and art's "revelation of divine substances," he was too much a temperamental dialectician to ignore the opposite pole or to turn from it entirely. During the period of the 1890s when he was most under the spell of Rosicrucianism, he kept on forming theoretical and imaginative antitheses and writing them down. The act of writing was itself an anchor for him, the material half of an antithesis the other half of which was the insubstantial matter of his mind. He speaks of writing, humorously, in his 1897 story "The Adoration of the Magi," as an exercise in safekeeping: "I have let some years go by before writing out this story, for I am always in dread of the illusions which come of that Inquietude of the veil of the Temple, which Mallarmé considers a characteristic of our times; and only write it now because I have grown to believe that there is no dangerous idea which does not become less dangerous when written out in sincere and careful English" (*Myth,* p. 309). This thought is meant to characterize the somewhat timorous pedantic narrator of the story, from whom Yeats keeps a fine ironic detachment. It also contains the idea that writing is by its nature a mask, an essentially artificial objectification and formalization of ideas that, in giving them the solidity of visible symbols upon something material, deprives them of part of their potential destructiveness, or "danger," by depriving them of the protean quality of formlessness.

The relationships between formlessness and form, or nonbeing and being, provides the basis of Hegel's dialectic, as we have seen. Nietzsche develops the dichotomy in *The Birth of Tragedy,* strengthening the nonbeing pole by endowing it with the energy of Schopenhauer's will, and making the whole concept primarily relevant to art. Yeats arrives at his own dialectical theory, which becomes the basis of his conception of life as tragedy, through a number of influences. They are genetic (marriage of Pollexfen and Yeats, which W. B. understood as a union of opposites in more than a sexual sense); literary (especially through Yeats's early heroes, Shelley's solitaries who are set against the rest of creation, the isolate self against necessity or nature, and through Blake's positive contraries); and theosophical (through the hermetic insistence on the existence of two realms, one material, one spiritual, and Blavatsky's description in *The Secret Doctrine* of the law of polarity of life as a conflict of opposites).

Yeats's first major formulation of his dialectical theory appears in his and Edwin Ellis's edition of the works of Blake (1893). Identified by Harold Bloom as "the seed of *A Vision,*"[51] the idea is that the mind has two poles, one contracting to hardness, the other expanding limitlessly:

> The mind or imagination or consciousness of man may be said to have two poles, the personal and impersonal, or, as Blake preferred to call them, the limit of contraction and the unlimited expansion. When we act from the personal we tend to bind our consciousness down as to a fiery centre. When, on the other hand, we allow our imagination to expand away from this egoistic mood, we become vehicles for the universal thought and merge in the universal mood. Thus a reaction of God against man and man against God . . . goes on continually.[52]

He sets forth the idea again, in a new form with an alchemical basis, in a review of a verse translation of Ibsen's *Brand* (1894):

> Certain alchemical writers say that the substance left behind in the retort is the philosopher's stone, and the liquid distilled over, the elixir or alkahest; and all are agreed that the stone transmutes everything into gold, while the elixir dissolves everything into nothing, and not a few call them the fixed and the volatile. One might take these contraries as symbols of the minds of Brand and Peer Gynt. Peer Gynt lets sheer fantasy take possession of his life, and fill him with the delusion that he is now this or that personage . . . until the true Peer Gynt is well-nigh dissolved. Brand, upon the other hand, seeks

to rise into an absolute world where there is . . . only God and his laws, and to transmute by the force of his unchanging ideal everything about him into imperishable gold. . . . His mistake is not less disastrous, though immeasurably nobler, than the mistake of Peer Gynt, for the children of the earth can only live by compromise, by half measure, and by disobedience to his impassioned appeal.

Yeats then quotes Brand's song, which urges the listener to be whole-souled, not piecemeal, and Yeats comments: "Poetry has ever loved those who are not 'piecemeal,' and has made them its Timons and its Lears, but Nature, which is all 'piecemeal,' has ever cast them out."[53]

The two principles represented by stone and elixir are ancient and, as Yeats might say, perpetually present in the anima mundi. Obviously they form an important part of magical lore, but they also form the bases of philosophical systems. Their appearance in this review demonstrates the tenacity of archetypes; it also shows that Yeats was assembling the parts of his "system" early, long before he saw it whole himself. The dialectic implicit in the Blake study, as the mind's journey between the poles, is developed in the *Brand* review. The two poles of static form and formlessness are set at the extremes, with the "earth" or "Nature" between as the *tertium quid*. Furthermore, Yeats introduces the concept of tragedy in connection with this dialectical model. He does so tangentially, marginally, and by implication only: the human beings who refuse to compromise, as nature demands, pay for their "mistakes" by death, "being cast out." Brand's mind seeks to "transmute everything into imperishable gold"; he is whole-souled, a tragic figure like Timon and Lear, who in striving to maintain his ideal without compromise is loved by poetry (as fit subject for tragedy), but cast out by nature. Brand's form of idealism is related to Parmenides's "pure being," to "the limit of contraction" in the Blake passage, and to the goal of the artist, who desires to transmute the images of piecemeal nature into imperishable gold, beauty. It can also represent the purposes of saint, patriot, or anyone who serves a fixed absolute as an "unchanging ideal." The "stone" of Brand's thought is the same as that of "Easter 1916":

Hearts with one purpose alone
Through summer and winter seem

Enchanted to a stone
To trouble the living stream.

(*VP*, p. 393)

The other pole, the elixir that dissolves everything into nothing, or formlessness, is the deindividuating principle; the shape-changer; persuader to chaos; flux; madness; Schopenhauer's will; and as beyond compromise as the stone principle. Total commitment to either principle means a casting out by nature. In this short review, Yeats establishes a structure that resembles Nietzsche's Apollonian-Dionysian duality of *The Birth of Tragedy*. He barely hints at the interrelation of the ideas he assembles, however; Nietzsche develops it elaborately, his main contribution (following Hegel) being to set the poles at war with one another. He can then assert that the confluence of the contrary forces of ideal form (human vision of a saving "truth," however it may appear) and of those forces that dissolve form, creating primal unity, are the basis of tragedy.

Yeats in 1894 is not ready to put the ideas he has associated—transmutation, dissolution, tragedy—into a scheme; he has not seen the implication of their juxtaposition. But in the next several years, he turns the stone-elixir dialectic to account in three short stories, where he examines it playfully, self-consciously. "Rosa Alchemica," "The Tables of the Law," and "The Adoration of the Magi" provide a counterpoint, if not a countertruth, to *The Wind among the Reeds,* poems that attempt, as Allan Grossman says, to exchange art for life.[54] The stories, written at roughly the same time as the poems, show Yeats ironically aware of the "danger" of following either stone or elixir to the limit and satisfied to remain, the self-conscious author, piecemeal in the middle, writing out his ideas in sincere and careful English.

By the late 1890s, the effect of another influence was beginning to appear in Yeats's work. It is mythology, or, as he put it in an article on "The Literary Movement in Ireland" (1899), "the new science of folklore and the almost new science of mythology."[55] The subject matter of these new "sciences" (which were indeed soon to take on scientific status as cultural anthropology) naturally interested Yeats, combining as it did magic and religion and, if the myths were Celtic, nationalism. In a series of six long essays on Irish folklore and supernatural experience, appearing in English journals from 1897 to 1902, Yeats cites his sources as Frazer's *The Golden Bough* (first two volumes published in 1890); Arbois de Jubainville's *Cours de littérature celtique* (1884); John Rhys's *Lectures on the Origin and Growth of Religion as Illustrated by Celtic Heathendom* (1886), and finally a book reviewed by Yeats, Alfred E. Nutt's and Kuno Meyer's *The Voyage of Bran* (1898). What Yeats reads in these books (added to what he reads in Blake, Shelley, and Arnold) helps him make by the turn of the century extravagant claims for the function of art, whose roots he discovers in primitive ritual and of which he finds traces still persisting in folk belief, myth, and poetic symbols. Expanding and explaining Matthew Arnold's interpretation of the Celtic element in literature, Yeats says: "When Matthew Arnold wrote, it was not easy to know as much as we know now of folk-song and folk-belief, and I do not think he understood that our 'natural magic' is but the ancient religion of the world, the ancient worship of Nature and that 'troubled ecstasy' before her, that certainty of all beautiful places being haunted, which it brought to men's minds." He then looks at the quotations Arnold makes from English poets to prove a Celtic influence, and identifies in each an allusion to "ancient religion," passages that demonstrate "the delight and wonder of devout worshippers among the haunts of their divinities" (*E&I,* pp. 176–77). If poetry grew from ritual incantation, might it not once again take on the office of religion?

At the turn of the century, Yeats's hopes for the role of poetry in society reached messianic heights, carrying the implications of Shelley's ideal of poet as unacknowledged legislator of the world and of Arnold's ideal of culture to their logical conclusion. Again and again in the essays he collected in *Ideas of Good and Evil,* Yeats calls upon poetry, or art in general, to assume the responsibility formerly held by religion. In "The Symbolism of Poetry" (1900): "How can the arts overcome the slow dying of men's hearts that we call the progress of the world, and lay their hands upon men's heartstrings again, without becoming the garment of religion as in old times?" (*E&I,* pp. 162–63). Or in "The Celtic Element in Literature" (1902): "The arts by brooding on their own intensity have become religious, and are seeking, as I think Verhaeren has said, to create a sacred book" (*E&I,* p. 187). Or in "The Autumn of the Body" (1898): "The arts are, I believe, about to take upon their shoulders the burdens that have fallen from the shoulders of priests, and to lead us back upon our journey by filling our thoughts with the essence of things, and not with things" (*E&I,* p. 193).

The art best suited to take upon its shoulders the burdens that had fallen from the shoulders of priests, Yeats felt, was drama. His increasing interest and involvement in the Irish theater from 1897 on had partly to do, therefore, with his moral commitment to help overcome "the slow dying of men's hearts" through the reinstatement of a ritual drama. Partly, too, it had to do with his alignment with the nationalist cause (from whatever motives—interest in Maud Gonne probably constituting the primary one), and partly with his own intrinsic penchant for opposition—a bias both ontological and epistemological—which made him naturally ironic, and therefore a natural dramatist.

He emphasizes the moral and national importance of his dramatic enterprise in newspaper and journal articles around the turn of the century. His essay in the Dublin *Daily Express* for January 14, 1899, following his announcement two days earlier of the formation of the Irish Literary Theatre, attributes the new theatre's genesis to Ireland's growing political consciousness after the fall of Parnell: "There is no feeling, except religious feeling, which moves masses of men so powerfully as national feeling, and upon this, more widely spread among all classes in Ireland to-day than at any time this century, we build our principal hopes."[56] In much of his writing about the Irish Literary Theatre, Yeats seems to be working toward a theory based on the synchrony of art, religion, and nationalism. References to the theater of ancient Greece occur frequently, as he expresses the hope that the theater might become the kind of unifying and civilizing force it once was: "Victor Hugo has said that in the theatre the mob became a people, and, though this could be perfectly true only of ancient times when the theatre was a part of the ceremonial of religion, I have some hope that, if we have enough success to go on from year to year, we may help to bring a little ideal thought into the common thought of our times."[57]

The romantic dichotomy between "this world" (mortal, mutable) and "the other world" (immortal, immutable) that informs much of Yeats's early poetry, supplies him with the concepts he tends to use when writing in aid of the Irish literary movement. Describing the new season of plays to be offered by the Irish Literary Theatre in 1900, he reports that the plays dramatize the conflict between the world of the faery on the one hand, and on the other, the human world where "even the most famous of the beautiful sink into querulous old age." He continues: "This thought of the war of immortal upon mortal life has been the moving thought of much Irish poetry, and may yet, so moving and necessary a thought it is, inspire many plays."[58] Earlier, in an 1895 essay called "The Moods," Yeats talked about "immortal moods in mortal desires" (*E&I,* p. 195); this phrase points back to the formulation of the 1893 Blake edition, where both "poles" are present at once and in conflict in the human mind—both the "fiery centre" of the individual ego, and the "limitless expansion" of aspiration toward "God." In the 1900 formulation, however, he separates the poles, giving the "immortal moods" not only an external, objective life or world of their own, but making this "life" an aggressive force as well. Immortal life fights *against* mortal life. In the plays Yeats himself writes under the inspiration of this thought, *The Land of Heart's Desire* and *Cathleen Ni Houlihan,* the battle is unequal, the dice are loaded. On the opening of *Cathleen Ni Houlihan* in Dublin, April 1902, Yeats furnished *The United Irishman* with an explanation of the conflict:

> My subject is Ireland and its struggle for independence. . . . I have described a household preparing for the wedding of the son of the house. Everyone expects some good thing from the wedding. . . . Into this household comes Kathleen Ni Houlihan herself, and the bridegroom leaves his bride, and all the hopes come to nothing. It is the perpetual struggle of the cause of Ireland and every other ideal cause against private hopes and dreams, against all that we mean when we say the world.[59]

In Yeats's plays of this period, the ideal cause is both aggressor or antagonist, and victor.

Yeats identifies his alignment on the side of the "ideal" as explicitly "Romantic" in an article written for the *North American Review,* "The Literary Movement in Ireland," 1899. Like the romantics, he too, with the literary movement in Ireland, is seeking "to bring again the Golden Age." By rediscovering Irish myths—and those who still believe in them, the Irish peasants who have kept them alive—the Irish literary movement hopes, Yeats explains, to "sanctify" the countryside, not through priests, but through their successors, the artists. Their opponent is the same one the romantics fought: "The Romantic movement, from the times of Blake and Shelley and Keats . . . has been battling with the thoughts of the good citizen."[60] The article draws up the battle lines, which extend and clarify the theme of "the war of immortal upon mortal life." On the "Romantic" side Yeats places Ireland; "traditional" (folk) belief; the ideal; the immortal ("imperishable"); symbolic art and artists, especially the romantic and pre-Raphaelite poets and painters who "labour to bring the Golden Age"; mysticism; and the Irish countryside. On the side of "the good citizen" he places such miscellaneous concepts as England; materialism; comfort and safety; moderation; vulgarity; insincerity; systems of morals (rather than "spiritual ardour"); art of imitation rather than revelation; cities, newspapers, noise, and "the sordid compromise of success."[61] The conflict in this essay is as clearly value-laden, and as oversimplified, and as much in accordance with the Victorian sages—Carlyle, Arnold, Ruskin—in their fight against Philistinism, as Yeats ever presents it. The thought reappears, of course, in many forms, again and again throughout Yeats's career—famously in a poem written thirty-two years later, "Coole Park and Ballylee":

> We were the last romantics—chose for theme
> Traditional sanctity and loveliness;
> Whatever's written in what poets name
> The book of the people.
>
> (*VP*, pp. 491–92).

Another piece of the 1900 period, in which the spiritual-material conflict appears in the context of literary criticism, is Yeats's "At Stratford-on-Avon" (1901), an essay that again makes explicit the parallel between art and religion and emphasizes the difference between art and nature or the "real world." Yeats praises the contemporary Benson production of six of Shakespeare's history plays as representing before the mind's eye "something almost mythological," akin to dreams: "The people my mind's eye has seen have too much of the extravagance of dreams, like all the inventions of art before our crowded life had brought moderation and compromise, to seem more than a dream, and yet all else has grown dim before them" (*E&I*, p. 97). London, in this essay, epitomizes crowded modern material life, while Stratford represents a life more "medieval," quiet, spiritual. "Surely a bitter hatred of London is becoming a mark of those that love the arts," Yeats says; "adventures like this of Stratford-on-Avon show that people are ready to journey . . . to live with their favourite art, as shut away from the world as though they were 'in retreat,' as Catholics say." In this sentence Yeats reveals, unconsciously it would seem, what he considers the real state of affairs. He would reinstate the "immortal" in art, because he feels that art is in fact "in retreat," along with religion, shut away from the world, alienated. Erich Heller contends that aestheticism itself, "the religion of Art, the deification of the 'artifice of eternity' . . . is supported—as, at its origin, the Christian religion was—by the sense of a condemned 'real world.' "[62] Certainly his claim would appear at first glance to be borne out by the dichotomy between art (Stratford) and reality (London) as Yeats develops it in this and other essays of the period. Yet the very next sentence of the Stratford essay indicates that he is at least half aware of the extremity of his position, and is determined not to be defeated by it, but to mock it: "Nobody but an impressionist painter, who hides it in light and mist, even pretends to love a street for its own sake" (*E&I,* p. 98). In this pronouncement, Yeats dramatizes the attitude of the privileged cultural elite whose view it expresses. *Nobody* contains the sense of exclusion, its meaning in context being "nobody who is anybody." The exceptions are artists, who are permitted to love the street because everybody (who is anybody) understands that artists are exceptional by nature, and anyway they love the street for *art's sake,* not its own, which is entirely different. Even impressionist painters, however, cannot bear too much reality, and so hide it in light and mist, both images suggestive of the romantic and the spiritual. The words "Nobody . . . *even pretends* to love a street" imply a hierarchy of emotional commitment—real, false, and nonexistent; their tone is ironic, their effect satiric, as Yeats gently castigates a social world where pretense is customary in matters emotional and (by association with the impressionist painter) aesthetic. "To love a street" is a vaguely absurd idea, its incongruity arising from investment of love in a material object, for, as Yeats repeats elsewhere and as this sentence implies, everybody (who is anybody) knows that love belongs on the side of the spiritual—with religion, nationality or race, dreams, and art. To love a street for its own sake is to take life literally, to be "objective," scientific, to deny the spiritual behind the material world. It is to be "modern," as Yeats comes to use the word, in contempt, frustration, or despair. For the sentence is structurally ironic; while it satirizes the aesthetic position as elitist, pretentious, and hypocritical, its context makes clear that even with its flaws, it is the only position anybody can reasonably endorse.

The horrendous possibility for Yeats at this time is that, finally, art may cease to be relevant. He defines "art" in the essay on Blake that appeared in the July 1896 number of *The Savoy* beside Ellis's "Nietzsche." He says that, for Blake:

> True art is expressive and symbolic, and makes every form, every sound, every colour, every gesture, a signature of some unanalysable imaginative essence. False art is not expressive, but mimetic, not from experience but from observation, and is the mother of all evil, persuading us to save our bodies alive at no matter what cost of rapine and fraud. True art is the flame of the Last Day, which begins for every man when he is first moved by beauty, and which seeks to burn all things until they become "infinite and holy." (*E&I,* p. 140)

There is a psychological as well as an aesthetic theory in this passage. Yeats's explanation of the genesis of true art, based on his reading of Blake, is that true art "begins" when one is "first moved by beauty." Thus the beholder, really experiencing beauty rather than merely observing it, becomes a part of its expressiveness—its forms, sounds, colors, gestures. True art makes a connection between the sensual world and the beholder that awakes in the beholder a kind of emotion (burning) in which he/she is, as Yeats implies, purified. All this is sound romantic aesthetic theory. Its psychological dimensions are fairly complex; they become clearer in comparison with those in another passage by Yeats on Blake written at about the same time:

> [Blake] cried again and again that everything that lives is holy, and that nothing is unholy except things that do not live—lethargies, and cruelties, and timidities, and that denial of imagination which is the root they grew from in old times. Passions, because most living, are most holy—and this was a scandalous paradox in his time—and man shall enter eternity borne upon their wings. (*E&I,* pp. 112–13)

"True art," interpreted in the light of the second passage, becomes a means of expressing or re-creating the joy that is in life, especially in the energy of passion, which is released, Yeats seems to suggest, by means of the work's signs, its forms. This kind of art finds, and persuades us to find, even death preferable to a nonlife of "rapine and fraud," cruelties, timidities, and denial of imagination. True art reconnects humans with their source, which in a mystical sense is both beginning and end, both "first-moved" and "the flame of the Last Day." Blake calls the source God, and Yeats follows. True art as defined by Yeats-Blake seeks the fulfillment of desire, the reuniting of love and death. False art is an instrument, not of death (which, as the dialectical counterpart of Eros, is part of "life"), but of "evil"—repression, desexualization, the deadened life, or the "modern" way of materialism, moderation, and morality as Yeats defines the "opponent" in "The Literary Movement in Ireland."

Because he feels that art—true, life-promoting art as the romantics define it, repository of religious sensibility, means to cultural unity—is embattled, Yeats creates his theme, the war of immortal upon mortal life, and makes God win. When the faery takes the child in *The Land of Heart's Desire,* when Cathleen Ni Houlihan as Ireland takes the bridegroom, Yeats is telling his audience that there is power or "life" on the immortal, "ideal" side. Some of them, at least, hear him and join the Easter Rising of 1916. Yeats knows what he is about in learning to use symbols and images that appeal to the deepest human desires. "The only two powers that trouble the deeps," he says in 1898, "are religion and love, the others make a little trouble upon the surface."[63] He will try to trouble those deeps—for art's sake, for Ireland's sake, for the sake of "traditional loveliness" and "ideal thought," all of which causes combine, as he comes to realize, in the cause of life itself, the struggle "to overcome the slow dying of men's hearts."[64] In his struggle he gains a powerful literary ally in Friedrich Nietzsche, a last romantic who thinks of himself at the same time as a first modern. Reading Nietzsche in 1902 provides Yeats with a stimulant whose effects are both immediate and permanent.

3.

"The Shock of New Material"

"Is not style," as Synge once said to me, "born out of the shock of new material?" —W. B. Yeats, *The Autobiography*

The Change in Yeats (1902–3)

Bibliographic evidence testifies, and critics agree, that the years from 1902 to 1909 were comparatively lean productively for Yeats. He wrote a few plays, a few lyrics, a batch of essays, some newspaper articles; but when the *Collected Works* began to appear in 1908, talk in literary circles in London and Dublin had it that Yeats was finished as a poet.[1] Richard Ellmann makes the case that these years were especially difficult for Yeats: "His *Autobiographies* end in 1902, and from that date until December, 1908, when he began a diary, we have no direct record of his thought or life. During almost six years, he wrote only one lyric, 'O Do Not Love Too Long.' In a man notoriously indiscreet about self-revelation . . . the silence about these years is significant. His fists were tightly clenched."[2] Yeats eventually reveals something of his thoughts about this era in his Diary of 1930, for he speaks of "the most creative years of my artistic life, when Synge was writing plays and Lady Gregory translated early Irish poetry with an impulse that interpreted my own" (*Ex,* p. 300). Synge's plays appeared from 1903 to 1907, and Lady Gregory's translations in 1902 and 1904. It is evident that this period of autobiographical lacuna is a most significant time in Yeats's development. He himself does not hesitate to use the superlative—"The most creative years of my artistic life" is positive enough—and probably enjoyed using it in connection with this maligned period of his life. He had been aware of the talk in literary circles in London and Dublin during these years, and was not above a bit of rubbing-in of its mistaken judgment.

But there is reason to think that his assessment is correct. When he made it, Yeats may have had in mind a similar assessment that he had made almost forty years earlier about a period of apparent unproductivity in the life of Blake. In the biographical chapter of the first volume of his and Edwin Ellis's edition of the works of Blake (1893), the authors offer this analysis of the twelve-year hiatus between Blake's writing the last of the *Poetic Sketches* and the printing of the first *Songs of Innocence:*

> He was thinking out his symbolic system, and considering how to make it the chief matter of his art. . . . His studies and meditations must have not only filled his working-time, but checked for a period the fluency of his compositions. He was going through a period of mental change. . . . Times of transition are seldom fruitful in creative impulse. Wonder, delight, perception of new beauty, take up all the mind. The will waits for direction, and the artistic harvest is prepared for another season. The reaper does not come until long after the sower has gone.[3]

However accurate these thoughts are as a description of the career of Blake, they show considerable foresight into that of Yeats who, ten years later, would himself live through a time of transition that "checked for a period the fluency of his compositions." The period may be understood as "the most creative," intellectually, of his artistic life, for during this time he was himself, as he had said of Blake, "thinking out his symbolic system, and considering how to make it the chief matter of his art."

Although there is no direct record of Yeats's thought during this time, there is plenty of indirect evidence to substantiate his claim of its importance. He himself first records an awareness of a change in his thought in a letter to Lady Gregory (January 15, 1903), when he says: "I was never so full of new thoughts for verse, though all thoughts quite unlike the old ones. My work has got far more masculine. It has more salt in it. I have several poems in my head" (*L,* p. 402). The Preface to the Dun Emer *In the Seven Woods,* written in the spring of 1903, tells of the development of *On Baile's Stand:* "The first shape of it came to me in a dream, but it changed much in the making, foreshadowing, it may be, a change that may bring a less dream-burdened will into my verses" (*VP,* pp. 814–15). In letters to George Russell and John Quinn written on May 14 and 15, 1903, about his just-published book of essays, *Ideas of Good and Evil,* Yeats says (to Russell): "The book is only one half of the orange for I only got a grip on the other half very lately" (*L,* p. 402); and (to Quinn): "I feel that much of it [the new book] is out of my present mood; that it is true, but no longer true for me. I have been in a great deal better health lately, and that and certain other things have made me look upon the world, I think, with somewhat more defiant eyes" (*L,* p. 403). Ellmann attributes the less dream-burdened will and the more defiant eyes solely to the effect upon Yeats of Maud Gonne's marriage in February 1903. Undoubtedly the unexpected collapse of his sustaining hope shocked Yeats thoroughly, but it is questionable whether this shock was sufficient to engender a new philosophical dispensation. In any case, the "change" did not occur suddenly in February 1903. The letter to Lady Gregory written in January, finding Yeats assured of "new thoughts for verse," proves that his transformation was already underway by the time of the marriage.

The marriage, however, was surely one of the "certain other things," as Yeats says vaguely in the letter to Quinn, responsible for his new outlook. Another thing, according to G. M. Harper, a student of Yeats's involvement with the Hermetic Society of the Golden Dawn, was his "disillusionment with the Golden Dawn."[4] Caused by internal power struggles in the organization and disagreement over its principles, this disillusionment preceded Maud Gonne's marriage by several months. Yeats had associated his esoteric studies with Maud, for they interested her, and union on an astral plane was better than no union at all.

Yet another thing disturbing Yeats at this time, according to Terry Eagleton, is his insecurity about his social class. Eagleton makes the case in *Criticism and Ideology* that Yeats was torn between his natural affinity with the Anglo-Irish Ascendancy and his acquired one with the Catholic nationalist movement "whose poetic mythologizer he attempted to become." This split meant that in fact he was "doubly dislocated," since his birthright placed him solidly among the Protestant bourgeoisie. Eagleton offers, as explanations for the famous "change" in Yeats, the following: "Yeats's consciousness of his social disinheritance is precisely what fuels the process of his poetic maturation, as his poetry turns in the early years of this century from narcotic fantasy to the stripped, toughened forms of a bitter yet defiant disillusion. *Fin de siècle* langour is transformed into combative oratory as the historical contradictions sharpen, forcing the progressively displaced Yeats into a compensatory ideology of aggressive poetic activities."[5] His attempts to establish aristocratic ancestry around 1906 suggest that his "consciousness of his social disinheritance" may have been a problem for Yeats especially as, after Maud Gonne's marriage, he broke with the nationalist movement. Social disequilibrium may have contributed some logs to the fire, but that it was "precisely" or exclusively what fueled the process of his poetic maturation is unlikely.

More amorphous than any specific historical event or social position, but nonetheless important as an influence on Yeats at this time, is his sense of history itself, of time and change steadily eroding the position of poetry, or art in general, relegating it to the periphery. "The arts have failed," he flatly states in 1901; "fewer people are interested in them every generation."[6] The new century had decidedly not brought the apocalypse anticipated by members of the Golden Dawn, but rather had intensified the sense of the march of "progress"—the mechanical and the prosaic. At the turn of the century, Yeats wrote much later, "everybody got down off his stilts."[7] This action was, from his point of view then and later, unfortunate. Getting down off stilts meant acquiescing in the march of progress, feet on the ground, sharing a worldview increasingly literal, material, and egalitarian.

Thus, coalescing for Yeats in the first two years of the 1900s were many forces: consciousness of decline of interest in the arts and of social displacement; disillusionment with the human agents of the Golden Dawn, if not with its superhuman purposes; disappointment in love—all would have been psychologically catalytic of change, but none would have been in itself intellectually substantive as a catalyst. These negative, disheartening forces in Yeats's life were offset by positive ones: growing friendships with Lady Gregory and John Synge in his objective, exterior world and increasingly passionate involvement with Nietzsche in his subjective, interior one. From the involvement with Nietzsche came Yeats's sense of excited discovery of which he writes Lady Gregory. The change in Yeats, as he records it in January 1903, is intellectual: he has "new thoughts." In an article on Yeats, Synge, and Nietzsche, Lorna Reynolds says that from the time of Yeats's first reading of Nietzsche, it seems to her "that the thinking of Nietzsche is entangled in most of Yeats's thinking."[8] It seems so to me, too.

Yeats's Introduction to Nietzsche

There has been a certain amount of biographical confusion about the time and circumstances of Yeats's first reading of Nietzsche, and about the appearance of Nietzschean influence in his work. The confusion originates with a misdated letter in Allan Wade's *The Letters of W. B. Yeats*. The letter, addressed to Lady Gregory, has been generally taken as the first hard evidence of a Yeats-Nietzsche connection. It begins: "Dear Friend, I have written to you little and badly of late I am afraid, for the truth is you have a rival in Nietzsche, that strong enchanter. I have read him so much that I have made my eyes bad again. They were getting well it had seemed. Nietzsche completes Blake and has the same roots—I have not read anything with so much excitement since I got to love Morris's stories which have the same curious astringent joy" (*L,* p. 379). Wade dated this letter "?Sept. 26, 1902," and his uncertainty about the date has proved to be well founded. From references in the same letter to other matters, David Thatcher argues that Yeats must have written it "between 27 December 1902, and 3 January, 1903."[9] The matter is of some importance because various critics have identified parts of Yeats's play *Where There Is Nothing,* written in August-September 1902, as "Nietzschean," assuming that Yeats's excited reading of Nietzsche coincided with the writing of the play.[10] But if Thatcher is right—and his case seems incontestable—the claim for influence cannot be made on the basis of the letter, because we know that the play was written before Yeats says he read Nietzsche. Yet there is a touch of Nietzsche in it; Ellmann in *The Identity of Yeats* speaks of its "rather Nietzschean hero"[11]—which is a vague enough designation, but in fact it is probably about as definite as it is possible to be, given the murky nature of the play's genesis.

Where There Is Nothing was meant to be the second collaboration of Yeats and George Moore (after *Diarmuid and Grania*); both claimed credit for the original idea, but according to J. B. Yeats, they'd both stolen it from George Russell.[12] This idea, which could well have been suggested by Russell, is essentially occult. Yeats took the play's title, and its antimaterialist theme, from his story in *The Secret Rose* called "Where There Is Nothing There Is God." Either Russell or Yeats himself could have invented a scenario in which the hero subscribes to the belief that, as Paul Ruttledge says in the play, "We must get rid of everything that is not measureless eternal life" (*VPl,* p. 1139). The idea of a hero who tries to attain the Kabbalistic goal literally, in the natural world, appealed to Yeats, as he put it in *Dramatis Personae,* as a "fantastic plot for a play" (*AU,* p. 274).

If the idea appealed to Yeats on account of its occult nature, it would have appealed to George Moore on account of its heroic heterodoxy. As we know, he admired Nietzsche, and he could well have seen Nietzschean possibilities in Yeats's scenario. As originally conceived, Paul's stance could be thought of as Nietzschean, by Moore or anyone, in its emphasis on destruction, since destruction of old values, for Nietzsche, necessarily accompanies creation of new ones. Moore and Yeats, from their opposite positions, were both enthusiastic about the projected play. As matters fell out, however, Moore could scarcely have contributed the Nietzschean element as it exists in the text, since he had nothing to do with writing it.

When Yeats quarreled with Moore over the presence of the Fays in the Irish National Theatre in the spring of 1902, he ended their collaboration on the play and told Moore that he intended to go ahead on his own.[13] He and Moore were still at loggerheads over the issue in August, when they met in Galway at a Gaelic *feis,* or fair. Also present at the *feis* was the American lawyer John Quinn, visiting Ireland for the first time and staying at Coole Park with Yeats. Quinn tried, unsuccessfully, to reconcile Yeats and Moore; when Moore returned to Dublin he telegraphed Yeats to say that he would get an injunction if Yeats used the scenario of the play "as he was writing a novel on the subject himself."[14] John Quinn was still present at Coole when the telegram arrived; he supported Yeats's rights to the material and, as his biographer informs us, agreed to see to the play's copyrighting in the United States.[15] Quinn's vigor and encouragement, added to Lady Gregory's, roused Yeats to action: he began the first draft of *Where There Is Nothing* while Quinn was still there and finished it in two weeks.

Quinn sailed back to New York on September 2. His biographer, B. L. Reid, tells us of his visit to Coole Park that, while there, "Quinn had talked much to Yeats of Nietzsche, and sent him now, in mid-September, his own copy of *Thus Spake Zarathustra* and copies of *The Case of Wagner* and *The Genealogy of Morals.*"[16] With the exception of *Thus Spake Zarathustra,* these copies are still in Yeats's library—cut, dog-eared, and marked in his hand.[17] Quinn explains the reason for the gift of *Thus Spake Zarathustra* in a letter to Yeats dated September 27 (evidence sufficient in itself to rule out Wade's tentative September 26 on Yeats's Nietzsche letter to Lady Gregory):

I mailed to you a week ago my copy of Nietzsche's *Thus Spake Zarathustra.* I don't know whether you are acquainted with Nietzsche's writings or not. While his so-called philosophy is utterly abhorrent to me—the philosophy of the "blond beast," of the exaltation of brutality, the philosophy that would make Bismarck and Chamberlain the greatest men of their time—nevertheless he has a wonderful epigrammatic style, and in recalling some of the dialogue of your play I was reminded of certain passages in *Zarathustra.* But since I sent the book to you I have received Lady Greogry's letter telling me the play is finished so that you probably will not want to bother with the book at all.

Another reason for my sending it was that I saw a copy of it in the French edition on Moore's library table when I called at his house. . . . *If* he is writing a novel on the subject, he may be reading *Zarathustra* with the plan of the novel in his mind. This is only a supposition on my part. The two things may have no connection. Now that your play is finished you will not of course care to waste time on Nietzsche's *rhetoric.*[18]

Quinn may have been under the influence of Nordau in his assessment of Nietzsche's "so-called philosophy," yet he knows *Zarathustra* well enough to have been "reminded" of it by some of the dialogue of Yeats's play, which supposes that he also knows Yeats's play, and knows it well enough to be alerted to the possibility of Moore's using *Zarathustra* in developing the same plot.

Quinn's books must have arrived in Ireland by October 9, for on that day Lady Gregory wrote Quinn that Yeats had arranged publication of the play with *The United Irishman* and that she was sending him "the M.S." so that he could organize the U.S. copyright. She concludes: "Is not the play splendid? I am glad Yeats had finished it before your Niedtsche [*sic*] (for which he is very grateful) came, for it is the more original."[19] Whatever else this comment implies, it indicates that Lady Gregory is herself familiar enough with Nietzsche to recognize a resemblance between his ideas and those of Yeats's play, and that she knows Quinn too will recognize it.

One begins to imagine the scene at Coole as the play is being written. Yeats's Dedication of *Where There Is Nothing* to Lady Gregory helps fill out the picture. Dated September 19, 1902, it reads: "I offer you a book which is in part your own. . . . My eyes were troubling me. . . . You said I might dictate to you, and we worked in the mornings at Coole, and I never did anything that went so easily and quickly, for when I hesitated, you had the right thought ready" (*VPl*, p. 1292).

The scene is further enlarged upon in an article by John Quinn, printed in *Outlook* in New York on December 16, 1911, entitled "Lady Gregory and the Abbey Theater." Quinn describes his meeting with Lady Gregory and Yeats at the Galway *feis* in August 1902, and his visit afterwards at Coole, where Douglas Hyde and Yeats were also staying. Of the composition of *Where There Is Nothing* he says cryptically: "Yeats and Lady Gregory made a scenario of a play and Hyde spent three afternoons 'putting the Irish on it.' "[20] (In a 1908 letter to A. H. Bullen, Yeats admits to Hyde's collaboration [L, p. 503]). Somewhat less cryptically, Quinn speaks of Yeats, illustrating his general impression of the poet's mind with a significant example: "His mind is one of the most subtle I have ever known. He delights in discussing art and philosophy, and will talk for hours and hours on politics, diplomacy, and international affairs. I remember how interested he became in a volume of Nietzsche that I had with me, and how in reading out from it he quickly pointed out the resemblance of some of Nietzsche's ideas to Blake."[21]

It looks as though Quinn's September 27 letter to Yeats, accompanying the volumes of Nietzsche, was a cover-up, designed to conceal Yeats's and Lady Gregory's adaptation of ideas from *Thus Spake Zarathustra*. Yeats had not read much Nietzsche when he wrote the play—a piece in *The Savoy* perhaps, a bit plagiarized by Moore in *Evelyn Innes*, a bit of Quinn's volume—yet its "Nietzschean element" exists, supplied through conversation with John Quinn and a look at his book. What is of most human interest in this tale of literary sources is not especially that John Quinn introduced some *Zarathustra* into *Where There Is Nothing,* but that he worried so much about it, to the point of needing to disguise his contribution; and further that the atmosphere at Coole during the writing of the play, for all the hours of subtle philosophizing, was fraught with ordinary one-upmanship against Moore.

"Team spirit" might more kindly describe the effort at Coole during that August fortnight. Yeats was a notoriously slow writer, a fact he frequently admitted himself. When he says, in "Adam's Curse," "A line will take us hours maybe," he is speaking the literal truth about his own manner of laborious composition. To write a five-act play in two weeks would be so exceptional as to seem miraculous. The near miracle is accounted for, I think, by the challenge provided by George Moore in the first place; then by the closing of ranks around Yeats—Lady Gregory's almost obsessive encouragement, Hyde's willingness to help with dialogue, John Quinn's charisma and support as an influential outsider; and finally by Nietzsche's "rhetoric," which on first impression, even in the execrable translation Yeats read out of, could have been dynamite.

Where There Is Nothing

More than most of Yeats's compositions, and in spite of revisions, *Where There Is Nothing* remains unsatisfying. Eclectic from the start, the speed with which it was written by various hands kept it from attaining the unity that Yeats usually managed to achieve. He recognized its weaknesses himself, and rather than reprint it in the *Collected Works,* he allowed Lady Gregory to rewrite it completely, in 1908, as *The Unicorn from the Stars.* His Notes to *The Unicorn* offer one of several accounts of his dissatisfaction with the earlier play: "I knew that my first version was hurried and oratorical . . . and I came to dislike a central character so arid and so dominating. We cannot sympathize with a man who sets his anger at once lightly and confidently to overthrow the order of the world" (*VPl,* p. 712). The reminiscence in this sentence of Davidson's description of Nietzsche as a man who set himself, smiling, to dislodge the old world from its orbit (see chapter 2), suggests an association of Yeats's hero with Nietzsche. Assuming that the association exists, Yeats's later "dislike" of his central character could indicate a disaffection from Nietzsche, as F. A. C. Wilson has suggested.[22] This is entirely possible, since Yeats vacillated between allegiances during these years. However, the central theme of *The Unicorn from the Stars,* if not the central character, is as "Nietzschean" as that of *Where There Is Nothing* in its espousal of ecstatic destruction and "the continual clashing of swords" (*VPl,* p. 703). The symbol of this warfare is the white unicorn, "a scourge from above," as Giorgio Melchiori says, "which will bring renewal, through ruin."[23] The unicorn returns, carrying the same emblematic burden, in Yeats's final version of *The Player Queen* in 1922.

In 1922, Yeats also returns briefly to *Where There Is Nothing;* in his Notes to *Plays in Verse and Prose,* he is still worrying at it, as at a problem not successfully solved; offering still another reason for his dislike of the play:

> [*Where There Is Nothing*] became hateful to me because, in desperation, I had caught up from a near table a pamphlet of Tolstoy's on The Sermon on the Mount, and made out of it a satirical scene that became the pivot of the play. The scene seemed amusing on the stage, but its crude speculative commonplaces filled me with shame and I withdrew the play from circulation. (*VPl,* p. 713)

If the second explanation blames the failure of the whole on its lump of unassimilated Tolstoy, the first, in effect, places the blame on its unassimilated Nietzsche. Both objections are valid and, taken together, indicate a central reason for the play's lack of coherence. The emphasis of the "Nietzschean" passages, which makes Paul a visionary and a poet, jars with that of the "Tolstoyan" ones, which makes him an Evangelical reformer. Yeats is right, I think, to single out the passages based on Tolstoy as discordant, for they destroy the single-mindedness of Paul's purpose, without which he, and the play with him, lose their force.

The first version of *Where There Is Nothing* was printed in Dublin and New York in October 1902; it contains only as much Nietzsche as Quinn's *Thus Spake Zarathustra,* which Yeats glanced through and compared to Blake, supplied during the two weeks of hurried composition at Coole. In my discussion of the play I shall quote from this earlier version, for the extensive revisions appearing in the 1903 text were made after Yeats really read *Zarathustra*.

Yeats must have conceived Paul Ruttledge as a descendant of Ibsen's Brand, the man who "seeks to rise into an absolute world where there is . . . only God," as Yeats puts it in his 1894 review.[24] Paul is an idealist, a neo-Platonist in his belief in the essence of God as pure spirit—literally, no-thingness. In the course of the play, Yeats sets him at war with all "things" of this world—first with social institutions, represented by his brother's middle-class marriage and family and by local government officials. Paul leaves home and joins some tinkers on the road, encouraging them in "excess." Then, because he grows ill, the tinkers leave Paul at a monastery, where he wars with the conventions of organized religion, makes some converts among the brothers, and preaches a sermon in which he symbolically extinguishes the lights of the Laws, the "towns," the Church, hope, memory, thought, the Sun, the Moon, and the World (*VPl,* pp. 1137–40). Finally, evicted from the monastery, he is killed by a mob.

Besides Brand, Paul has behind him as a model Blake's Jesus, the moral revolutionary. When, at the end of act 4, as he is being evicted from the monastery, Paul says, "Do as you like to me, but you cannot silence my thoughts. I learned them from Jesus Christ, who made a terrible joy, and sent it to overturn governments, and all settled order" (*VPl,* p. 1140n), he is echoing a passage from Blake's *Everlasting Gospel,* which Yeats and Ellis printed in a kind of variorum form with commentary in the second volume of their Blake edition:

> He scorned earth's parents, scorned earth's God
> And mocked the one and the other rod;
> His seventy disciples sent
> Against religion and government.

Yeats's plot also echoes Blake's:

> He left his father's trade to roam
> A wandering vagrant without home,
> And thus he others' labour stole
> That he might live above control.[25]

If Ibsen's Brand and Blake's Jesus were in Yeats's mind during the gestation of *Where There Is Nothing,* it is easy to see how a look at Zarathustra might have fired Yeats, adding impetus to the creation of his already antisocial nonconforming hero. There are great differences between Blake and Nietzsche, but it is not surprising that Yeats, on first looking into Nietzsche's *Zarathustra,* would seize on the great similarities, and would regard Nietzsche as a powerful ally on the side of life and joy—and, like Blake, "against religion and government" and all institutionalized forms of spiritual death. Instead of seventy disciples, Paul would send, against religion and government, a "wild beast of laughter." He tells Father Jerome in act 2: "I have taken to the roads because there is a wild beast I would overtake, . . . a very terrible wild beast, with iron teeth and brazen claws that can root up spires and towers. . . . My wild beast is Laughter, the mightiest of the enemies of God. I will outrun it and make it friendly" (*VPl,* pp. 1098–99). This particular means of revolution—laughter—is the most obvious, uniquely Nietszchean device in the play.

Almost wherever Yeats might have looked at Quinn's *Thus Spake Zarathustra,* he would have found references to laughter. Zarathustra insists on laughter as an antidote to the tradition of *lacrimae mundi,* as a means of spiritual revolution and psychological release. Thus, for example:

> And when I saw my devil, I found him earnest, thorough, deep, solemn: he was the spirit of gravity—through him all things fall. Not through wrath but through laughter one slayeth. (*Z,* p. 50)
>
> And be every truth called false with which no laughter was connected! (*Z,* p. 306)
>
> The laughter I have proclaimed holy. Ye higher men, *learn* how to laugh! (*Z,* p. 432)

He associates laughter with apocalypse; the superman will laugh: "No longer a shepherd, no longer a man—a changed one, one surrounded by light, who *laughed!* Never on earth hath a man laughed as *he* did. . . . My longing for that laughter gnaweth at me" (*Z,* p. 229). Lions are also apocalyptic, especially when they are laughing: "First of all the signs must appear unto me that it is *mine* hour—namely, the laughing lion with the flock of doves" (*Z,* p. 285). Paul's vision of

Laughter as a "brazen beast" is also apocalyptic, his imagery based on that of the Book of Revelation: "I think they have seen my wild beast, Laughter. They could tell me if he has a face smoky from the eternal fires, and wings of brass and claws of brass—claws of brass" (*VPl,* p. 1102).

This imagery held Yeats's imagination. In his Introduction to *The Resurrection* (1934), he recounts the "myths" that dominate his work, and asks: "Had I begun *On Baile's Strand* or not when I began to imagine, as always at my left side just out of the range of the sight, a brazen winged beast [Yeats's note at *beast:* "Afterwards described in my poem 'The Second Coming' "] that I associated with laughing, ecstatic destruction? Then I wrote, spurred by an external necessity, *Where There Is Nothing,* a crude play with some dramatic force" (*VPl,* pp. 932–33). His chronology is slightly skewed, for the brazen winged beast belongs to *Where There Is Nothing,* the revisions of which in early 1903 would have coincided with the writing of *On Baile's Strand.* Laughter, in association with ecstatic destruction, is what Paul Ruttledge has in mind.

Two other, related, Nietzscheanisms that found their way into *Where There Is Nothing* are the qualities of coldness and hardness. As laughter is antithetical to conventional Christian wisdom, so coldness and hardness are offered as antithetical virtues. Zarathustra preaches a mental rigor that he often describes in these terms:

> Every perception floweth cold. As cold as ice, are the innermost wells of the spirit,—a refreshment for hot hands and doers. (*Z,* p. 144)

> Thou goest the way of thy greatness. Hither no one shall steal after thee! Thy foot itself extinguished the path behind thee, and above it there standeth written: "Impossibility."
>
> And if thou now lackest all ladders, thou must know how to mount thine own head. . . .
>
> Thine own head, and past thine own heart! Now what is mildest in thee must become hardest. (*Z,* p. 218)

> All creators are hard. (*Z,* p. 122)

In Yeats's play, Paul attributes coldness and hardness to the wild beast of laughter: "Sabina, would you like to see a beast with eyes hard and cold and blue, like sapphires?" (*VPl,* p. 1102). And in a passage added in the revisions, Yeats produces a dialogue in which the repetition of the phrase "colder than ice and harder than diamonds" takes on ritual significance:

Paul: I am led by hands that are colder than ice and harder than diamonds. They will lead me where there will be hard thoughts of me in the hearts of all that love me, and there will be a fire in my heart that will make it as bare as the wilderness.

Aloysius: We will go with you. We too will take those hands that are colder than ice and harder than diamonds.

Patrick: Bring us to the hands that are colder than ice and harder than diamonds. (*VPl*, p. 1141)

Paul's ultimate goal is to "get rid of everything that is not measureless eternal life" (*VPl*, p. 1139). Speaking to Father Jerome in the first scene, he says: "It is not religion I want. I'm not even sure that I am a Christian. I don't love anything. I want to pull down all this—what do you call it—the building of the world—to put a crowbar under the gates and a grappling iron over the towers and uproot it all" (*VPl*, p. 1171n.). When Jerome sensibly replies, "I don't see that would do you any particular good," Paul answers: "Oh! yes, it would. When the stones are out of the way there will be more room to get drunk—not with wine, for that has never amused me, though it may suit other people—I want to get drunk with life, and I don't care whether it is good or bad so long as it is life" (*VPl*, p. 1071–72n). These two ideas, pulling down the building of the world and getting drunk with life, are Nietzschean, whatever else they may also be.

Zarathustra insists on the destruction of old values as the necessary preliminary to the creation of new ones:

> And he who must be a creator in good and evil—verily he must first be a destroyer, and break values into pieces.
>
> Thus the highest evil is part of the highest goodness. But that is creative goodness. . . .
>
> And whatever will break on our truths, let it break! Many a house hath yet to be built! (*Z*, p. 162)

As a refrain to passages in his long recapitulating chapter, "Old and New Tables," Nietzsche has Zarathustra chant: "Break up, break up, ye knowing, the old tables!" (*Z*, p. 291). The old tables in our culture, Zarathustra makes clear, are the ones created and preserved by the institutions of Judeo-Christian tradition, now not only outworn but positively harmful in this time of spiritual decadence and world-weariness. He would speed their downfall: "The All of to-day—it falleth, it decayeth. Who would keep it? But I—I *will* strike down it [*sic*] besides! . . . and him whom ye do not teach to fly, teach—how to *fall quicker!*" (*Z*, pp. 303–4).

In the second "Nietzschean" passage, on drunkenness, Paul endorses values Yeats has espoused elsewhere, principally in his *Savoy* articles on Blake: exuberance, excess, and passion or "life"—the fruit of the Tree of Life, as opposed to that of the Tree of Knowledge of Good and Evil. Zarathustra also praises drunkenness in several passages, culminating in the penultimate chapter of the book called "The Drunken Song." Drunkenness in Nietzsche is a metaphor—as it is explicitly for Paul: ("not with wine . . . I want to get drunk with life")—for unity with life's sources, primal energy; a related metaphor for the same thing is music. Music and drunkenness together help describe the "Dionysian" side of human nature as Nietzsche expounds it, first in *The Birth of Tragedy*. In "The Drunken Song" Zarathustra says, "What am I! A drunken sweet lyre" and finally makes explicit what the entire four parts of the book have adumbrated: that the meaning of life is joy, which also includes death and eternity:

> Thou vine-plant! Why praisest thou? Did I not cut thee? I am cruel, thou bleedest. What meaneth thy praise of my drunken cruelty?
>
> "Whatever hath become perfect, all that is ripe, wanteth to die!" thou sayest. Be the vine-knife blessed, blessed! But all that is unripe, wanteth to live! . . .
>
> Everything that suffereth wanteth to live in order to become ripe and gay and longing,—
>
> Longing for what is more distant, higher, brighter. "I want heirs," thus saith everything that suffereth, "I want children, I want *not myself*."
>
> But delight wanteth not heirs, not children. Delight wanteth itself, wanteth eternity, wanteth recurrence, wanteth everything to be eternally equal unto itself. (*Z*, pp. 471–72)

Death is one with perfection, perfection with joy, joy with life, life with death, in Nietzsche's circular conception of truth in this passage—a conception profoundly indebted to both Christian and romantic ideas.

Yeats shares these ideas and passes them on in the final scene of

Where There Is Nothing, in which Paul chooses martyrdom at the hands of a mob, saying: "Death is the last adventure, the first perfect joy, for at death the soul comes into possession of itself, and returns to the joy that made it" (*VPl,* p. 1160). As he disappears into the angry crowd, Paul says, "I go to the invisible heart of flame"; the penultimate words, as he is dying, are, "O plunge me into the wine barrel, the wine barrel of God"; and his last words are, "Coleman, Coleman, remember always where there is nothing there is God" (*VPl,* pp. 1162, 1164). Yeats here associates death, joy, flame, drunkenness, God, and "nothingness." His nothingness is hardly a vacuum. Like Schopenhauer's will, it is full of energy; like Nietzsche's (and Blake's) energy, it is positive; and like the goal of mystics, it is essential, absolute, and eternal. Heat or fire, drunkenness, song—mystics have traditionally used these concepts as symbols to describe their certain but ineffable experience of union with Godhead. When Zarathustra chooses drunkenness and song to convey his intuitions about time and eternity, he appeals to this ancient tradition in the service of his own end, the transvaluation of values from the other world to this one, from the absolute to the relative. Yeats himself has not made the transvaluation; he uses the symbols for their ancient purpose.

He conceived *Where There Is Nothing* as a tragedy. Paul, like Brand, refuses the piecemeal lot of bourgeois comfort and hypocrisy, remains whole-souled and so, according to Yeats's sense of tragic plot as enunciated in the *Brand* review, must be cast out by nature. For Paul, the road of Blakean excess is the only one; his commitment to an ideal, once taken, is absolute; and as he pushes restlessly along this road, nothing resists him. Yeats has not created a countertruth in this play; there is nothing on the material side, corresponding to the hearth and home of earlier plays, to cause Paul hesitation or regret. Like revolutionaries after him whom Yeats regards more critically, he has a heart with one purpose alone. He takes time out to castigate his neighbors in the Tolstoyan scene, and to learn to mend pans with the tinkers on the road, in the scenes Hyde put the Irish on, but these do not significantly hinder him from his quest of the wild beast of "laughing, ecstatic destruction." Paul's motivation in desiring the destruction of all things is unclear, which is a major flaw in a play having some pretensions to realism, as this one does. If *Where There Is*

Nothing is not a good play, however, it is an interesting play and of critical importance in the history of Yeats's development. As its main character is an extremist, so Yeats is himself at an extreme, the end of a phase, like one of his gyres about to reverse itself. Never before or after this play does Yeats commit himself so unequivocally to the "fabulous darkness," the spiritual, the surrender of the things of this world.

Yet the embodiment of Paul's quest as a wild beast of laughter proves that contradictions are present even at this extreme—or that perhaps the next phase has already begun. The laughter, Zarathustran, is meant to be the agent of destruction, as the wild beast will "root up spires and towers," symbols of church and state. In his speedy perusal of *Thus Spake Zarathustra,* Yeats took in the "destruction" half of Nietzsche's message only, and in some dim way he linked the creative joy he found there to Blake and both to his original occult plot. Had he thought about it, he would have seen that laughter is not an appropriate vehicle for the destruction of the material world; had he really read *Zarathustra,* he would have heard him say, "I conjure you, my brethren, *remain faithful to earth.* . . . Now the most terrible of things is to offend earth and rate the intestines of the inscrutable one higher than the significance of earth!" (*Z*, pp. 5–6). For Nietzsche, nothing could have been less meaningful than destruction without its counterpart, creation; the kind of joy he preaches in "The Drunken Song" is only possible when one embraces all of life's contradictions. Total affirmation of existence is his highest goal—whereas Yeats's, or rather Paul's, in *Where There Is Nothing,* is total negation. Yet because Yeats and Nietzsche both take extreme positions, the distance between them is finally not great. They meet in a state of mind that in 1902 Yeats calls death, and Nietzsche calls "delight," or joy. In 1932, however, when he writes "Vacillation," Yeats has absorbed the other half of Nietzsche's message:

> The body calls it death,
> The heart remorse.
> But if these be right
> What is joy?
>
> (*VP*, p. 500)

Yeats's Reading of Nietzsche (1902–3)

Soon after finishing the first draft of *Where There Is Nothing,* Yeats began to read Nietzsche. We know from Lady Gregory's letter to Quinn that his gift of books to Yeats had arrived by October 9, 1902. If Yeats read right through the three volumes Quinn sent him—Tille's translation of *Thus Spake Zarathustra;* Common's translation of *The Case of Wagner, Nietzsche contra Wagner, The Twilight of the Idols,* and *The Antichrist;* and Haussmann's and Gray's translation of *A Genealogy of Morals*—he encountered most of the major ideas of Nietzsche that were to be important to him. Both *The Case of Wagner* and *Nietzsche contra Wagner* contain, in a witty and caustic mode, an analysis of modern Europe's decadence; a case for "appearance" or the superficial; and a description of, and prescription for, self-overcoming. *The Twilight of the Idols* adds Nietzsche's longest argument for tragedy outside *The Birth of Tragedy,* and for art as an answer to the problem of decadence. *The Antichrist* analyzes the Judeo-Christian tradition as a two-thousand year period of decline (with a slight halt at the Renaissance) and asserts that a reversal of direction must occur.

Much would have appealed to Yeats in these works in 1902. When he found Nietzsche describing the "great lassitude" and depression induced by the draughts of pessimism in Schopenhauer and Wagner, and characteristic of the modern age in general, he might well have identified with it, and in the need to fight this depression, with Nietzsche's means. "For such a task," Nietzsche says in the Preface to *The Case of Wagner,* "I required some self-discipline:—I had to engage in combat *against* whatever was morbid in me, including Wagner, including Schopenhauer, including all modern 'humanity' " (*CW,* p. 2). In *Nietzsche contra Wagner,* he amplifies: "Lonely, henceforth, and sadly mistrustful of myself, I then, not without indignation, took sides *against* myself, and *for* everything which gave pain to, and was hard upon me; I thus found the way again to that brave pessimism which is the antithesis of all idealistic falsity, and also, it would appear to me, the way *to myself,*—to *my* task" (*CW,* p. 83). To find oneself through one's antithesis, of course, becomes an increasingly interesting idea to Yeats as a strategy in his work, and maybe in his life as well.

The tracts of *The Case of Wagner* volume are also full of statements, related to those on self-overcoming, that emphasize the importance of form or appearance in art and life. The Epilogue to *Nietzsche contra Wagner,* an essay that develops the idea of a cultural need for an antidote to the Wagnerian, or modern, disease of heaviness and loss of will, proposes the approach of antithesis or self-overcoming in the arts. The Epilogue as a whole must have been extraordinarily seminal for Yeats, struggling with his sense of art's isolation and possible atrophy, and convinced that realism or naturalism lacked the aesthetic power to "overcome the slow dying of men's hearts," as he puts it in "The Symbolism of Poetry" (*E&I,* p., 162). In this conviction he is reinforced by Nietzsche's Epilogue, which also suggests solutions to the problem of artistic representation in the modern world:

> No, if we convalescents still need an art, it is another art—an ironical, easy, fugitive, divinely untrammelled, divinely artificial art, which, like a pure flame, blazes forth in an unclouded heaven. Above all, an art for artists, *only for artists!* We afterwards understand better what is first of all necessary thereto: gaiety, *all* gaiety, my friends. . . . And as regards our future: we will scarcely be found again on the paths of those Egyptian youths who at night make the temples unsafe, embrace statues, and absolutely want to unveil, uncover, and put into clear light everything which for good reasons is kept concealed. No, this bad taste, this will to "truth at any price," this madness of youths in the love of truth, has become disagreeable to us. . . . We no longer believe that truth remains truth when the veil is pulled off it. (*CW,* pp. 91–92)

The notion of an "artificial art" is not new to Yeats in its substance, for he had advocated symbolism in poetry throughout the 1890s. In 1897, he had written to Fiona McLeod about symbolic representation in stage design: "My own theory of poetical or legendary drama is that it should have no realistic, or elaborate, but only a symbolic and decorative setting. A forest, for instance, should be represented by a forest pattern and not by a forest painting" (*L,* p. 280). The use of "veils" to *reveal* the truth, then, is an idea Yeats already subscribes to and will develop further. Other Nietzschean solutions to the problem of moral and aesthetic decadence—irony, ease, purity, confidence, gaiety, and exclusivity—are qualities Yeats will also recommend and develop in his own work.

Nietzsche's audacity in his treatment of art may have struck Yeats, since he himself at this time treats art as sacred, expressive of "the essence of things." It is one thing to talk about symbolic representation and another to talk about "artificial art." So put, the phrase is a redundancy (enjoyed by Nietzsche, and later by modernists, futurists, expressionists, and surrealists). Yeats was accustomed to audacity—after all, he had enjoyed Oscar Wilde's description of nature as artifice in *The Decay of Lying*. However, although Wilde reverses the conventional wisdom that nature is real and art an imitation of nature, his attitude to art remains devout. Nietzsche is more irreverent. If his irreverence shocked Yeats, the shock was presumably therapeutic. Instead of flinging the book across the room, Yeats read on, in the Epilogue to *Nietzsche contra Wagner;* there are his characteristic marginal strokes beside the following paragraph in his copy:

> Oh those Greeks! They knew how to live! For that end it is necessary to remain bravely at the surface, the fold, the skin, to worship appearance, to believe in forms, in tones, in words, in the whole *Olympus of appearance!* These Greeks were superficial—out of profundity. . . . And do we not just come back thereto, we adventurers of intellect, we who have climbed up the highest and most dangerous peaks of present thought and have looked around us therefrom? Are we not just therein—Greeks? Worshippers of forms, of tones, and of words? And just by virtue of that—artists? (*CW*, p. 93)

In *The Case of Wagner, Nietzsche contra Wagner,* and *The Twilight of the Idols,* despite his irreverent tone, Nietzsche gives art high importance. In a time of decadence—ebbing will to live, creeping nihilism, or plain boredom—we need stimulation. "Art," he says, "is the great stimulus of life" (*CW*, p. 186). This, one of the underlying ideas of these volumes, must have accorded with Yeats's hopes for the future of art as he expressed them in his turn-of-the-century essays. Also useful to Yeats is Nietzsche's stress on the connections between art and subjectivity, or aesthetics and psychology, and on the connection of both with history.

The Antichrist links psychology and history (as does, more radically, *A Genealogy of Morals*), arguing that human kind has lost touch with its bases of power, its instincts: "I call an animal, a species, an individual, depraved, when it loses its instincts, when it selects, when it *prefers,* what is injurious to it. . . . Life itself I regard as instinct for growth, for continuance, for accumulation of forces, for *power:* where the will to power is wanting, there is decline. My assertion is that this will is *lacking* in all the highest values of mankind,—that values of decline, *nihilistic* values, bear rule under the holiest names" (*CW,* p. 245). Nietzsche's condemnation of Christianity is an extravagant demolition job, but it is not offered without reason or without alternative. The alternative to faith in God and an afterlife is faith in (or "will to") humanity and its future generations on earth. He has said in *The Twilight of the Idols:* "What justifies man is his reality,—it will forever justify him. How much more worthy is actual man, compared with any merely wished, dreamt, or shamelessly falsified man! compared with any ideal man whatsoever" (*CW,* pp. 191–92). The problem is the creation, or willing, of the "right" kind of human, the kind who will ensure that the race will survive: "The problem which I here put is not what is to replace mankind in the chain of beings (man is an end), but what type of man we are to *cultivate,* we are to *will,* as the more valuable, the more worthy of life, the more certain of the future" (*CW,* p. 243). At a strategic moment of uncertainty and hesitation in his own life, and in a time of comparative historical innocence, Yeats must have found Nietzsche's confident prescriptions for the "more valuable" and "more worthy" types of humans heartening. They would have accorded, too, with his interest in Irish heroes—for Nietzsche prescribes heroism.

The Antichrist, like *Thus Spake Zarathustra,* insists on the spiritual qualities of coldness and hardness, especially coldness: "We are Hyperboreans . . . Beyond the north, beyond ice, beyond death—*our* life, *our* happiness. . . . Better to live in the ice than among modern virtues and other south winds. . . . We were brave enough, we spared neither ourselves nor others" (*CW,* p. 241). The cold acts as stimulant and bracer, and Nietzsche links it with the unmodern and heroic virtue so much needed by modern humanity, courage; and with the unmodern and heroic social organization, aristocracy: "By the order of castes, the *order of rank,* the supreme law of life itself is formulated . . . .—The *inequality* of rights is the very condition of there being rights at all.—A right is a privilege. Let us not undervalue the privilege of the mediocre. Life always becomes harder towards the *summit.*—The cold increases, responsibility increases. A high civilization is a pyramid" (*CW,* p. 341). Though it is impossible, and maybe undesirable, to escape the conventional connotation of the word *cold* as "unfeeling," for Nietzsche it is an attribute not so much of peoples' affectional natures as of their moral ones. For him it contains a whole web of positive associations. Nietzsche does not oppose all feelings—on the contrary; only those he feels are lukewarm, sentimental, pitying because self-pitying, defeatist. In 1902, writing to Lady Gregory of his "enchantment" with Nietzsche, Yeats also calls him "astringent" (*L,* p. 379).

Warfare is a constant metaphor in these books. The term *countermovement* occurs often; the "on the one hand . . . on the other hand" construction is used constantly. *A Genealogy of Morals* develops the concept of self-overcoming through appeal to one's opposite by internalizing the conflict, setting self against soul or conscience. The opening words of the Preface are: "We are strangers to ourselves, we perceivers,—we ourselves to ourselves" (*GM,* p. 1), and continues its exploration of the origins of morality by equating the development of self-consciousness with that of guilt (or original sin). Internal warfare then gives rise, as this pre-Freudian hypothesizes, to creativity of all sorts—to civilization. Nietzsche sets at war in this book not only instinct and conscience, but also knowledge and power, and the "master" virtues of the Classical world against "slave" virtues associated with the Christian. The battle occurs both subjectively, within the individual (as instinct vs. conscience) and objectively or historically (as era vs. era). Warfare will become a central metaphor for Yeats also, and along Nietzsche's lines.

Thus Spake Zarathustra is the work Yeats always quotes when he refers to Nietzsche explicitly. It contains in symbolic and dramatic form what the other works contain more discursively, themes and images that Yeats returns to, elaborates, or comes to regard as important: loftiness, courage, "tragic joy," laughter, flux, conflict of opposites (war, maternity), masks, the dance, a hunchback, a fool, an ass. Blake provides the groundwork in Yeats's theoretic and poetic love of opposition and the certainty that somewhere contraries are equally true; *Zarathustra* builds on that groundwork, asserting that the power or energy of opposition creates all things. The governing artistic device of the book is oxymoron: burning ice, weeping laughter, tragic joy, silent speech, abyss of light, beautiful terribleness (but not "terrible beauty"), and life, whose "coldness enflameth," whose "hatred seduceth" (*Z,* p. 328). Contraries linked in paradox form truth for Zarathustra, and that truth is, at bottom, moral. "Ye shall seek your own enemy, ye shall wage your own war, and for your own thoughts," he counsels; "let your work be a fight, your peace a victory!" (*Z,* pp. 59–60). In a world in which God is dead, as Zarathustra proclaims on page one, man, now free, has the chance to make what he will of himself. As prophet of the superman ("beyond-man," in Yeats's translation), Nietzsche is simply asking humans to try ("will") to be perfect in asking them to "surpass" themselves. In this demand he resembles the God whose death he proclaims in announcing the end of the Christian era, an irony that Nietzsche enjoys. "This Zarathustra," the wizard says, "he himself seemeth often unto me to be like a beautiful mask of a saint" (*Z,* p. 434). His articles of perfection differ from Christ's: Zarathustra asks for strength, pride, hardness, laughter, and in this respect is the saint's anti-self, in Yeats's sense, which *Thus Spake Zarathustra* surely did much to develop.

Zarathustra fractures consciousness: "The creative self created for itself valuing and despising, it created for itself lust and woe. The creative body created for itself the spirit to be the hand of its will" (*Z,* p. 40). Nietzsche is using terms that sound like Yeats's four faculties, and his urge to analyze, like Yeats's, arises from its opposite, the will to synthesize. His choice of oxymoron is appropriate, for oxymoron is dialectical; it insists on synthesis from analysis. In a prophetic passage, Zarathustra makes this implicit aim of the book explicit: "I walk among men as among the fragments of the future, of that future which I see. And all my thought and striving is to compose and gather into one thing what is a fragment and a riddle and a dismal accident" (*Z,* p. 199). In this aspiration Nietzsche is a child of romanticism—as is Yeats, for whom Unity of Being is the summit of possibility (*V,* p. 88).

Nietzsche's aspiration toward unity produces his theory about time. Two roads, Zarathustra explains, or preaches (for his form is parable), stretch forward and backward into eternity:

> They contradict each other, these roads; they knock each other directly on the head. And here, at this gateway, they meet. The name of the gateway standeth written above: "Moment." . . .
> And are not thus all things knotted fast together that this moment draweth behind it all future things? *Consequently*—draweth itself, as well?

For what *can* run of things—in that long lane *out there,* it *must* run once more! (*Z,* pp. 225–26)

The present includes all past and all future, which are joined at the gateway of becoming, the present moment. Here the bias toward wholeness, or continuity, romantic as it may be, nevertheless predicts (appropriately enough) or points toward "modern" speculations about time—toward Bergson's hypothesis about *durée* and twentieth-century physicists' excursions into the space-time continuum. When he first reads this passage, Yeats's concept of time is Blakean; he has come to think, with Blake, that six thousand years may be encompassed in one pulsation of a poet's artery.[26] Later, as he charts his own system, he will try to follow Nietzsche into the paradox of the Eternal Return, which demolishes sequential or linear time altogether.

Of all the ideas Yeats encounters in his initial reading of Nietzsche, probably the most significant is Nietzsche's complete acceptance and affirmation of human and natural life as what there is. The conflict of opposites, on aesthetic, moral, and even historical levels, is not a strange or foreign idea to Yeats. His basic poles of opposition, however, have hitherto posited God (the "immortal" or "universal") at one extreme and man ("mortal," "personal") at the other. Now, reading Nietzsche, he finds that the supernatural is gone. He hears Zarathustra say, in the persona of a past "creator":

Brethren, that God whom I created was man's work and man's madness, like all Gods!

Man he was, and but a poor piece of man and the I. From mine own ashes and flame it came unto me, that ghost, yea verily! It did not come unto me from beyond! (*Z,* pp. 33–34)

To "despisers of the body," Zarathustra says:

"Body I am and soul"—thus the child speaketh. And why should one not speak like children?

But he who is awake and knoweth saith: body am I throughout, and nothing besides; and soul is merely a word for something in body.

Body is one great reason, a plurality with one sense, a war and a peace. . . .

There is more reason in thy body than in thy best wisdom. (*Z,* pp. 38–39)

The supernatural, the "quietude of wisdom," contemplation, trance, "the essence of things"—these have dominated Yeats's intellect and imagination in the decade before he reads Nietzsche. He has preserved his body chaste for "the most beautiful woman in the world," Maud Gonne, until well into adulthood. Now, rather than being repelled by Nietzsche's antithetical perspective, he is "enchanted"—partly, no doubt, because much of what he finds in Nietzsche is familiar. "Nietzsche completes Blake and has the same roots," he says, grasping at the known in defense against the shock of new material.

Even as he reads, the assault of the new continues in his human world. In October 1902, after Quinn's books have arrived, he meets James Joyce. In his biography of Joyce, Richard Ellmann says that this meeting "has a symbolic significance in modern literature,"[27] taking his cue from Yeats, who says at the end of the essay he wrote but never published describing the meeting, "The younger generation is knocking at my door as well as theirs."[28] The accounts of the meeting that have been handed down by Joyce, Yeats, Stanislaus Joyce, and George Russell all describe the event as a generational, even Oedipal, contest. But Yeats takes the advent of the next literary generation well, in his essay, treating both himself and Joyce with good-humored irony, perhaps because he is confident that in fact he is far from the state he has Joyce attribute to him, of "the cooling of the iron; of the fading out of inspiration."[29] He is, on the contrary— and if he senses himself to be so it accounts for his equanimity—on the very brink of renewal and self-remaking, about to become modernist in ways Joyce might have appreciated. The appearance of an idea Yeats purportedly used in conversation with Joyce at this meeting, which recurs in the letter to Lady Gregory about reading Nietzsche, suggests that there exists an associative link in Yeats's mind between the two events. According to Stanislaus Joyce, Yeats compared Joyce's "joyous vitality" to that of William Morris.[30] In the letter to Lady Gregory, Yeats says of Nietzsche: "I have not read anything with so much excitement since I got to love Morris's stories which have the same curious astringent joy" (*L*, p. 379). It seems to me that Morris is somewhat of a red herring, and that the most likely connection for Yeats is that between Nietzsche and Joyce—both irreverent, both iconoclasts, both self-appointed prophets of a new day simultaneously assaulting the ascendancy of occultism and the metaphysical on Yeats's philosophical horizon.

"Adam's Curse"

The effect of the assault by Nietzsche appears sporadically in Yeats's work, more often in his prose and plays than in his poetry, during the next decade. It does appear, however, in the poem "Adam's Curse," written in October-November 1902 (*The Monthy Review* had sent a proof sheet of the poem to Yeats by November 20).[31] Many critics have called "Adam's Curse" remarkable among Yeats's poems. Richard Ellmann sees in the poem a "new development," indicating a change of style in the direction of "verisimilitude" and maturity. On the other hand, Harold Bloom announces as "myth" the chronological interpretation that divides Yeats "the twilight crooner" from Yeats "the modern poet" at "Adam's Curse." He believes, though, that in "Adam's Curse," a "dialectical process" produced "one of the undoubted poems of the language."[32]

I agree with Ellmann that "Adam's Curse" is pivotal, and with Bloom that it is part—as what is not?—of a dialectical process. Yeats is himself at the vortex of the tensions he sets "at war" in the poem, and out of the vortex he voices a prophecy. Intuition precedes reason, practice precedes theory; in good Shelleyan fashion, Yeats in "Adam's Curse" is a mirror of the shadows that futurity casts upon the present. The intuition that Yeats produces in this poem involves the concept he is to name "the mask," or the dialectical relationships between art and nature and between objectivity and subjectivity, as they interact in the individual subject, in society, and in history.

The background of the poem is well known: Yeats, still in love with Maud Gonne, has come to understand that his love is hopeless. He meets her at the house of her sister ("that beautiful mild woman" of the poem) in Dublin, and the two women and Yeats live the scene that Yeats later dramatizes as "Adam's Curse." It is an ambitious and daring poem, and I do not believe Yeats could have written it when he did without having begun his reading of Nietzsche. Intuition tells me that he was reading through the volume containing the four short works (*The Case of Wagner* volume) and that he had read into *The Twilight of the Idols* when "Adam's Curse" seized him. Nietzsche's subject is the connection between art, decadence, and the individual will, and his dialectical method embodies his theory; much of Yeats's poem deals with the same ideas, in the same way.

Nietzsche's emphasis on self-overcoming through the means of a powerful, heroic, creative will, may have given Yeats, despondent about his love, the impetus to try to overcome his feelings of despair about Maud Gonne by recreating them as art, but as art closer to nature or "real life" than he had ever dared before. He is taking sides against himself, as Nietzsche recommends, in speaking of the world of commerce, limitation, and despair when, as the title indicates, the ideal paradisiacal world still attracts him. In presenting the fallen world with the implied other behind it, he sets up one of the poem's major oppositions. The principal opposition, however, the one on which the poem turns from line to line, is the ironic one of shifting perspectives. In *Nietzsche contra Wagner,* Nietzsche stresses the importance of "the whole *Olympus of appearance*" in reaching the profound. Yeats's poem begins:

> We sat together at one summer's end,
> That beautiful mild woman, your close friend,
> And you and I, and talked of poetry.
>
> (*VP,* p. 204)

By recasting his experience as a scene from a play, or a fiction, Yeats objectifies it—or brings it, to use Nietzsche's term, to the surface. In *The Case of Wagner,* Nietzsche describes the sorts of masks people will adopt to hide their own pain and so to overcome themselves: "There are scientific minds which make use of science, because it gives a gay appearance and because the scientific spirit suggests that a person is superficial . . . There are free, insolent minds which would fain conceal and deny that at the bottom they are disjointed, incurable souls. . . . Folly itself may be the mask for an unhappy *over-assured* knowledge" (*CW,* p. 88). In "Adam's Curse," Yeats becomes a player, wearing the mask of a poet. This self-dramatization bifurcates him—one part is the "disjointed, incurable soul" Nietzsche talks about; the other the practicing poet, expounding his trade, putting on, as Nietzsche recommends, "a gay appearance." Having stepped into the role of poet, Yeats is free from the self-consciousness that makes him hide his face in remote symbols of stars and roses in the earlier poetry. Once disguised or distanced from himself, he can *be* himself; paradoxically, because the situation described in the poem is "artificial," the poem can proceed to real discovery and self-disclosure.

The first discovery is about the work of the poet, which is more laborious than that of the stonebreaker, though it must "seem a moment's thought":

> I said: "A line will take us hours maybe;
> Yet if it does not seem a moment's thought
> Our stitching and unstitching has been nought.
> Better go down upon your marrow bones
> And scrub a kitchen pavement, or break stones
> Like an old pauper, in all kinds of weather;
> For to articulate sweet sounds together
> Is to work harder than all these, and yet
> Be thought an idler by the noisy set
> Of bankers, schoolmasters, and clergymen
> The martyrs call the world.

In *The Case of Wagner,* Nietzsche advocates a principle of aesthetics based on the appearance of ease: " 'What is good is easy; everything divine runs with light feet'—the first proposition of my Aesthetics" (*CW,* p. 6). Yeats is later to encounter with delight Castiglione's concept of *sprezzatura,* which Nietzsche echoes in this proposition, and Yeats reechoes in "Adam's Curse."[33] Yeats establishes an opposition between the work of the pauper and that of the poet, his diction working to define the contrast ("break stones" sounds strong and deep; "articulate sweet sounds," shallow and superficial); yet appearance, Yeats says, masks the reality of effort in the case of the poet's labor. Effort and self-discipline; in *The Case of Wagner,* Nietzsche prescribes these, too, as ways out of depression: "I require some self-discipline:—I had to engage in combat *against* whatever was morbid in me . . . including all modern 'humanity' " (*CW,* p. 2).

In "Adam's Curse," Yeats engages in combat with "modern humanity": bankers, schoolmasters, and clergymen represent hard reality, and it is "self-discipline" for Yeats to put them into a poem. Once in, however, they form the pole of another opposition: modern humanity or "the noisy set" against "the martyrs," who have renounced "the world." Yeats is experimenting with perspectives, which places him in a new position, a middle position between contraries, holding the balance of power. The power generated by his control of his antitheses moves him forward to the next section of the poem. (I quote the lines as Yeats wrote them in 1902; they are the only ones in the poem he revised, and not until 1921):

> That woman then
> Murmured with her young voice, for whose mild sake
> There's many a one shall find out all heartache
> In finding that it's young and mild and low:
> "There is one thing that all we women know,
> Although we never heard of it at school,
> That we must labour to be beautiful."

A passage in *The Twilight of the Idols* in a chapter checked by Yeats in the Contents repeats Nietzsche's emphasis on form and adds a thought about the provenance of beauty. It is my guess that Yeats read through this passage and then wrote "Adam's Curse":

> *Beauty no accident.* —Even the beauty of a race or family, the pleasantness and kindness of their whole demeanour, is acquired by effort; like genius, it is the final result of the accumulated labour of generations. . . . What labour and effort in the service of beauty had the Athenian males required of themselves for centuries! . . . It is decisive for the future of a people and of humanity, that civilization begin at the *right place—not* at "soul." . . . The right place is body, demeanour, regimen, physiology; the rest follows therefrom. (*CW*, pp. 215–17)

If Kathleen Gonne in fact said, in conversation with Yeats, that it was hard work being beautiful,[34] then Nietzsche's thought would have reinforced hers. Yeats theorizes about "the heroic discipline of the looking-glass" in *Discoveries*, 1906 (*E&I*, p. 270), but the beautiful mild woman in "Adam's Curse" knows about it in 1902: *beauty no accident*, she says.

The poet continues the dialogue, linking male and female by demonstrating that, since poet (male) and woman labor separately in the service of beauty, they may labor together in the service of love:

> I said: "It's certain that there is no fine thing
> Since Adam's fall but needs much labouring.
> There have been lovers who thought love should be
> So much compounded of high courtesy
> That they would sigh and quote with learned looks

> Precedents out of beautiful old books;
> Yet now it seems an idle trade enough."

The pull of opposites exists here, on one level, between past and present, with the balance swinging to the medieval past, when courtly lovers studied the art of love. For these lovers, Yeats says, the ideal of high courtesy demanded the practice of formal patterns of behavior, whose precedents out of beautiful old books the lovers had to strive (labor) to emulate. If, for Yeats, courtly love is compounded of high courtesy, it is all the finer for the fact that high courtesy is itself a compound that yokes Apollonian form (the rules or precedents, quoted with learned looks) and Dionysian energy (the lovers' sighs of passion). High courtesy is a fine thing—a form of beauty energized and sexualized because it has been created through the union of opposites.

The opposite of courtly love is the modern world of the noisy set, which Yeats evokes in the last line of the stanza by repeating its word for the poet's trade: *idle*. Perspectives shift again. "It," courtly love, *seems* from the modern world's point of view an "idle trade," like the poet's. *Seems* is, of course, a key word in this line as in the poem. Poems must "seem a moment's thought," poets seem idlers, bankers seem the noisy set, women seem naturally beautiful, high courtesy seems an idle trade. So much consideration of seeming gives it validity. In *The Twilight of the Idols,* Nietzsche says, "Heraclitus will always be right in this that being is an empty fiction. The 'seeming world' is the only one; the 'true world' has been *deceitfully invented* merely" (*CW,* p. 118). Yeats does not accept at this point that reality is perspectival, subjective, and constructed, although he begins, in this Janus-faced poem, to show an interest in Nietzsche's view of the seeming world. However, the polarity between the fallen world and its implied opposite—Yeats's mortal-immortal opposition—controls the final two stanzas of the poem.

"Since Adam's fall" the human condition has required labor; the ideal of the courtly lovers and of the poet supposes a paradise where everyone's trade would be idle enough. But the human condition commits man and woman to conflict and labor—the delving in the earth, the bringing forth of children in pain. The latter kind of labor connects the human condition and time, connects especially woman and the changing of the moon, and it is to the human circumscription by time, such a predominant theme in his earlier poems, that Yeats now turns in "Adam's Curse":

> We sat grown quiet at the name of love;
> We saw the last embers of daylight die,
> And in the trembling blue-green of the sky
> A moon, worn as if it had been a shell
> Washed by time's waters as they rose and fell
> About the stars and broke in days and years.

Except for the first line, which is dramatic, this stanza looks backward to the symbolic remoteness of the earlier poetry. It is perfect of its kind—truly the articulation of sweet sounds. The stanza is effective partly because its formal elegance, which makes it seem easy, is set in contrast with the world of labor whose diction—"poetry," "stitching and unstitching," "kitchen pavement," "bankers, schoolmasters, and clergymen"—makes it seem difficult, intractible.

Yeats used the word *seem* one more time in the poem. The natural, fallen world (Nietzsche's "seeming world"), with its cycles of time, defeats the will of the poet laboring to enter an ideal world with his beloved, and he admits defeat. The last *seem* occurs in the penultimate line:

> I had a thought for no one's but your ears:
> That you were beautiful, and that I strove
> To love you in the old high way of love;
> That it had all seemed happy, and yet we'd grown
> As weary-hearted as that hollow moon.

The words "it had all seemed happy" refer both to earlier times in the characters' lives, and to the earlier part of the poem. In its investigation of appearance and its experimentation with perspective, the earlier part of the poem had remained "bravely at the surface," as Nietzsche recommends (*CW,* p. 93); it had seemed happy because it had been happy. The dramatization of himself, his personal situation, and his art had given Yeats the energy and courage to forget his own pain, or to change it temporarily for the joy of remaking the experience of one summer's end. "I had to engage in combat against whatever was morbid in me," says Nietzsche in *The Case of Wagner.* In "Adam's Curse," Yeats creates his own antithetical self, another poet from the dreamy, mystical, lonely, weary-hearted poet who has dominated his life and verse until now. The anti-self in "Adam's Curse" is gregarious and, within limits, powerful. This second poet will reappear in Yeats's work from this point on, under various names: the day (as opposed to the night); the self (as opposed to the soul); *Hic* (as opposed to *Ille*); *anima hominis* (as opposed to *anima mundi*). Yeats's anti-self is never called Nietzsche, but that is his real name.

4.

The Mask in the Making

What does it mean when an artist turns into his antithesis?
—Nietzsche, *A Genealogy of Morals*

When Yeats first reads Nietzsche, he finds Nietzsche's ideas exciting, and his excitement stimulates his thoughts, "quickens" him, and generates the beginnings of his theory of the mask. As Richard Ellmann says in *Yeats: The Man and the Masks:* "The doctrine of the mask is so complex and so central in Yeats that we can hardly attend to it too closely."[1] Rather than produce generalizations about the mask theory at this point, I am going to trace its development as it becomes increasingly central to Yeats's thought. During the same years that ideas about the mask begin to coalesce for Yeats, his ideas about the nature of tragedy also change and mature. This chapter will consider the developing mask theory; the next, its relation to Yeats's concept of tragedy. The relationship is crucial to an understanding of the synthesis of mask and tragedy that informs *A Vision* and the later poems and plays. The interconnected concepts of mask and tragedy are also, for Yeats, connected to ideas and events in the world around him. This historical influence subtly moves the direction of Yeats's philosophy and, with the passing of time, makes the ideas of Nietzsche more, rather than less, important to his thought.

Nietzsche in England, 1903

In 1903, Nietzsche's ideas gained wider circulation in England. Early in the year, the publication in translation of his *The*

Dawn of Day gave occasion for Arthur Symons, its reviewer in *The Athenaeum* (March 7, 1903), to scold the British public for its conservatism, its indifference to intellectual innovators like Nietzsche who had taken Europe by storm, and its willingness to accept condensations like Ellis's *Savoy* series without clamoring for the thing itself. In a statement that refuses to isolate philosophical currents from (literally) technological ones, Symons says: "Nietzsche, for good or evil, has spoken to his end of the century with a formidable voice. He may be fought, he cannot be disregarded. To disregard him is like disregarding the motorcar because you prefer your carriage and pair. He is a new force, like electricity in its modern development."[2] Symons's analogy between the new force of electricity and that of Nietzsche's formidable voice suggests that both kinds of power possess a charge discernible in 1903, and a potential energy whose effects are unknown. The analogy is apt; Nietzsche's power, like electricity's, has been and may yet be used for good or evil. Symons's very choice of words and construction—"for good or evil"—indicates how little he has absorbed Nietzsche's message, how fixed in conventional patterns of language and culture he is. This is important, for Symons was a fairly avant-garde representative of his time, willing to accept, if not to celebrate, the appearance of new forces like motorcars, electricity, and Nietzsche.

Yeats read *The Dawn of Day* in 1903 without needing Symons's bidding. There is a copy of the 1903 translation in his library today, inscribed "W. B. Yeats from A.G." "A.G." is of course Augusta Gregory, who must have hoped to keep Yeats's recently kindled interest in Nietzsche alive through the gift of this latest edition. *The Dawn* would have underscored for Yeats ideas he had met in the books of Nietzsche's he already knew. In *The Dawn,* written in 1883, before *Zarathustra* and the other books owned by Yeats, Nietzsche is working out his concept of "antithetical optics"—the presence of opposition in all things, even in values. Periodicity, he finds, underlies the notions of "good" and "evil," making these moral values both impure and relative. For example: "The moral fashions reverse themselves. . . . [Egoists'] selfishness differs from that of the compassionate; but to call them, in the highest sense, evil, and the compassionate ones good, is nothing but a moral fashion, which is having its run, and a long run too" (*Dawn,* 135). The idea of "moral fashions" reversing themselves will become part of Yeats's concept of history, which he will extend to include not only morals but "all things," as he puts it in "The Gyres":

> . . . and all things run
> On that unfashionable gyre again.
>
> (*VP*, p. 565)

Nietzsche also makes connections between ancient Greece and modern Europe in *The Dawn*. The characteristic wit of his antitheses in the following sentences helps account for Yeats's "enchantment" with his work: "The Greeks, in a life which was surrounded by great dangers and upheavals, sought a feeling of safety and last refuge in meditation and knowledge. We, in a state of unparalleled safety, have introduced insecurity into meditation and knowledge, and seek ease in the struggles of life" (*Dawn*, p. 158). He also equates the ability to face the consequences of ethical relativity with characteristics of strength, courage, and "manliness": "Our weak, unmanly social conceptions of good and evil, and their enormous ascendancy over body and mind, have at last weakened all bodies and minds and crushed all self-reliant, independent, unprejudiced people, the pillars of a strong civilisation. . . . Thus let paradox fight against paradox! It is impossible for truth to be on both sides: is it really on either side? Examine for yourselves" (*Dawn*, p. 161). Though Nietzsche's "antithetical optics" make it impossible for him to call the strong and manly "the true," they do not prevent him from valuing these qualities. For him, but even more for followers like D. H. Lawrence, courage and strength indicate, and rely on, virility. Yeats too, during these "most creative" of his artistic years, comes to emphasize the masculine as a moral and aesthetic virtue.

While some people, including Yeats, were reading *The Dawn of Day* in 1903, others (no doubt many of the same) were being introduced to Nietzsche's concept of the Übermensch in G. B. Shaw's publication of *Man and Superman*. Shaw gives explicit credit to Nietzsche in the play's Dedicatory Epistle, in its "Don Juan in Hell" scene, and in "The Revolutionist's Handbook," which he appends to the play proper and in which he mentions the "vogue" for Nietzsche. He also asserts that Nietzsche's ideas are not new, that they clothe old moral vigor (of which he approves) with new names (of which he also approves). "The despair of institutions," he says, "and the inexorable 'ye must be born again,' with Mrs. Poyser's stipulation, 'and born different,' recurs in every generation. The cry for the Superman did not begin with Nietzsche, nor will it end with his vogue." Shaw's purpose is more Darwinian than Nietzschean, however, and reflects the new century's growing interest in eugenics. The cry for the Superman will not be forlorn, Shaw says, in "The Revolutionist's Handbook," if we work for "the socialization of the selective breeding of Man; in other terms, of humane evolution. We must eliminate the Yahoo, or his vote will wreck the commonwealth."[3] Though this interpretation of Nietzsche seems far from Yeats's more aesthetic interests of 1903, it is "in vogue," and its vogue had some effect on Yeats. He too will take up the cry for the Superman, in his admiration and depiction of heroic men and women, in his bidding God to fill the cradles right, and—in Shaw's sense—in his explicit references to eugenics in *On the Boiler* (1939).

Closer to Yeats's immediate interests of the time come two other cases of Nietzschean promulgation in England. Arthur Symons, again, wrote an article on "Nietzsche and Tragedy" that appeared in *The Academy* in August 1902, and was reprinted in his 1903 collection of essays, *Plays, Acting, and Music.* The Nietzsche essay gives an account of the main scheme of *The Birth of Tragedy* (which appeared in French translation in 1901 but was still untranslated in English). Symons's opening sentence expresses an idea Yeats is later to express himself: "I have been reading Nietzsche on the Origin of Tragedy with the delight of one who discovers a new world, which he has already seen in a dream." Symons then defines the two chief concepts of the book: "Art arises, [Nietzsche] tells us, from the conflict of the two creative spirits, symbolized by the Greeks in the two gods, Apollo and Dionysus; and he names the one, the Apollonian spirit, which we see in plastic art, and the other the Dionysiac spirit, which we see in music. Apollo is the god of dreams, Dionysus the god of intoxication."[4] Yeats could have encountered these concepts Apollonian and Dionysiac in Nietzsche's own recapitulation in *The Twilight of the Idols,* along with his idea, quoted by Symons, that " 'the object of the tragic myth is precisely to convince us that even the horrible and the monstrous are no more than an aesthetic game played with itself by the Will in the eternal plenitude of its joy.' " The prodigal will is, by another name, an artist-god: "To Nietzsche the world and existence justify themselves only as an aesthetic phenomenon, the work of a god wholly the artist."[5] The idea of the artist-god and of the justification of life as an aesthetic phenomenon, deriving from Flaubert and Gautier, lay hold on artists' imaginations, forcing an attitude of objectivity toward their work antithetical to that of romantic lyricism. James Joyce's Stephen Dedalus in *A Portrait of the Artist as a Young Man* offers the definitive explanation of the relation of the artist to "the dramatic form" that, based on a passage of Flaubert, describes the stance of the artist-god: "The artist, like the God of creation, remains within or behind or beyond or above his handiwork, invisible, refined out of existence, indifferent, paring his fingernails."[6] The indifference is a pose or mask, both a defense and methodology, for Joyce, as for Yeats, as for Nietzsche.

Related to the aestheticism of *The Birth of Tragedy* as retold by Symons, is the anthropology of tragedy as told in another book first published in 1903, *Prolegomena to the Study of Greek Religion* by Jane Ellen Harrison. Harrison's book lent substantial support to the myths of Frazer's *Golden Bough,* and it acknowledged both directly and indirectly the influence of Nietzsche on its principal discoveries. Harrison, like Nietzsche, places the greatest historical emphasis on the arrival of "Dionysos," at a point when the Greek Olympians had passed their heyday and threatened to become mechanical, lifeless. Dionysos meant a "return to nature,"[7] to earlier ritual more magical than religious, whose "main gist is purification" and which "furnished ultimately the material out of which 'mysteries' were made."[8] She follows Nietzsche precisely in her revaluation of the Wincklemann tradition that held that the Greeks knew no fear: "Greek religion for all its superficial serenity had within it and beneath it elements of a darker and deeper significance." In a footnote, Harrison summarizes more succinctly than Symons, and from the German rather than the French, *The Birth of Tragedy's* basic dichotomy: "Nietzsche has drawn a contrast, beautiful and profoundly true, between the religion and art of Apollo and Dionysos. Apollo, careful to remain his splendid self, projects an image, a dream, and calls it *god.* It is illusion (*Schein*), its watchword is limitation (*Maass*), know thyself, nothing too much. Dionysos breaks all bonds: his motto is the limitless excess (*Ubermaas*), Ecstasy."[9]

Whereas *The Birth of Tragedy* is abstract and hypothetical, *Prolegomena to the Study of Greek Religion* is empirical, adding the strength of material evidence to Nietzsche's intuition. Symons's article emphasizes the aesthetic and Harrison's book the anthropological aspects of *The Birth of Tragedy*. Together they represent two broad strands of influence that help create a climate in which the use of myth in art in the early twentieth century could become self-conscious.

The Other Half of the Orange

Both strands were of utmost importance to Yeats in 1903. Maud Gonne's marriage in February bent but did not break him; his first written response to it occurred in the Preface to the Dun Emer edition of *In the Seven Woods* that he wrote shortly thereafter: "I made some of these poems walking about among the Seven Woods, before the big wind of nineteen hundred and three blew down so many trees, & changed the look of things; and I thought out there a good part of the play [*On Baile's Strand*] which follows. The first shape of it came to me in a dream, but it changed much in the making, foreshadowing, it may be, a change that may bring a less dream-burdened will into my verses" (*VP,* p. 814). The key word in this paragraph is *change.* If we take the storm that "changed the look of things" to represent Maud Gonne's marriage—a change imposed from without—the change in the making of *On Baile's Strand* and the projected one in his verses are changes originating within Yeats, self-created. The change bringing a less dream-burdened will into his verse has already manifested itself in "Adam's Curse." Now, after Maud Gonne's marriage, the change will be self-conscious and willful.

At this time Yeats was also making his final additions and revisions for the book of essays Bullen was to publish in May, *Ideas of Good and Evil.* His interest in Nietzsche appears in print for the first time in this book. In one of the Blake essays written for the *Savoy* in 1896 to be included in *Ideas of Good and Evil,* Yeats changes a paragraph to add his observation that Nietzsche is a follower of Blake. He places Nietzsche with Blake on the side of the Tree of Life, the new dispensation that was to take the place of the Kingdom of the Tree of Knowledge, now passing. Blake, Yeats says, is the "first" to announce the change, and he does so "with a firm conviction that the things his opponents held white were indeed black, and the things they held black were white; with a strong persuasion that all busy with government are men of darkness and 'something other than human life.' " This much exists in the 1896 text, and it is easy to see how a cursory look into, say, *The Antichrist,* which seems simply to reverse values, would remind Yeats of the black-white reversal he found in Blake. So he adds to the description of Blake's convictions this comment: "One is reminded of Shelley, who was the next to take up the cry, though with a less abundant philosophical faculty, but still more of Nietzsche, whose thought flows always, though with an even more violent current, in the bed Blake's thought has worn" (*E&I,* p. 130). That the word *always* here is an extravagance, he must himself have realized soon after reading more deeply in Nietzsche. The Blake he describes and quotes is a dualist: " 'I know of no other Christianity,' " Yeats quotes Blake as saying, " 'and of no other gospel, than the liberty of both body and mind, to exercise the divine arts of imagination, the real and eternal world of which this vegetable universe is but a faint shadow' " (*E&I,* p. 135). For Nietzsche at all times, this vegetable universe *is* the real and eternal world, full circle and full stop. The differences between Blake and Nietzsche help define the shift in Yeats's thought from transcendental to material, essence to substance. When he revises the Blake essay again in 1924, he adds a Post Script that indicates he is aware of the changes passing time has brought to his style and to his own apprehension of experience. Having been made aware by Ezra Pound of "the movement against abstraction" (of which he was aware long before Pound came on the scene), he says: "in writing these essays I am ashamed when I come upon such words as 'corporeal reason,' 'corporeal law,' and think how I must have wasted the keenness of my youthful senses" (*E&I,* p. 145).

Yeats also produced for publication in *Ideas of Good and Evil* the second part of his essay "The Philosophy of Shelley's Poetry," which discusses Shelley's "ruling symbols."[10] In this new section, Yeats returns to the description of a set of contraries that has long interested him, the opposition of sun and moon. It will assume increasing symbolic importance for Yeats during this decade, as the ideas behind his mask theory begin to take shape. The moon will represent one conceptual extremity, the sun the other, between which Yeats will run his vacillating course.

In "The Philosophy of Shelley's Poetry," Yeats says that Shelley dislikes both those heavenly lights, sun and moon. He gives an authoritative version of the moon's symbolism founded upon his occult studies and his study of Blake: "The Moon is the most changeable of symbols, and not merely because it is the symbol of change. As mistress of the waters she governs the life of instinct and the generation of things . . . ; and, as a cold and changeable fire set in the bare heavens, she governs alike chastity and the joyless idle drifting hither and thither of generated things. . . . Because she only becomes beautiful in giving herself, and is no flying ideal, she is not loved by the children of desire" (*E&I,* p. 91). Yeats piles up quotations to prove that Shelley, a child of desire if ever one lived, distrusts the moon or sees it at best as an object of pity: "The Moon's lips 'are pale and waning,' it is 'the cold Moon,' or 'the frozen and inconstant Moon,' . . . or it is like a 'dying lady' who 'totters' 'out of her chamber led by the insane and feeble wanderings of her fading brain' " (*E&I,* p. 92). Nietzsche has no love of the moon either. He associates it, in *Thus Spake Zarathustra,* with deceit, covetousness, and stealth:

> When the moon rose yesternight, I fancied she would give birth unto a sun. So broad and big she lay on the horizon.
>
> But a liar she was with her childbearing; and I shall rather believe in the man in the moon than in the woman.
>
> To be sure, there is little of man either in the moon, that shy dreamer of the sky. Verily, with a bad conscience she strideth over the roofs.
>
> For he is lascivious and jealous, the monk in the moon, lascivious for earth and all delights of the loving. . . . Behold, like a cat, dishonestly the moon strideth on. (*Z,* p. 171)

Zarathustra's major light is the sun. The "perfect" hour is the Great Noontide; the symbol of the "new virtue," the will to power, is a "golden sun." The night with its stealthy moon, gathering historical overtones, becomes associated with eras of religion and the love of God; the day, with eras of humanity and the love of life:

> The moon's flirtation is at an end! Look there! Dejected and pale she standeth there—before the dawn of the day!

There it cometh already, the glowing one,—its love unto earth cometh! All sun-love is innocence and creative desire. . . .
Verily, like the sun I love life. (*Z,* pp. 174–75)

Yeats's exegesis of the sun, in the Shelley essay, sounds like an interpretation of Nietzsche. If it is based on Blake alone, one can see why he found Blake and Nietzsche so similar:

The sun is the symbol of sensitive life, and of belief and joy and pride and energy, of indeed the whole life of the will, and of that beauty which neither lures from far off, nor becomes beautiful in giving itself, but makes all glad because it is beauty. . . . It was therefore natural that Blake, who was always praising energy, and all exalted overflowing of oneself, and who thought art an empassioned labour to keep men from doubt and despondency, and woman's love an evil, when it would trammel man's will, should see the poetic genius not in a woman star but in the sun, and should rejoice throughout his poetry in 'the Sun in his strength.' " (*E&I,* p. 93)

For Shelley, poetic genius resides in the Morning and Evening Star, symbol of Intellectual Beauty and infinite desire. In this second part of the essay, Yeats separates himself from Shelley, condemning him to the limbo of dreams from which Yeats himself wants so badly to awaken. Surely, while approving Blake, he creates the Shelley of the passage in his own image: "In ancient times, it seems to me that Blake, who for all his protest was glad to be alive, and ever spoke of his gladness, would have worshipped in some chapel of the Sun, but that Shelley, who hated life because he sought 'more in life than any understood,' would have wandered lost in a ceaseless reverie, in some chapel of the Star of infinite desire" (*E&I,* p. 94).

The moon (with some attributes of Shelley's Star of infinite desire) holds ascendancy over Yeats's imagination in the 1890s, standing for dreams and spirit, the unseen life, beauty, the whole complex of associations with the ideal. Another set of associations is added through contact with Macgregor Mathers, then Magus of the Golden Dawn. In *The Trembling of the Veil,* Yeats recalls: " 'Solar,' according to all that I learnt from Mathers, meant elaborate, full of artifice, rich, all that resembles the work of a goldsmith, whereas 'water' meant 'lunar,' and 'lunar' all that is simple, popular, traditional, emotional" (*AU,* p. 223). Through the backdoor of the Kabbalah, the Irish peasant enters the lists of Yeats's ideal. At the turn of the century, Yeats speaks of "the art of the people" and of marrying sun and moon, aristocratic and popular, castle and hut.[11] In a letter to George Russell (1899) analyzing a "symbol," Yeats says: "You are perhaps right about the symbol, it may be merely a symbol of ideal human marriage. The slight separation of the sun and moon permits the polarity which we call sex, while it allows of the creation of an emotional unity, represented by the oval and the light it contains" (*L,* p. 324). Merely, indeed. This "symbol" with its interpretation contains yet another embryonic version of Yeats's major symbols, the gyres and the Great Wheel—the interaction of opposites creating light or unity.

Sun and moon in this symbolic representation balance each other, making unity possible. Mostly Yeats does not achieve this balance in the 1890s and the early 1900s. Overbalancing on the moon's side in the nineties, he compensates in the other direction in the first decade of the 1900s. Rereading his short story "John Sherman" in 1908 when he was preparing his *Collected Works,* Yeats notes that the story, written when he was a "young man" ("Was I twenty-three?"), prophesied a shift in his thought from moon to sun: "I can see," he says of the narrative, "the young man's struggle with the still all-too-unconquered Moon, and at last, as I think, the summons of the prouder Sun."[12] By the time he writes the second part of the Shelley essay, the moon's connotations are mainly negative, for "the moon's love affair," as Nietzsche has it, is, for Yeats, temporarily at an end. In "Adam's Curse," the moon is hollow.

In May of 1903 Yeats wrote two letters on successive days, to George Russell and to John Quinn, announcing the gift of his new book *Ideas of Good and Evil* and apologizing for its contents. To Russell:

> The book is only one half of the orange for I only got a grip on the other half very lately. I am no longer in much sympathy with an essay like "The Autumn of the Body," not that I think that essay untrue. . . . The close of the last century was full of a strange desire to get out of form, to get to some kind of disembodied beauty, and now it seems to me the contrary impulse has come. . . . The Greeks said that the Dionysiac enthusiasm preceded the Apollonic and that the Dionysiac was sad and desirous, but that the Apollonic was joyful and self-sufficient. (*L,* p. 402)

And to Quinn:

> I feel that much of it [*Ideas of Good and Evil*] is out of my present mood; that it is true, but no longer true for me. I have been in a great deal better health

lately, and that and certain other things have made me look upon the world, I think, with somewhat more defiant eyes. . . . I have always felt that the soul has two movements primarily: one to transcend forms, and the other to create forms. Nietzsche, to whom you have been the first to introduce me, calls these the Dionysiac and the Apollonic, respectively. I think I have to some extent got weary of that wild God Dionysus, and I am hoping that the Far-Darter will come in his place. (*L,* p. 403)

The concepts Yeats uses in these letters to describe the shift in his "sympathy" from the half of the orange that represents the desire to transcend forms, to the half that represents the desire to create forms, are the same ones he has used in the Shelley essay to describe the sun-moon polarity. He is speaking in these letters of "the summons of the prouder Sun." In the letter to Quinn he attributes his understanding of the change in his sympathy, if not the change itself, to Nietzsche, whose works have helped lift him out of a state or mood of sad, desirous passivity to a more defiant one of will to creation, action, and the possibility of joy. In the letter to Russell, he attributes his change of sympathy to history, the cultural or aesthetic zeitgeist ("the close of the last century was full of a strange desire to get out of form, . . . now . . . the contrary impulse has come"). Both the version to Quinn and the one to Russell are true; the change he feels is both in and around him. But the change in him did not occur visibly—in his work—until he read Nietzsche, and Nietzsche's thought also helped create the change in mood around him.

He refers to the concepts Apollonic and Dionysiac from *The Birth of Tragedy*—a book he hasn't read, as his definition of its major terms shows. One can see in fact how much Yeats projects his own ideas onto Nietzsche's, how he simply appropriates them for his own purposes. None of the possible sources of Yeats's definitions—Nietzsche himself in *The Twilight of the Idols,* Ellis, or Symons—talks of Dionysus as sad and desirous or of Apollo as joyful and self-sufficient; none talks about the Dionysian state as "transcendent." It seems clear that Yeats, having established a connection between Nietzsche and Blake in his mind, proceeds to connect the Apollonian-Dionysian duality with the duality he has "always felt" about the soul's two movements, expressed in the sun-moon dichotomy and in the 1893 Blake edition, where the two "poles" are the "personal" and the "universal."[13] Ten years later the universal pole has lost some of its attraction for Yeats. It has become "sad and desirous"—descriptive qualities not apparent in the passage from the Blake edition, qualities neither Nietzschean nor Blakean, but qualities of Yeats himself in the late nineties. The words indicate that Yeats, now conscious of his former state, is in the process of transvaluing his halves of the orange.

He makes one other explicit reference to Nietzsche at this time in a review in the May 1903 *Bookman* of Lady Gregory's *Poets and Dreamers: Studies and Translations from the Irish*. This book, he says, is "canonical" for the "new Irish movement"; it presents love songs and stories that are "fruits of the Tree of Life." The Tree of Life as Yeats explicates it here represents passion or energy; the Tree of Knowledge represents intellect. He contends that "modern poetry" cannot be read at all when one is deeply stirred by passion, because it is "full of thoughts, and when one is stirred by any deep passion one does not want to know what anybody has thought of that passion, but to hear it beautifully spoken, and that is all." Then, into what is an old theme for Yeats—passion as designated by Blake as most holy because most living—enters a new note: "Sometimes, indeed, being full of the scorn that is in passion, one is convinced that all good poems are the fruit of the Tree of Life, and all bad ones apples of the Tree of Knowledge."[14] I do not think that Yeats has talked about "the scorn that is in passion" before this. He has equated passion with energy, but also with spirit, as in "divine love in sexual passion" in "The Moods" (*E&I*, p. 195). "Scorn" is bitter, violent, "defiant"—Yeats's self-descriptive word in the letter to Quinn—and Nietzschean. Smarting from Maud Gonne's marriage to a man of action, a soldier, Yeats might have taken these lines from *Thus Spake Zarathustra* to heart: "Brave, unconcerned, scornful, violent—thus wisdom would have us to be: she is a woman and ever loveth the warrior only" (*Z*, p. 49). Nietzsche is, of course, yoking violence with sexual love in a metaphor for the kind of passion he expected from thinkers, from the process of thought; but as so often happens, the metaphor is lost for the vividness of the literal image. It is not a long step from Nietzsche's metaphor to Sylvia Plath's famous thought "Every woman adores a Fascist" in her poem "Daddy"—a line that for all its bitterness is, I believe, to be read without irony. One of the things Nietzsche liberates, and the new note in Yeats is symptomatic of its liberation, is a conscious recognition of the presence of "evil" in "good"—of scorn, for example, in passion, of beastliness in beauty, of hate in love.

To return to the review: Yeats then resumes his aesthetic stance in arguing for the quality of Lady Gregory's Irish country verses, saying that he is "content that they offer me no consolation but their beauty." Of the critic who insists on literature's didacticism, he says, making the explicit reference to Nietzsche I announced earlier: "He [the didactic critic] could hardly come to understand that the poet was too full of life to concern himself with that wisdom, which Nietzsche has called an infirmary for bad poets. . . . The end of wisdom is sometimes the beginning of heroism, and Lady Gregory's country poets have kept alive the way of thinking of the old heroic poets that did not constrain nature into any plan of civic virtue, but saw man as he is in himself, as an amorous woman has seen her lover from the beginning of the world."[15] Nietzsche's "infirmary for bad poets" appears in a chapter of *Thus Spake Zarathustra* called "Of The Famous Wise Men," in which Nietzsche castigates the wordly-wise who have earned honor and reverence from the people in cities by serving the "virtues" or values of the people rather than by creating their own values. He charges the famous wise ones: "Ye have frequently made out of wisdom an alms-house and infirmary for bad poets" (*Z,* p. 144). This is one of many charges laid against them in a passage dense with figures, which proves that Yeats was reading attentively to have picked it out. Nietzsche, like Yeats, praises the virtue of passion, and condemns the virtue of wisdom, in poetry.

They are talking about the relation of power and knowledge, a subject that fascinates them both. Nietzsche makes it clear that knowledge without power breeds pestilence, poverty, and sterility of the spirit; power is helpless without knowledge as its vehicle. In *Thus Spake Zarathustra* he speaks of the "new virtue" that will replace traditional notions of good and evil: "It is power, that new virtue; one dominating thought it is, and round it a cunning soul: a golden sun, and round it the serpent of knowledge" (*Z,* p. 105). Though he hasn't yet the terminology in 1903, Yeats has been working with the power-knowledge antinomy for years. In the 1892 poem "Fergus and the Druid," Fergus exchanges kingly power for druidical knowledge and loses everything. Robartes and Aherne in the stories of the nineties each bargains away his soul trying to attain, through opposite means, absolute knowledge. The "all-too-unconquered moon" is related to knowledge in occult lore, for esoteric knowledge is the goal of the Adept on the journey on the Tree of Life from sun to moon.[16] The sun comes to represent power for Yeats—as well as energy, joy, and the other positive qualities he gives it in his Shelley essay. Now, in 1903, the sun-moon, power-knowledge polarities enter not only Yeats's letters and essays, but two new plays, *On Baile's Strand* (first published by the Dun Emer Press in August 1903) and *The King's Threshold* (produced by the Irish National Theatre Society in Dublin in October 1903). Nietzsche is very much in Yeats's thoughts during this time. In a letter he writes to the *Irish Times* (October 8, 1903), he complains of the national library's policy of censorship. It has only just added books by Flaubert, and "at this moment 'The National Library' refuses to have any book written by Nietzsche, although it has a book upon his genius" (*L*, p. 305).[17]

In everything Yeats writes for the next five years the effects of his admiration of Nietzsche become increasingly apparent. S. B. Bushrui establishes, in *Yeats's Verse Plays: The Revisions, 1900–1910,* that in successive revisions of his plays during these years, Yeats works toward terseness, concreteness, faster action, coarser and more masculine dialogue and characterization, and forcefulness.[18] Making the revisions of *The King's Threshold* and *On Baile's Strand* coincides with further development of the sun-moon theory in his prose, and with his reading and annotating Thomas Common's anthology of Nietzsche, loaned him on his lecture in America in 1904 by John Quinn. Isolating a chronology for Yeats during these germinal years (to use his own organic metaphor from the Blake edition) seems arbitrary, mechanical, and untrue to the quixotic process of mental growth. Nevertheless, there are some statements about order and structure that can safely be made without imposing too heavily authoritative a hand on a delicate matter. The prose essays of *Samhain,* for instance, which Yeats writes as "occasional publications" for the Irish Theatre between 1903 and 1906, and the Preface to Lady Gregory's *Gods and Fighting Men,* written in late 1903, anchor some of his flying thoughts, as do even more vividly the annotations in the Common anthology. Yeats then, or simultaneously, works these thoughts into his plays and the few lyrics he writes—or the thoughts come out of the working of the plays and verse, or both.

In the *Samhain* articles, written in the autumn of 1903 before he sails for America in November, Yeats carries on his battle for the freedom of the theater from moral and political restraints. Now he has Nietzsche as an ally, and his influence begins to pervade Yeats's prose. Sometimes it is not especially obvious or remarkable and serves only to remind us that Yeats has been reading Nietzsche with absorption. On this very question of careful reading, for example, Yeats furnishes a disgression on the habits of readers of Douglas Hyde's poetry: "They read plenty of pamphlets and grammars, but they disliked . . . serious reading, reading that is an end and not a means, that gives us nothing but a beauty indifferent to our profuse purposes" (*Ex,* p. 104). Nietzsche is constantly encouraging the almost-forgotten art of slow reading; at the end of the Introduction to *A Genealogy of Morals,* he says: "To practice reading in this manner, as an *art,* one thing of course is necessary, which today has been best forgotten . . . for which thing it is almost necessary to be a cow and certainly *not* a modern man: chewing the cud is necessary" (*GM,* p. 12).

Yeats's emphasis on masculinity in this period may also be traced to Nietzsche. In the letter to Lady Gregory early in the year, telling of "new thoughts for verse," Yeats's first comment on this change is, "My work has got far more masculine. It has more salt in it" (*L,* p. 397). In *Thus Spake Zarathustra* Nietzsche praises a kind of Spartan stoicism: "When ye despise what is agreeable and a soft bed, and know not how to make your bed far enough from the effeminate: there is the origin of your virtue" (*Z,* p. 104). In *A Genealogy of Morals* he links "the swamp of modern morality" and effeminacy: "the sickly effeminacy and moralisation by means of which the animal 'man' is taught to feel ashamed at last of all his instincts" (*GM,* p. 76). Yeats uses this argument in *Samhain* to condemn the effect of "moral" plays: "The English theatre is demoralising . . . because the illogical thinking and insincere feeling we call bad writing make the mind timid and the heart effeminate" (*Ex,* p. 112). More affirmatively, he follows Nietzsche's line in *The Case of Wagner,* for logic and integrity of line in art: "Whatever method one adopts, one must always be certain that the work of art, as a whole, is masculine and intellectual, in its sound as in its form" (*Ex,* p. 109). As Yeats remakes his plays, this aesthetic theory gets translated into practice. He works consciously for an increase of strength in the bony structure, and "the search for more of manful energy . . . for clean outline," as he puts it in 1906 (*VP*, p. 849).

In the final essay of the 1903 *Samhain* series, "The Theatre, the Pulpit, and the Newspapers," the effect of Nietzsche is both obvious and remarkable. Yeats names his adversaries as "those enemies of life, the chimeras of the Pulpit and the Press" (*Ex*, p. 119). It is well known that the pulpit is a chimera of Nietzsche's. His most cogent criticism of institutionalized Christianity occurs in the third book of *A Genealogy of Morals* on Ascetic Ideals. Priests, he says, maintain their power by encouraging and exploiting mass guilt: "It is the instinct of importance which willed, and the policy of the priest which organized, herds," he says on a page that is dog-eared in Yeats's copy (*GM*, p. 185). In the *Samhain* essay Yeats gives what reads like a summary of Nietzsche's central idea of this book: "The priest, trained to keep his mind on the strength of his Church and the weakness of his congregation, would have all mankind painted with a halo or horns" (*Ex*, p. 119). Newspapers are another of Nietzsche's chimeras; as conformity-breathing monsters, they are vilified in *Thus Spake Zarathustra*. Nietzsche puts his criticism in the mouth of a "foaming fool" so as to allow his vitriol full reign, but it is clear that Zarathustra agrees in principle:

> Dost thou not see the souls hang slack like filthy rags? And they make even newspapers out of these rags!
>
> Dost thou not hear how in this place the spirit hath become a play upon words? Loathsome word-dishwater is vomited by it. And they make even newspapers out of that dishwater of words. (*Z*, p. 254)

In his essay, Yeats uses both the central Zarathustran tenet of the need for destruction of old values, and the means of destruction suggested by Nietzsche's subtitle, *The Twilight of the Idols: or How to Philosophize with a Hammer*. One passage brilliantly dresses thoughts from Nietzsche in original imagery:

> We cannot linger very long in this great dim temple where the wooden images sit all round upon thrones, and where the worshippers kneel, not knowing whether they tremble because their gods are dead or because they fear they may be alive. In the idol-house every god, every demon, every virtue, every vice, has been given its permanent form, its hundred hands, its elephant trunk, its monkey head. The man of letters looks at those kneeling worshippers who have given up life for a posture, whose nerves have dried

up in the contemplation of lifeless wood. He swings his silver hammer and the keepers of the temple cry out, prophesying evil, but he must not mind their cries and their prophesies, but break the wooden necks in two and throw down the wooden bodies. Life will put living bodies in their place till new image-brokers have set up their benches. (*Ex*, pp. 120–21)

In the Preface to *The Twilight of the Idols,* Nietzsche says, "This little work is a *grand declaration of warfare:* and as regards the ascultation of idols, it is no temporary idols, but *eternal* idols which are here touched with a hammer as with a tuning fork" (*CW,* p. 98). Yeats makes his hammer "silver," and his "man of letters" the warrior, who destroys the lifeless in order to create "living bodies" until the next cycle comes round.

In *A Genealogy of Morals,* Nietzsche's diagnosis of and prognosis for mankind's illness is of a loss of instinctual life-force and for a future of meaninglessness:

We see, today, nothing which will grow larger; we divine, that it goes still downwards, downwards into the thinner, into the more good-natured, the more prudent, the more comfortable, the more mediocre, the more indifferent, the more Chinese, the more Christian. Man, no doubt whatever, grows ever "better." . . . Even here lies the doom of Europe—with the fear of man, we have lost also the love and reverence for man, the hope in man, in fact, the will to man. The sight of man now makes tired. What, today, is nihilism, if not *this?* . . . We are *tired of man.* (*GM,* p. 43)

The "man of letters" of Yeats's passage is Nietzsche, swinging his silver hammer over those kneeling worshippers whose nerves have dried up in the contemplation of lifeless wood. Nietzsche advocates, in all he writes, smashing the idols (with a tuning fork, or a philosophical hammer), thereby restoring "life"; he also says that new image-brokers will appear, as they have in every age, to begin a new fashion in morals. But the present has its work cut out. Its business is resistance of the mediocre and the introduction of the new virtue, power, to reinstate fear, reverence, and love of man. Its need is great because the danger is great; the risks are high. "By my love and hope," says Zarathustra, "I conjure thee: throw not away the hero in thy soul" (*Z,* p. 55). Heroes of old, of the "noble races," are described in *A Genealogy of Morals* as possessing "indifference and contempt for safety, life, body, comfort . . . terrible gaiety and profundity of delight in all destruction, in all blisses of victory and cruelty" (*GM,* pp. 39–40). Yeats goes on, in the essay under consideration:

"And if the priest or the politician should say to the man of letters, 'Into how dangerous a state of mind are you not bringing us?' the man of letters can but answer, 'It is dangerous, indeed,' and say, like my Seanchan, 'When did we promise safety?' " (*Ex,* p. 121). (The first draft of *The King's Threshold,* with Seanchan as hero, has been written at this point.) "The air rarified and pure, danger near, and the spirit full of a gay wickedness: these agree well together," says Zarathustra (*Z,* p. 48). In this *Samhain* essay, Yeats's spirit is eager for combat.

"Ye shall seek your own enemy, ye shall wage your own war, and for your own thoughts! . . . Let your work be a fight, your peace a victory," says Zarathustra (*Z,* pp. 59–60). Yeats speaks often in these years of his need for, and delight in enemies. And he writes a long preface to a book about warrior heroes, Lady Gregory's adaptation of old Irish myths, *Gods and Fighting Men.* Nietzsche's *A Genealogy of Morals* presents the "noble races" as heroic, active, whole people, not given to thinking (knowledge) as separate from acting (power): "The chivalric-aristocratic valuations presuppose a powerful corporality, a vigorous, exuberant, ever-extravagant health, and all that is necessary for its preservation—war, adventure, hunting, dancing, sports, and in general, all that involves strong, free, and cheerful activity" (*GM,* p. 27). Yeats, describing the Fianna in his Preface, speaks of their "power," and then says:

> They have no speculative thoughts to wander through eternity and waste heroic blood . . . whatever they do, whether they listen to the harp or follow an enchanter over-sea, they do for the sake of joy, their joy in one another, or their joy in pride and movement; and even their battles are fought more because of their delight in a good fighter than because of any gain that is in victory. They live always as if they were playing a game, and so far as they have any deliberate purpose at all, it is that they may become great gentlemen and be worthy of the songs of poets. (*Ex,* pp. 20–21)

The dreamy, childlike game-playing quality that Yeats ascribes to Lady Gregory's heroes is unlike the exuberant joy in cruelty that Nietzsche is at pains to expose in his "blond beasts." Both versions, however, romanticize life in the Heroic Age until their historical reality disappears.

In this Preface Yeats shows himself to be a soul divided. On the one hand he approves the aristocratic values and the art of the ideal, edenic world of the Fianna. He repeats the word *delight* many times as he describes the heroes' attitude toward their bucolic world. On the other hand, he expresses his sense of the value of the heroic existence by providing a contrast, derived from Nietzsche, with values of a later, more complicated time. This contrast adds an intellectual complexity to what would otherwise be a vapid account of fairyland; it adds conflict. The Round Table, he says, later in time than the Fianna, faces divisions unknown to Finn: "There the four heroic virtues are troubled by the abstract virtues of the cloister" (*Ex,* p. 21). The world of the Fianna sounds like Yeats's earlier descriptions of Tir na nog, Land of the Living Heart, and so represents, as it were, the first half of the orange, an ideal. "No thought of any life greater than that of love, and the companionship of those that have drawn their swords upon the darkness of the world, ever troubles their delight in one another," he says, and adds—returning to the thought about "the abstract virtues of the cloister"—"as it troubles Iseult and her love, or Arthur amid his battles" (*Ex,* p. 21). He is working toward a power-knowledge split (concrete, active vs. abstract, contemplative), but only hints at it.

He quotes for the first time in this Preface—he'll do so again—Nietzsche's list of "noble virtues" from *The Dawn of Day*. Aphorism 556 goes: "*The four noble virtues.*—Honest towards ourselves and all who are friendly to us; valiant in face of our enemy; generous to the vanquished; polite—always in all cases" (*Dawn,* p. 378). Yeats, with typical vagueness about attribution, or perhaps for other reasons, says: "It has been said, and I think the Japanese were the first to say it, that the four essential virtues are to be generous among the weak, and truthful among one's friends, and brave among one's enemies, and courteous at all times" (*Ex,* p. 21). He has the virtues almost right, if out of order. It seems to me that this almost correctly quoted, misattributed inclusion of an idea from Nietzsche acts as a symbol for what is going on in the essay as a whole, or even in all of Yeats's work at this time. Thoughts of Nietzsche's have entered his mind, causing some confusion, some disorder, some disorientation. They have not destroyed the old idealizations or the symbolic, occultist, "moony" Yeats, but they are putting some pressure on them to move over and make place, and he is doing so.

One can see his accommodation of new ideas in the additions to the sun-moon theory that occur in the Preface. Again Yeats puts forth the idea of a marriage of sun and moon, but adds the phrase, "in the arts I take most pleasure in." The symbolic marriage now represents an aesthetic theory, explicitly, and for that reason the concepts take on new meaning. Yeats first defines them according to the version he says he learned from Mathers, with a slight but significant difference. In the Mathers version, "solar meant elaborate . . . lunar meant all that is simple, popular, traditional" (*AU,* p. 223). In the *Gods and Fighting Men* version, sun and moon are less important than the human agents they represent: "To the lunar influence belong all thoughts and emotions that were created by the community, by the common people, by nobody knows who, and to the sun all that came from the high disciplined or individual kingly mind" (*Ex,* p. 24). Later in the essay Yeats enlarges on the idea behind this change: "[The sun's] discipline is not of the kind the multitudes impose on us by their weight and pressure, but the expression of the individual soul turning itself into a pure fire and imposing its own pattern, its own music, upon the heaviness and dumbness that is in others and in itself" (*Ex,* p. 26). There is a new emphasis on cause and effect, subject and object: under "lunar influence," the community creates thoughts and emotions, the multitudes impose a discipline by their weight and pressure. The new phraseology suggests or hints at a connection between the lunar influence and the herd (the multitudes) or the "slave morality" of *A Genealogy of Morals* and *The Case of Wagner.* Similarly, the influence of the sun is felt when "the individual soul" imposes its own pattern upon inert matter (here presented psychologically as human heaviness and dumbness). The individual soul has taken on characteristics of the creators of noble or "master" morality. Yeats's new version adheres to a fundamental Nietzschean distinction between those who cannot create and so have a discipline imposed on them, and those who create their own discipline.

The very next sentence of the Preface, after the one about the imposition of disciplines, returns to Yeats's early distinction between moon and sun as symbols of transcendence and immanence, with an addition: "When we have drunk the cold cup of the moon's intoxication, we thirst for something beyond ourselves, and the mind flows outward to a natural immensity; but when we have drunk from the hot cup of the sun, our own fullness awakens, we desire little, for wherever we go our heart goes too; and if any ask what music is the sweetest, we can but answer, as Finn answered, 'what happens' "

(*Ex,* p. 26). The addition to these familiar characteristics of sun and moon is the acceptance of "what happens" as an attribute of solar virtue. Fullness of heart implies a strength and confidence that reconciles itself completely with reality. Finn may have answered that what happens is the sweetest music (I cannot find the episode in *Gods and Fighting Men*), but it is one of Zarathustra's theme songs. "I carry my yea-saying with its blessing even into all abysses," he says (*Z,* p. 237); "To redeem what is past in man and to transvalue every 'It was' until will saith: 'Thus I willed!' " (*Z,* p. 288). Zarathustra epitomizes the great bestower, the overflowing "hot cup of the sun." His creator says in the Epilogue to *Nietzsche contra Wagner,* underlined by Yeats: "*Amor fati:* that is my innermost nature" (*CW,* p. 88).

In *Nietzsche contra Wagner,* Nietzsche establishes an antithesis in which he presents the aesthetic conditions as twofold. The distinction he makes between "advancing" and "decaying" life, and the art required by each, nourishes Yeats's sun-moon dichotomy. The passage reads:

> Every art, every philosophy, may be regarded as a medicine and assistance to advancing or decaying life; suffering and sufferers are always presupposed. But there are two kinds of sufferers: on the one hand, [n.b. this characteristic construction] those suffering from the *superabundance* of life, who want a Dionysian art, and consequently a tragic insight and outlook; on the other hand, those suffering from the *impoverishment* of life, who seek repose, tranquillity, smooth seas, or perhaps ecstatic convulsion and langour from art and philosophy. (*CW,* pp. 73–74)

By the time Nietzsche writes this tract, he has left the Apollonian-Dionysian antithesis of *The Birth of Tragedy* behind. Dionysian art is now a synthesis of the two, the one word standing for the marriage of Dionysian energy and Apollonian form that Nietzsche's first book declares conceived tragedy. The Dionysian art of this passage possesses many of the characteristics that Yeats has ascribed to the solar influence—abundance and, indeed, superabundance. The other type of art corresponds, confusingly, to the type Yeats has labeled Dionysiac in the letter to Russell—lunar, sad and desirous. The first type is also heroic or classical, the second romantic and Christian, for implicit in the words "advancing or decaying life" is a cyclical theory of the history of civilizations. Other passages in *Nietzsche contra Wagner* make the theory explicit and label the periods classical vs. romantic, or classical vs. Christian. *A Genealogy of Morals* puts it unequivocally: "The symbol of this struggle [for power], written in letters which remained readable, above the entire history of man until now, is called 'Rome against Judea, Judea against Rome' " (*GM*, p. 53). The passage from *Nietzsche contra Wagner* is important because it presents the idea of cycles (advancing and decaying life) on two levels, the individual and the historical, and because it incorporates aesthetics on both levels. The sufferers of each tendency, or historical period, "want" or "seek" an art that reflects the opposite tendency. The superabundant individuals and ages (or races?) want impoverishment—disaster, tragedy; the impoverished ones want either the calm and repose of plenty or superabundance—heaven, the ideal; or an infusion of energy—"ecstatic convulsion"—both of which, plenty and energy, the superabundant possess. Thus the advancing and decaying lives and periods draw strength from each other, and must be seen as dialectically related and interdependent. A question that this Nietzschean scheme raises for Yeats, who must have taken it into his subconscious as well as his conscious mind, is what happens to the superabundant individual in an impoverished age? Or to put it differently, what happens when "race" and "soul" are out of synchrony? Nietzsche's Zarathustra is one answer—the heroic individual striving on, alone, against odds. Yeats, however, needs to see the whole—individuals and periods of time subsumed under one scheme. Hence, fifteen years later, *A Vision*.

In the Preface to *Gods and Fighting Men* there are signs and portents of a vision to come. Yeats indicates, for instance, that the ideas behind the solar-lunar opposition apply not only to the aesthetic realm, but also the the historical. Solar and lunar at the most literal level of interpretation, of course, mean day and night, and Yeats muses: "It sometimes seems as if there is a kind of day and night of religion, and that a period when the influences are those that shape the world is followed by a period when the greater power is in influences that would lure the soul out of the world, out of the body" (*Ex*, p. 24). Though he has "always felt" that the soul has "two movements primarily: one to transcend forms, and the other to create forms," as he tells John Quinn (*L*, p. 403), he now connects those movements to periods of history in definite sequence. The transcendent one follows the creative one, as the Christian period follows the classical. This particular historical sequence, his obsessive antithesis, appears in much that Nietzsche writes, sometimes with clear polemical intentions and biases. One of this kind appears in *The Antichrist,* and we can be positive that Yeats read it because there are marginal strokes beside it in his own characteristic manner in his copy: "Parasitism as the *sole* praxis of the church; drinking out all blood, all love, all hope for life, with its anaemic ideal of holiness; the other world as the will to the negation of every reality; the cross as the rallying sign for the most subterranean conspiracy that has ever existed—against healthiness, against beauty, *well*-constitutedness, courage, intellect, *benevolence* of soul, *against life itself*" (*CW,* p. 353). The "night" of religion in Yeats's version moderates Nietzsche's hyperbole, but talking about influences that "lure the soul out of the world, out of the body" is capturing Nietzsche's essential idea—without, however, conveying the negative connotations that accompany it.

As Nietzsche moves on from *The Birth of Tragedy* to his late work, his bias swings increasingly toward the art of superabundance, the "Dionysian" art of tragedy. He comes to discount the art of "repose" as that of "impoverishment" and decadence. Yeats is surely aware of this bias, but in 1903 he is far from discounting the "first half of the orange," transcendence. Nietzsche's bias does give him a grip on the second half, however, which makes it possible for him to begin setting the halves at war—or marrying them, which is much the same thing, as he has begun to see. In the Preface to *Gods and Fighting Men,* he advocates impartiality and balance between the halves: "The songs and stories that have come from either influence are a part, neither less than the other, of the pleasure that is the bride-bed of poetry" (*Ex,* p. 26). He arranged such a marriage in his own "Adam's Curse," setting the "solar," individual, laboring, disciplined joyous life of the will next to the "lunar" life of the emotions (sad and desirous) and of natural process. The problem for him will be how, in the "arts he takes most pleasure in," to get the marriage consummated.

The Common Anthology

In November 1903, Yeats began his first visit and lecture tour in the United States. He stayed with John Quinn, his unofficial manager, using Quinn's Manhattan apartment as his home base.

While he was with Quinn, we know that he wrote many letters and one lyric, "Never Give All the Heart"; that he presented Quinn with the page proofs of Lady Gregory's *Gods and Fighting Men* before he left, in March 1904;[19] and that he took Thomas Common's anthology, *Nietzsche as Critic, Philosopher, Poet, and Prophet: Choice Selections from His Works,* with him on his tour and brought it back to Quinn, with many comments penciled in the margins. Other commentators on these marginal notes assume, following Ellmann in *The Identity of Yeats,* that Yeats "discovered" the Common anthology in the summer of 1902 as part of his initial exposure to Nietzsche.[20] I find no proof of this; there is no mention of the book's existence in B. L. Reid's biography of Quinn, or in letters to or from Yeats. The book surfaces in the catalogue of the auction of John Quinn's library (1923–24), among the books of special interest, as item 11404. Its description reads: "This is the copy which Mr. Quinn lent to Mr. Yeats when he was in America as a guest of Mr. Quinn on his first lecture tour. Mr. Yeats took the book with him. It was his first introduction to Nietzsche. The marginal notes on fifteen pages of the book were made by Mr. Yeats while on his tour."[21] Aside from the assertion that this book was Yeats's "first introduction to Nietzsche," I am inclined to accept the catalogue's account. The information must have come from Quinn himself (who was as far as he knew the first to introduce Yeats to Nietzsche, though not with this book), and the content of the marginal notes corresponds to ideas Yeats was expressing at about the same time.

Yeats's attraction to Nietzsche must have been strong indeed for him to have borne with Common's abridgment—an argument for the book's not being his introduction to Nietzsche. Working on the assumption that the book was among Quinn's original gifts, Otto Bohlmann, in *Yeats and Nietzsche,* wonders why Yeats's pencil ignores the passages most likely to appeal to him: "Yeats gives little evidence of having been struck by Nietzsche the poet."[22] The answer is of course that Yeats had seen Nietzsche's poetry and his views on aesthetics in the volumes he already knew. Not surprisingly, he begins his markings at a passage from the as-yet-untranslated *Beyond Good and Evil,* which he would not have seen before. Relatively speaking, a good deal of critical attention has been paid to these markings, for they provide rare firsthand evidence of the working of a major influence. A fair amount of attention has even been paid to the attention.[23] I will therefore resist the temptation to discuss each note in detail and confine myself to specific observations that I feel are new, and to generalizations needed for the sake of continuity.

For the sake of continuity, then, I shall take up the two diagrammatic notes that grow logically from Yeats's sun-moon distinction as it appears in transition in the Preface to *Gods and Fighting Men,* and from the matter of the anthology's selections—much of it, after all, either similar to or identical with ideas of Nietzsche Yeats has already got a grip on. In the selection called "Master and Slave Morality," for example, Nietzsche defines the "noble" and the "good" as "antithetical" types. Yeats's marginal note shows how deeply he is following the concept of antithesis: "In the last analysis the 'noble' man will serve or fail the weak as much as the 'good' man, but in the first case the noble man creates the *form* of the gift, in the second the weak."[24] This distinction sounds very like the one Yeats makes between the sun's and the moon's discipline in the Preface to *Gods and Fighting Men.*[25] The first of the two diagrammatic notes is briefer than the second and unrelated except by extension to the content of the passage, "Asceticism" from *A Genealogy of Morals,* beside which it appears. It follows the note about the noble, the good, and the weak, and the important passage from *The Case of Wagner* that contains the statement that "Master morality *affirms,* just as instinctively as Christian morality *denies,* the world."[26] It reads:

> The night—knowledge—inaction, in the night dreams, from dreams the day's work
> The day—power—action.[27]

Yeats's second diagram follows, four pages later:

	Socrates	One god—denial of self in the soul turned towards spirit, seeking knowledge.
Night		
	Christ	
Day	Homer	Many gods—affirmation of self, the soul turned from spirit to be its mask and instrument when it seeks life.[28]

The two diagrams complete each other, the first relating the concepts knowledge and power to night and day respectively, and adding the crucially important subheading of "dreams" to the category of night—Yeats's own fecund world that makes possible his own day's work at least, if not everyone's, by bringing him the images from which to begin the labor of stitching and unstitching his poetry.

In the second diagram, the dreams have disappeared from the night. This note has attracted more critical attention than any of the others, the best coming from Patrick Keane in his doctoral dissertation. Keane's major thesis is based on this diagram, of which he says: "The firm Nietzschean basis of Yeats's contrast, and the consequent similarity of the Yeatsian *antithetical* to Nietzschean Master Morality, could hardly be clearer. Indeed, the operative terms in Yeats's diagram are all, and equally, Nietzschean."[29] He maintains that Yeats later turns Socrates into Plato, so that the primary-antithetical conflict is also the Platonic-Homeric, also Nietzschean, and that the matrix of *A Vision* is here in this diagram.[30] I had come to his general conclusions independently, and I say to his work, Yea and Amen. He quotes a passage from *A Genealogy of Morals* as possibly contributing "most to Yeats's formulation": "Plato versus Homer: that is the complete, the genuine antagonism—there the sincerest advocate of the "Beyond," here the instinctive deifier, the *golden* nature. To place himself in the service of the ascetic ideal is therefore the most distinctive corruption of an artist that is at all possible."[31] Incidentally, to the lists on either side of the primary-antithetical antagonism (to use Nietzsche's word) may be added "there" and "here" as Nietzsche uses them in this passage.

The attributes of night and day in Yeats's scheme are clear, obvious, and as Keane says, "all Nietzschean"; their interrelationships, however, are complex. Night includes Socrates as well as Christ; there is a long passage in the anthology from *The Birth of Tragedy* about Socrates as destroyer of instinct in favor of reason, abstract knowledge. "One god" is the universal mind that absorbs individuality (paradoxically it is the dispensation of "the many"); "denial of self" (as in "Christian morality *denies*") entails denial of the world—"soul turned toward spirit." Homeric Day is the time of "many gods" as symbol of the plenitude of the world, of the necessity of form, of individuation, of the Apollonic as Yeats uses the word in his letters to Russell and Quinn; its condition is the prerequisite for beauty—especially as defined by Nietzsche in *The Case of Wagner* and *The Twilight of the Idols.* "Affirmation of self" ("Master morality *affirms*") is followed by Yeats's brilliant, cryptic, seminal explanation: "the soul turned from spirit to be its mask and instrument when it seeks life."

Here, for the first time, Yeats uses the word *mask* in the sense he is about to develop so productively as it becomes his central aesthetic, historical, and psychological concept.[32] The very first selection of Common's anthology, entitled "Artists and Philosophers in General," is my choice for chief contributor to Yeats's formulation (although for Keane's more historical purposes, his choice of the "Plato versus Homer" passage is excellent, and surely also contributed to Yeats's concept). My passage comes from the Epilogue to *Nietzsche contra Wagner* which, as we have seen, took Yeats's eye in its original context. Excerpted here in Common, preceding new passages that emphasize antithesis in aesthetic, social, and historical matters, this key passage would have passed in review in Yeats's mind, deepening his insight through repetition of the idea. I have quoted it before, but in the hope of following Yeats, I quote it once more:

> Every art, every philosophy, may be regarded as a medicine and assistance to advancing and decaying life; suffering and sufferers are always presupposed. But there are two kinds of sufferers: on the one hand, those suffering from the *superabundance* of life, who want a Dionysian art; . . . on the other hand, those suffering from the *impoverishment* of life, who seek repose. . . . In respect to artists of every kind, I now make use of this main distinction: has the *hatred* of life, or the *superabundance* of life, become creative in them?[33]

Yeats applied "this main distinction" to his analysis of Blake and Shelley, earlier.[34] He now applies it to his analysis of night and day. The life-seeker of day is actually the one who "hates" life and so must seek it as medicine and assistance to his own decaying life. Already a doctrine of the will is implied in the causal circumstances of the relationship of the "seeker" to the "mask."

In this diagram Yeats offers a very subtle compilation and interpretation of many pieces of Nietzsche he has read. The phrase about the mask turns what might have been a reasonably uncomplicated two-part analysis—a set of dichotomies between spiritual and material, passive and active, knowledge and power, Christ and Homer (or Socrates and Homer)—into a complex idea which is, at its heart, psychological and dialectical. Yeats's definition of day turns upon a psychological paradox—as does the one of night, only day is appropriately clearer. When Yeats links self and soul so closely ("affirmation of self, the soul turned from spirit to be its mask and instrument when it seeks life"), he seems to say that the affirmation of the self depends upon the denial of the soul, as "denial" of the self (in night) in effect affirms the soul. In day, the time of self in its glory, the soul is made passive and yet remains, for all that, the motivating force.

The dialectical scheme and the idea of seekers or "sufferers" ("suffering and sufferers are always presupposed") desiring their opposite numbers come from Nietzsche and feed directly into Yeats's diagram. But so too do his value judgments. In night, the self is "denied," in day it is "affirmed." Furthermore, the day's positive connotations continue at the expense of night in the description of the objects sought by the subjects of each. In the first night-day diagram, day has represented power; in the second, the soul-turned-towards-spirit at night seeks knowledge. Then it would follow that the "life" sought by the soul-turned-self in day is power. In other words, Yeats equates power and life, explicitly following Nietzsche (Christianity, he says in *The Antichrist,* is "against life itself," [*CW,* p. 353]) and puts them both on the side of day. To compensate for the overbalance, and because he is maybe not quite happy with making night as negative as he has, he makes the soul the principal actor, or willer, in the scenario, and articulates the concept of the mask. This is fitting, for the concept of the mask is itself a compensatory theory in one of its manifestations—since Nietzsche finds that "all art, all philosophy" is compensation for suffering, for a lack, a "want," a desire.

Yeats tries, probably subconsciously, to compensate for Nietzsche's lack of sympathy with the values of night—his whole first half of the orange—in this diagram. He tries twice more in this book, the first time on the next page. His marginal comment is related to the matter of the passage on which the second night-day diagram is written, which proves that Yeats was reading as well as thinking and writing. In this passage Nietzsche is writing about the "wretched" Christians with their ideal of deferral of "payment" until Afterlife: "their wretchedness may be a preparation, a test, a schooling, perhaps even more—something which will one day be adjusted and paid for with immense interest in gold, no! in happiness. They call that 'bliss.' "[35] On the next page, Yeats has written in the margin: "Did Christianity create commerce by teaching men to live not in the continuous present of self-revelation but to deny self and present for future gain, first heaven and then wealth? But why does Nietzsche think that the night has no stars, nothing but bats and owls and the insane moon?"[36]

This note bewilders Erich Heller. In his *Encounter* article on Yeats's marginalia in the Common anthology, he remarks on the lack of correspondence between Nietzsche's passage and Yeats's comment on Christianity and commerce; it is "strange, very strange," he says, and goes on: "But even stranger is the question that Yeats asks immediately afterwards: 'But why does Nietzsche think that the night has no stars . . . ?' Now, Nietzsche does not think anything of the sort, and besides, nowhere near this Yeatsian query does Nietzsche's text mention any such nocturnal apparitions. . . . Only a mind, kept very busy by its own poetic affairs, would read another writer's writing with such imaginative impatience."[37] To take the last phrase first: Harold Bloom would say that a poetic mind always reads another writer's writing with imaginative impatience, and the greater the threat of an overpowering influence, the greater the impatience. Something of the sort is going on here, and I am grateful to Heller for pointing to it through his own impatience with Yeats. The Christianity-commerce part of Yeats's annotation I take to be more brilliant than strange, as it goes one step farther than Nietzsche in an almost Marxian interpretation of his implications. As to the second "even stranger" part of the annotation, Heller's comment itself is stranger still. He is right to maintain that Yeats's mind is busy with its own poetic affairs, but he does not see that that very condition answers his question. As recently as the page before, Yeats has been schematizing night and day in the margin. And as shortly as two pages later, Nietzsche says: "Christianity was the vampire of the *imperium Romanum*—in the night it undid the immense achievement of the Romans of obtaining the site for a grand civilization."[38] Now, as Yeats wonders about the connection between Christianity and commerce in words and tone sympathetic to Nietzsche's argument, he suddenly breaks out, impatiently to be sure, with his question about Nietzsche's dismissal of the stars. The "nocturnal apparitions"

Heller speaks of, "bats and owls and the insane moon," are an interesting lot. As we have seen, Nietzsche has no love of the moon, and he speaks of bats and owls with disgust in the Second Dance Song of Zarathustra (*Z,* p. 328). The "insane moon," however, is not Nietzsche's apparition, but Shelley's. Yeats quotes Shelley on the moon in his Shelley essay: the moon is "like a 'dying lady' who 'totters' 'out of her chamber led by the insane and feeble wanderings of her fading brain' " (*E&I,* p. 92). Yeats has identified Shelley and Nietzsche, mixed them up. Shelley is his first poetic "father" (he acknowledges it) from whose influence—if Shelley can be allowed to take major responsibility for Yeats's loyalties of the first half of the orange—he is trying to free his poetry. Nietzsche is a new father figure—potent, forceful, fascinating, an "enchanter." In identifying Nietzsche with Shelley, Yeats seems to be doing two opposite things. First, he is indicating a subconscious fear of being engulfed or enchanted by a second powerful influence. Second, by asking "Why does Nietzsche think the night has no stars?" he is asking, in effect, Why is Nietzsche *not* Shelley (bearing in mind that Shelley's central symbol, for Yeats, is a star)? Shelley is not fond of the moon, but he does not dismiss the entire night, the realm of the unseen, the spirit. Richard Ellmann comments on this note that Yeats objects to "Nietzsche's blanket condemnation of Socratic-Christian spirituality. . . . The utter rejection of the spirit meant the unpardonable exclusion of an important human mood."[39] I am not sure myself that at this point Yeats would have thought so "humanistically"; he may have been concerned at the rejection of spirit, full stop. It seems clear in any case that he is questioning his own identity—and, because history is involved, that of his culture.

He seems almost consciously aware of Nietzsche's power and attractiveness to himself, and of his bias in favor of master morality, Homer over Socrates or Plato, Rome over Judea, power over knowledge. It is a bias that Common's *Choice Selections* reinforces. As Heller implies, there are indeed passages in which Nietzsche shows that he thinks the night has stars; there are many passages in which he shows that without "night," day would be an impossibility. "Only where there are graves are there ressurrections," he says in *Zarathustra* (*Z,* p. 157). Still, as this aphorism shows, his bias is for the resurrection, as it is undeniably for the sun, the day. It proves to be Yeats's bias in the end, according to Keane, who takes as a declaration of faith Yeats's line, "Homer is my example and his unchristened heart."[40] At the moment, however, in the pages of the Common anthology where it is being nurtured, the bias is also being resisted. Whole-souled Yeats's heroes may be, but he himself is no more willing to embrace a single position than Nietzsche is, or even to commit himself to a bias. He leans instinctively toward the side of a dichotomy that needs more weight and, as Common has presented Nietzsche slightly out of balance, Yeats's occasional anti-Nietzschean leanings may be partly to correct Common's one-sidedness, as well as to ease his own anxieties.

Something that strikes me about the marginal notes is their form, or style. Rather than consisting of single words or phrases, abbreviations, colloquialisms, or other such casual jottings, they are almost always written out in sincere and careful English (Yeats's phrase from a story of the 1890s), and often they are elegant. Their completeness and elegance indicates not so much that Yeats was aware of their value to future book collectors, critics, biographers, and other literary epiphytes, as that he was seriously engaged with the subject—Nietzsche's ideas and his own—and was treating it carefully, thoughtfully, and deliberately. As an example of both elegance and thoughtfulness, as well as of compensation, this sentence appears, eight pages after the "insane moon" comment: "A sacred book is a book written by a man whose self has been so exalted (not by denial but by intensity like that of the vibrating vanishing string) that it becomes one with the self of the race."[41] The page of the Common anthology on which this note appears contains on its upper half the ending of an excerpt from *Thus Spake Zarathustra* entitled "NOW THE FUTURE OPENS." Its last paragraph reads: "Take heart, ye higher men! Now for the first time the mountain of man's future is in travail. God is dead; we want now—the overman to live." Then there is a space of two lines, then a new selection (and it is beside this that the notation is written): "Such a law-book as that of Manu sums up the experience, sagacity, and experimental morals of long centuries, it comes to a final decision, it does not devise expedients any longer. . . . At a certain point in the development of a nation, the book with the most penetrative insight pronounces that the experience according to which people are to live—*i.e.* according to which they *can* live—has at last been decided upon."[42] Nietzsche says nothing about an individual author—in fact he rather implies that the people themselves write the book; nowhere does he call it "sacred," though he implies it. But Yeats, in a sentence ready for transcription to the publisher, creates his own synthesis of Nietzschean and Yeatsian ideas. In previous passages, underlined by Yeats, Nietzsche has talked about the "noble type of man," the creator of values, who "determines the conception of 'good'; it is the exalted, proud disposition." He repeats the word *exalted* to describe a characteristic of "master morality."[43] Furthermore, Nietzsche uses the word *denial* as a characterization of "slave morality." So Yeats's author of the sacred book possesses qualities of master morality. He is creative to such an extreme, however, that he loses his "self" in the "self of the race." He is like the vibrating, vanishing string—the sound thereof, losing itself in air. Yeats the mystic appears here, Yeats the lyric poet, Yeats the epigone of Shelley, proponent of the first half of the orange, finding a way from the individual soul back to the universal mind.

The elegance and careful formality of most of the marginal notes, or Yeats's style itself, may be acting as a mask in the same two ways, negative and positive, that the "insane moon" comment masks a double concern about Shelley. In the first place, the formal style may mask (in the ordinary sense of hide or disguise) an insecurity about or a defensiveness against Nietzsche's ideas, even when the note's content is sympathetic to them, as it usually is. Second, more positively, Yeats is himself, as man and artist, in a position analogous to that of the soul in day: he is seeking "life." He must recognize himself as one of the impoverished, one of the passive, whose verses, sad and desirous like his personal life, have shown too much aspiration after remote ideals, too much dream-burdened will. Formal elegance or control is one of the requirements of Apollo, the Far-Darter; in these marginal notes, as in "Adam's Curse," the labor to be beautiful is also a labor, or will, to power.

"Never Give All the Heart"

The idea of willing appearances is beginning to surface in several places at once in Yeats's writing. He has been steadily busy with his plays, and it is no coincidence that his ideas about the mask begin to emerge at this time. Furthermore, he is beginning to conceive the process of *living* as in some ways analogous to acting. Representation on stage may be like representation of oneself in real life. In the Epilogue to *Nietzsche contra Wagner,* with Yeats's marginal strokes beside it, appears the thought that in order to know how to live like the Greeks, "it is necessary to remain bravely at the surface, the fold, the skin, to worship appearance" (*CW,* p. 93). An important word here is *bravely*. To remain at the surface, it may be necessary to put on a mask, an "appearance," an act. To put on an act requires courage; action itself requires courage sometimes. Some such thoughts may have been Yeats's as he wrote "Never Give All the Heart" while staying at Quinn's in New York.[44]

> Never give all the heart, for love
> Will hardly seem worth thinking of
> To passionate women if it seem
> Certain, and they never dream
> That it fades out from kiss to kiss.

In these first lines of the poem, love takes two forms: the whole-hearted, certain and, by implication, eternal or permanent; and the uncertain or chancy, risky, and temporal or mutable. Yeats implies that the "certain" love (even though it only "seem" certain) bores the passionate women, who prefer an element of the unknown, of mystery, of the dream of nostalgia with the possibility of loss. These passionate women are so far romantic women. Two lines later, Yeats varies the theme:

> O never give the heart outright,
> For they, for all smooth lips can say,
> Have given their hearts up to the play.
> And who could play it well enough
> If deaf and dumb and blind with love?
>
> (*VP,* p. 202)

The consequences of giving all the heart (as Yeats did, to Maud Gonne) are incapacity, inability to "play" or to act, loss of self. The passionate women are committed to the drama that their values—uncertainty, change or process, mutability—oblige them to play in. They are now self-consciously romantic. To interest them, the lover is in turn obliged to join the cast, play a part, and play it well.

But because his great love robs him of his individuality (he has given all) and thus his power to act, he cannot even play himself.

The oppositions established in the poem are like those of the night-day diagram of the Common anthology, the moon-sun and the Dionysiac-Apollonic antitheses as Yeats has talked about them. The poet ("he who made this") as protagonist exemplifies characteristics of night-moon-Dionysiac: inaction (or stasis), knowledge (or certainty), and formlessness (or senselessness; he is deaf, dumb, and blind). The passionate women exemplify day-sun-Apollonic: action (drama) and, by extension, power. Their acting involves self-consciousness and formal control. They also stand for process and time, and thus for life. The poet is singular, one, the Christ of total self-sacrifice; the passionate women are plural, or many, Homeric. One of the ironies of the poem depends upon a reversal that is at the base of the mask idea as Yeats sketches it in the night-day diagram. The women, who dream of or "want" loss or risk—the fading out of love from kiss to kiss as the plot of the play to which they have given up (sacrificed) their hearts—do not lose, at least not here. The poet, who stands for and "wants" the eternity and certainty of love, loses. Each seeks what the other possesses.

The two halves represent in an early form something that Joyce Carol Oates has described as characteristic of Yeats's genius: "Yeats's genius lies not in his ability to hammer his multiple thoughts into unity, but rather in his faithful accounting of the impossibility—which may lead one to the edge of madness—of bringing together aesthetic theory and personal experience."[45] The women in the poem, because of their commitment to the play, embody the aesthetic and even the aesthetic theory, as it is beginning to take shape under the "shock of new material" Nietzsche provides. They are heroic because they embrace change; they wear masks (play parts), do not break up their lines to weep; they are liars (as art is said to be); they are passionate, like all art of which Yeats approves. Like the art of which Yeats is coming to approve, they are committed to life—to mutability, to what is past, and to come. They may even represent ritual art, according to John Vickery in *The Literary Impact of the Golden Bough,* who maintains that Yeats put Frazer's "revelations about the sacred nature of ancient and primitive ritual drama" to use in this poem. "For it is clear," he says, "that the women's 'offering their hearts up to the play' is a dedicatory rite by which they approach their own reason for existence."[46] Vickery's reading adds substance to my sense that the women are involved in—indeed, dedicated to—the play, as a game or a drama with rules, and that their meaning or "reason for existence" depends on playing.

The poet on the other hand is excluded. He is dumb, an unpoet; he is chaos. He represents personal experience, unmolded, unredeemed by the energy of the creator in himself, to use Nietzsche's thought. His condition echoes the one Yeats suggests as awaiting the "sun's discipline" in the Preface to *Gods and Fighting Men;* he embodies "heaviness and dumbness . . . in itself." Yet—final irony—Yeats makes us feel that this unredeemed personal experience is valuable—that the poet's commitment (as a lover) is more serious than the women's because it is not a game, not a play, not "art"; and because it is a commitment to another individual human, while theirs is a commitment, however passionate, to a generalization called life.

Self-remaking

No one except a masochist wants to stay a loser, and Yeats was no masochist. The poet in "Never Give All the Heart" gives the impression that he would take a part in the play if he thought he could "play it well enough." In short, he lacks confidence in his acting. But on the tour of America the "poet," Yeats himself, gets plenty of experience and is applauded by enthusiastic audiences, and he reads Nietzsche—both confidence-building enterprises. The crowning appearance of his tour in March 1904, before 4,000 of "the cream of the Irish race in New York and vicinity," as the *Gaelic American* reported,[47] is a speech in honor of the Irish patriot Robert Emmet. The speech combines his nineties idealism about Ireland and his twentieth-century insistence on action and will—the two halves of the orange in fairly even proportion. Another speech given in New York at roughly the same time (quoted by Richard Ellmann) does the same thing, only it implicitly acknowledges the inspiration of the second half. The speech concludes:

> Yes, we desire to preserve into the modern life that ideal, a nation of men who will . . . remember always the four ancient virtues as a German philosopher has enumerated them: First, honesty among one's friends. Second,

courage among one's enemies. Third, generosity among the weak. Fourth, courtesy at all times whatsoever. . . . We must so live that we will make that old noble kind of life powerful amongst our people. We must be careful that we shall pass it on, fed by our example and not weakened by our example. . . . we will pass on into the future the great moral qualities that give men the strength to fight, the strength to labor. It may be that it depends on us to call up into life the phantom armies of the future.[48]

This speech has been written by someone who has himself begun to acquire "the strength to fight, the strength to labor." Yeats now repeats Nietzsche's list of "four noble virtues" in Nietzsche's order—and using his short simple sentences, rather than the interminable Paterian compounds whose very diction weakens the effect. He attributes the list more precisely than in the Preface to *Gods and Fighting Men,* where he had made "the Japanese" its originators. The call to the future is Zarathustra's, repeated in the Common anthology, and the "noble kind of life," "powerful" in its affirmation of instinct, breeding, and heroism, is also, of course, prominently featured in Common's selections. To paraphrase Whistler on Wilde, Yeats is acquiring the courage of Nietzsche's convictions.

The change in Yeats begins to show on the outside when he returns to Dublin and London in March 1904. George Moore's account, in *Hail and Farewell,* of the "externalization" of Yeats is both amusing and no doubt reasonably accurate: "As soon as the applause died away, Yeats who had lately returned to us from the States with a paunch, a huge stride, and an immense fur overcoat, rose to speak. We were surprised at the change in his appearance, and could hardly believe our ears when, instead of talking to us as he used to do about the old stories come down from generation to generation, he began to thunder like Ben Tillett against the middle classes, stamping his feet, working himself into a great temper."[49] Other outer manifestations of an externalized Yeats, described by Ellmann in *Yeats: The Man and the Masks* and by others, are well known: how he puts on the "habiliments of arrogance and power," as Ellmann says; looks for aristocratic ancestry and for quarrels, cries down all base blood, reads Castiglione's *The Courtier,* "damns all Celtic Christmases now and forever," and quotes Nietzsche in the letter to his father in which he declares his independence from "family affection."[50] In his fur coat, Yeats has turned into the rough beast, and Nietzsche's exhortations to courage, manliness, love of enemies, more wickedness, nobility, action, have encouraged this rather strange metamorphosis.

Moore's account also, with the quiet understatement of a conscious masterstroke, states that after the speech, "the difficult question was broached why Yeats had ceased to write poetry."[51] The answer is, I think, that his inner self was also raging, seeking, and his aesthetic energy was going into his plays and into theory. He knows very well by now what he does not like in poetry, and he says so in a letter to George Russell in April 1904. He is commenting on Russell's volume of lyric selections, *New Songs:*

> Some of the poems I will probably underrate . . . because the dominant mood in many of them is one I have fought in myself and put down. In my *Land of Heart's Desire,* and in some of my lyric verse of that time, there is an exaggeration of sentiment and of sentimental beauty which I have come to think unmanly. . . . I have been fighting the prevailing decadence for years, and have just got it under foot in my own heart—it is sentimental and sentimental sadness, a womanish introspection. My own early subjectiveness rises at rare moments and yours nearly always rises above sentiment to a union with a pure energy of the spirit, but between this energy of the spirit and the energy of the will out of which epic and dramatic poetry comes there is a region of brooding emotions full of fleshly waters and vapours which kill the spirit and the will, ecstasy and joy equally. . . . We possess nothing but the will and we must never let the children of vague desires breathe upon it nor the waters of sentiment rust the terrible mirror of its blade. . . . Let us have no emotions, however abstract, in which there is not an athletic joy. (*L,* pp. 434–35)

As Yeats has berated the middle class in society, so he berates the middle ground in the poetic landscape between the "energy of the spirit" that, he implies, creates lyric poetry, and the "energy of the will," creator of epic and dramatic poetry. The middle ground creates, or nourishes, the "prevailing decadence": it is brooding, desirous, womanish, deadly to spirit and will. In just such language Nietzsche berates Wagner and "modern decadence" in *The Case of Wagner.* Yeats equates spirit with ecstasy, will with joy, in a distinction that he takes for granted as meaningful. At the end of the letter, however, spirit drops out and will takes over: "We possess nothing but the will": and the will possesses a blade that is a "terrible mirror." Twenty-five years later, in "A Dialogue of Self and Soul," Yeats will make "Sato's ancient blade . . . still like a looking-glass" emblematic of conflict and, explicitly, "of the day," "against the tower / Emblematical of the night" (*VP*, pp. 477–78). Self, speaker for "the day," has the final word in the poem, about which more in chapter 7; in the letter to Russell, Yeats is preparing the "mirror" of the will's blade—now emerging, as in the Common night-day diagrams, as the mask. The mask, like the will's mirror, will be a "terrible" weapon for defense and aggression. Finally, the "athletic joy" he calls for suggests the Olympians—or the Olympics. In the earlier letter to Russell, Yeats has called the "Apollonic" half of the orange "joyful." Zarathustra's joy is almost always athletic; "acrobatic" might be a more appropriate word for it: "Raise your hearts, my brethren, high, higher! And forget not your legs! Raise also your legs, ye good dancers! Moreover it is better still, if ye stand on your heads!" (*Z*, p. 430).

In the autumn of 1904, Yeats's articles for *Samhain* are full both of Nietzsche and of the incipient mask theory. Yeats's about-face in sympathy from the first half to the second half of the orange may be measured by two statements he makes on "influence"—one from his 1901 essay "At Stratford-on-Avon," one from the 1904 *Samhain* series. In the earlier essay, he says: "I can never get it out of my head that no man, even though he be Shakespeare, can write perfectly when his web is woven of threads that have been spun in many lands" (*E&I*, p. 109). He has gotten it out of his head three years later, when he says: "A writer is not less National because he shows the influence of other countries and of the great writers of the world. . . . One cannot say whether it may not be some French or German writer who will do the most to make him an articulate man" (*Ex*, pp. 157–58). He is paying an implicit debt to Nietzsche, I think, the writer who has surely done the most to cause his about-face and to make him articulate, at the least, many of the ideas in the essay at hand.[52]

Because of Nietzsche's addiction to oppositions, or antagonisms, it is necessary to read every statement he makes as only one half of the orange, with the other half, if not given, always understood. In these 1904 essays, Yeats sometimes demands that he too be read this way. In a statement of obvious Nietzschean derivation, for instance, Yeats who has been condemning the creation of stereotypes of "typical characters" in drama says: "Everything calls up its contrary, unreality calls up reality, and, besides, life here [in Ireland] has been sufficiently perilous to make men think. I do not think it a national prejudice that makes me believe we are harder, a more masterful race than the comfortable English of our time" (*Ex,* p. 147). The principal contraries here are abstraction of character vs. individuality, or "strength of personality"; English (comfortable, unreal) vs. Irish (hard, masterful, real). The master morality vs. slave morality distinction of *Beyond Good and Evil* sounds through the passage. Yeats says that although the comfortable conformity of the English makes for tedious, morally impoverished literature (the literature of "unreality"), yet its very unreality will "call up" Ireland's "reality." The wording of the passage suggests a causal sequence, and references to night and power in the sentence directly preceding indicate that the night-day dichotomy is operating behind the text. There may exist in Ireland, Yeats says, "an energy of thought about life itself, a vivid sensitiveness as to the reality of things, powerful enough to overcome all those phantoms of the night." It looks as though Yeats has joined Nietzsche in his devaluation of the night. The bats and owls of the Common annotation are now "phantoms" or abstractions; the day is now boldly "life itself," the "reality of things," and power, mastery.

Two pages later, Yeats says that life itself is becoming a thing of the past—the life of concrete reality, instinct, freedom, "living imagination," giving way "more and more" each generation to "theories and opinions"—to knowledge, in short. Nietzsche has an aphorism in *The Dawn of Day* on the nature of knowledge—in this case, of epistemology: "*The two directions.*—When we try to examine the mirror in itself we eventually detect nothing but the things reflected by it. When we wish to grasp the things reflected, we touch nothing but the mirror. This is the general history of knowledge" (*Dawn,* p. 233). Nietzsche has also, most notably in *Thus Spake Zarathustra,* spoken about tables of values: "A table of values hangeth over each people. . . . Behold, it is the voice of its will unto power" (*Z,* p. 76). Yeats combines these ideas and images in his description of our civilization's decline: "We lose our freedom more and more as we get away from ourselves, and not merely because our minds are overthrown by abstract phrases and generalizations, reflections in a mirror that seem living, but because we have turned the table of values upside-down, and believe that the root of reality is not in the centre but somewhere in that whirling circumference" (*Ex,* pp. 149–50).

The "centre" is associated with "intense feeling," "pure life," and therefore, by a paradox Blake and Nietzsche both would enjoy, with eternity. Yeats associates the whirling circumference with abstraction, utility, and politics. As he turns the essay in the direction of aesthetic theory, he personifies life as a passionate woman, reminiscent of the "passionate women" and their commitment to life in "Never Give All the Heart":

> Indeed, is it not that delight in beauty which tells the artist that he has imagined what may never die, itself but a delight in the permanent yet ever-changing form of life, in her very limbs and lineaments? When life has given it, has she given anything but herself? Has she any other reward, even for the saints? If one flies to the wilderness, is not that clear light that falls about the soul when all irrelevant things have been taken away, but life that has been about one always, enjoyed in all its fullness at length? It is as though she had put her arms about one, crying, "My beloved, you have given up everything for me." If a man spend all his days in good works till there is no emotion in his heart that is not full of virtue, is not the reward he prays for eternal life? (*Ex*, pp. 152–53)

"The permanent yet ever-changing form of life" as eternity seems to me a good interpretation of Nietzsche's Eternal Return; and for Zarathustra, as for the artist of this passage a bit further on, life is a "jealous mistress." Nietzsche, personifying life as a passionate woman, has her tease Zarathustra, who has asserted that she is impenetrable. She replies:

> This is the speech of all fish. . . . What *they* do not penetrate is impenetrable.
>
> But I am only changeable and wild and a woman in all respects, and not a virtuous one—
>
> Although I am called by you men "the deep one" or "the fruitful one" or "the eternal one" or "the mysterious one."
>
> But ye men always present us with your own virtues. Alas, ye virtuous! (*Z*, p. 150)

Nietzsche insists in this passage, as he often does, on the importance of perspective, point of view, "optics"; life is all things to all men, but to herself, "changeable only"—yet permanent in that changeability. Yeats has picked up this idea and clothed it in Nietzsche's figure of speech. In this particular section of the *Samhain* essay, the oppositions at work—permanence and change, form and flux, saint and lover (chastity and sensuality)—are linked, like life-in-death and death-in-life, in a sequence whose linguistic limitations belie their essential conceptual unity.

This union of opposites is the very "bride-bed of poetry" Yeats has talked about in the Preface to *Gods and Fighting Men*. He ends the *Samhain* article with a variation on that theme that develops, as well, thoughts from the night-day diagram and, clearly, from Nietzsche's "two kinds of sufferers" (the impoverished and the superabundant) passage:

> There are two kinds of poetry, and they are commingled in all the greatest works. When the tide of life sinks low there are pictures, as in the *Ode on a Grecian Urn* and in Virgil at the plucking of the Golden Bough. The pictures make us sorrowful. We share the poet's separation from what he describes. It is life in the mirror, and our desire for it is as the desire of the lost souls for God; but when Lucifer stands among his friends, when Villon sings his dead ladies to so gallant a rhythm, when Timon makes his epitaph, we feel no sorrow, for life herself has made one of her eternal gestures, has called up into our hearts her energy that is eternal delight. In Ireland, where the tide of life is rising, we turn, not to picture-making, but to the imagination of personality—to drama, gesture. (*Ex,* p. 163)

In this passage Yeats adopts Nietzsche's distinction between the art of advancing life that is created by (and about) those suffering from superabundance—Lucifer, Villon, and Timon, energetically seeking and representing disaster out of their own vitality; and the art of decaying life, created by and about those suffering from impoverishment, who seek the repose and plenty of beautiful pictures. The poetry of "low tide" is imitative and, Yeats says, reflective of the poet's sadness at his separation from the life he imitates. Nietzsche has addressed the question of the psychology of aesthetics and its historical motivation in the "two kinds of sufferers" passage; in this *Samhain* passage Yeats shows that he has understood him. The passage also shows that Yeats has understood Nietzsche's use of antithesis ("These antithetical forms," says Nietzsche of master and Christian morality, "are *both* indispensable" [*CW,* p. 57]). Whether mimetic or expressive, the two kinds of art, says Yeats, are "commingled" in all the greatest works. He implies that the greatness of these works arises precisely from the commingling of antithetical tendencies.

However, still following Nietzsche, Yeats is beginning to express the thought that one half of the orange may be more important than the other, depending on historical circumstances. In Ireland, he says, where the people are "a more masterful race" than the English (*Ex,* p. 147; see above), the tide of life is rising. It is hard to think of the Irish at any time in their history as sufferers from superabundance, but the superabundance Nietzsche describes has to do with intellectual and physical qualities and not economic and political ones; Yeats clearly feels that Irish vitality, on the rise in 1904 *because of* the perilous political and economic condition of that nation, will create the art of superabundance: drama; quintessentially, tragedy.

By 1906 Yeats is fully aware that he has made a choice, if not a permanent one, in favor of the dramatic, superabundant art symbolized by the sun. He is busy changing his style in the effort of will Nietzsche calls self-overcoming. The quatrain he writes at this time sums it up:

> The friends that have it I do wrong
> Whenever I remake a song,
> Should know what issue is at stake:
> It is myself that I remake.[53]

He repeats the idea (or originates it) in his Preface to *Poems, 1899–1905,* reprinted in 1906: "Some of my friends, and it is always for a few friends one writes, do not understand why I have not been content with lyric writing. . . . to me drama . . . has been the search for more of manful energy, more of cheerful acceptance of whatever arises out of the logic of events, and for clean outline, instead of those outlines of lyric poetry that are blurred with desire and vague regret" (*VP,* p. 849). This is no more than he has been saying again and again since the letters to Russell and Quinn of May 1903, inspired by Nietzsche's battle against decadence in art, his age, and himself. But in this Preface, Yeats also talks about the fusion of the dramatic and the lyric in the creation of "dramatic verse": "In dramatic prose one has to prepare principally for actions, and for the thoughts or emotions that bring them about or arise out of them; but in verse one has to do all this and to follow as well a more subtle sequence of cause and effect, that moves through vast sentiments and intricate thoughts that accompany action, but are not necessary to it" (*VP,* p. 849).

As he describes it, dramatic verse has its major division between action on the one hand, and "mood" or spirit (the "more subtle sequence of cause and effect, that moves through vast sentiments") on the other. This sort of poetry would seem to be the very form Yeats needs to consummate the marriage of sun and moon, energy of will and energy of the spirit. The parts of dramatic verse, Yeats implies, form an intricate organic whole that is both sui generis and aesthetically determined or necessary. He explains that a prose play to which verse has been added later—in which the verse did not grow naturally with the action—"will never move us poetically, because it does not uncover, as it were, that high, intellectual, delicately organized soul of men and of an action, that may not speak aloud if it do not speak in verse" (*VP,* p. 849). The "verse" in dramatic verse provides the "soul" of the action. This idea is consistent with Yeats's earlier insistence on poetry's providing for the human soul in general, taking on the burdens that had fallen from the shoulders of priests. In this Preface he continues the theme of art's relationship or responsibility to the ideal: "All art is in the last analysis an endeavour to condense as out of the flying vapour of the world an image of human perfection, and for its own and not for the art's sake" (*VP,* p. 849). In the turn of the century essays he has spoken of art for art's sake; now Yeats thinks of creating images of human perfection for "its own sake," under Nietzsche's tutelage, who is explicit on the question of art for art in *The Twilight of the Idols:* "Art is the great stimulus to life, how could art be understood as purposeless, as aimless, as *l'art pour l'art?*" (*CW,* p. 186). Yeats's purpose from now on will be to serve life. The Preface continues, picking up again the subject of the switch from lyric to dramatic: "an image of human perfection, and for its own and not for the art's sake, and that is why the labour of the alchemists, who were called artists in their day, is a befitting comparison for all deliberate change of style" (*VP,* p. 849).

On the face of it, this chain of thought is not linked by logic. It moves instead by association. The notion of putting images of human perfection in the service of life is Nietzschean, but the alchemists are related to Yeats's hermetic study, in the "moon" phase. Yeats has not been talking about that phase; rather he has been describing his search for "more of manful energy" and "clean outline." He declares that he has made "a deliberate change of style." Alchemists turn lead into gold. Nietzsche equates gold and power in *Thus Spake Zarathustra;* the "new virtue" is a "golden sun." Its essence is power—overflowing, creative power. In his chapter "Of Giving Virtue," Zarathustra says to his disciples:

> "Tell me, how came gold to be valued highest? Because it is uncommon and of little use and shining and chaste in its splendour; it ever spendeth itself.
>
> Only as an image of the highest virtue gold came to be valued highest. Gold-like shineth the glance of him who giveth. The glitter of gold maketh peace between moon and sun. (*Z,* p. 102)

As Yeats considered his change of style, the sun-moon polarity must have been in his mind. The hermetic tradition also talks about uniting sun and moon, in a symbol that Yeats identified in the letter to Russell (1899) quoted above as representing "the ideal human marriage." In the passage in his Preface, he is ascribing the possiblity of a marriage between image and reality to the alchemy of style—linking, by association, his former study of the occult with his more recent one of Nietzsche. Nietzsche is the catalyst in the reaction. He is teaching Yeats how to work the alchemy necessary to transform his own leaden spirits and sad, desirous, remote images into an heroic will and "images of the highest virtue," golden handiwork.

5.

The Ceremony of Tragedy

Tragic Theory and Essays, 1903–4

As Yeats remakes his style and himself in 1903 and 1904, he faces a contradiction between his concepts of mask and tragedy. He has associated tragedy with "the beyond": with transcendence, stasis, perfection, the ideal, the absolute; and with values represented by night in the Common anthology diagram: one God, the soul, and knowledge. The mask, on the other hand, is associated with immanence, conflict, strength, creativity; with values represented by day in the Common anthology diagram: many gods, the self, and power. The contradiction between mask and tragedy becomes a wholescale philosophical dilemma for Yeats. It arises because Yeats, enchanted by Nietzsche's ideas, is beginning to question the validity of his faith in the beyond. On the aesthetic level alone, if the beyond ceases to be important, what happens to tragedy?

The dilemma appears unresolved in the expository prose pieces Yeats writes from 1903 to 1910, where he vacillates between placing tragedy on the side of night and placing it on the side of day. He comes closer to resolving it as he makes and remakes his plays from 1903 to 1906. In his revisions and the new plays of these years, the influence of Nietzsche's thought—and thus the swing to the side of day—is decisive. The mask idea, as Yeats learns it from Nietzsche, does not exclude the night; rather, it makes peace between sun and moon, day and night, by joining them in a dialectical process in which each side has more or less equal value in the long run. One side may dominate temporarily, but the other will have its day sooner or later. The aesthetic and ethical comprehension of the centrality of the conflict of opposites, which is the basis of Nietzsche's ontology and the basis, also, of Yeats's mask theory, dominates Yeats-the-playwright, and substantially alters his earlier conception of tragedy.

To recapitulate: he summarizes the earlier conception of tragedy in the 1902 essay "The Freedom of the Theatre." In that piece, he defines drama as "a picture of the soul of man, and not of his exterior life." He then defines tragedy's main element as passion: "It is the same with all tragedies, we watch the spectacle of some passion living out its life with little regard for the trouble it is giving." Finally, he says that his own heroes' passions in *The Countess Cathleen, The Shadowy Waters, Cathleen ni Houlihan,* and *Where There Is Nothing* "become through their mere intensity a cry that calls beyond the limits of the world."[1] On the one side Yeats places "exterior life," society, the world; on the other, the soul, the beyond. Passion, at its intensest, furnishes the jet propulsion that lifts the soul out of the world, beyond its limits. This is my inelegant paraphrase of Blake's thought, loved and more elegantly paraphrased by Yeats, that "passions, because most living, are most holy . . . and man shall enter eternity borne upon their wings."

In the *Brand* review (1894), Yeats distinguishes between poetry (tragedy) and nature: "Poetry has ever loved those who are not 'piecemeal,' and has made them its Timons and its Lears, but Nature, which is all 'piecemeal,' has ever cast them out."[2] Then in an essay on William Morris, written in the beginning of 1903 after he had begun to read Nietzsche, Yeats again distinguishes between "nature" and "out-of-nature" in the art of Morris, on the natural side, and Rossetti and Shelley on the side beyond nature. His description of "Rossetti's genius," which like Shelley's "can hardly stir but to the rejection of Nature," sounds like his earlier descriptions of the state necessary to tragedy:

> [Rossetti] desired a world of essences, of unmixed powers, of impossible purities. It is as though the Last Judgment had already begun in his mind and that the essences and powers, which the Divine Hand had mixed into one another to make the loam of life, fell asunder at his touch. . . . If he painted a woman's face he painted it in some moment of intensity when the ecstasy of the lover and the saint are alike, and desire becomes wisdom without ceas-

ing to be desire. He listens to the cry of the flesh till it becomes proud and passes beyond the world. (*E&I,* p. 53)

Added to these ideas are others that fill out the concept Yeats associates with tragedy at this stage. Morris's men and women, in love with the natural world, "are not in love with love for its own sake, with a love that is apart from the world or at enmity with it . . . as all men have imagined Helen. They do not seek in love that ecstasy which Shelley's nightingale called death, that extremity of life in which life seems to pass away like the phoenix in the flame of its own lighting" (*E&I,* p. 53). The ecstasy Yeats offers for consideration is Dionysian in its dissolution of individuality and of form itself; lover and saint are one, wisdom and desire are one. This state is self-referential; it is "love for its own sake," "the flame of its own lighting." It is a world of "unmixed powers," pure, essential; it is like death. It is apart from the world, or at enmity with it.

In contrast, Morris's nature lovers possess "a gentle self-surrender that would lose more than half its sweetness if it lost the savour of coming days." The women's love is "less a passion for one man out of the world than submission to the hazard of destiny, and the hope of motherhood and the innocent desire of the body. The women accept changes and chances of life as gladly as they accept spring and summer and autumn and winter" (*E&I,* p. 57). In the letter to Lady Gregory describing his first response to Nietzsche, "that strong enchanter," Yeats associates Nietzsche with Morris, perhaps as much on the grounds of their mutual loyalty to the earth as on the grounds of their "astringent joy." In the Morris essay, Yeats accepts nature as a legitimate source of artistic energy and as a repository of value for artists. He still feels that there is more energy or passion on Shelley's side, but his understanding of Nietzsche is beginning to convince Yeats of the value for art of natural process. He remains convinced that the instinct of tragedy, the intensest art, must "reject Nature," but this essay marks the beginning of his serious ambivalence toward the values of immanence and transcendence. It is unclear in the essay, for instance, which pole represents "self," and which "soul." Shelley and Rossetti represent the ideal and the romantic, the cry that calls beyond the limits of the world, but in the description of Rossetti's genius, in the midst of phrases about unmixed powers and impossible purities, Yeats talks about the moment when "desire becomes wisdom without ceasing to be desire." This moment of unity arrives *in* time, *in* the world, not beyond it; but Yeats is not yet content to have it here. He wants it *there*.

He persists in maintaining that escape from the wheel of time into "the integrity of fire" is the business of the arts in general, tragedy in particular. A passage from the 1904 *Samhain* series shows him working with a set of ideas on tragedy very like those of the 1902 essay on the "Freedom of the Theatre," yet not entirely like. He has been talking about the dangers to the arts of "habit, routine, fear of public opinion, fear of punishment here or hereafter," and goes on:

> The arts are at their greatest when they seek for a life growing always more scornful of everything that is not itself and passing into its own fullness, as it were, ever more completely as all that is created out of the passing mode of society slips from it; and attaining that fullness, perfectly it may be—and from this is tragic joy and the perfectness of tragedy—when the world has slipped away in death. We, who are believers, cannot see reality anywhere but in the soul itself, and seeing it there we cannot do other than rejoice in every energy, whether of gesture, or of action, or of speech, coming out of the personality, the soul's image, even though the very laws of Nature seem as unimportant in comparison as did the laws of Rome to Coriolanus when his pride was upon him. Has not the long decline of the arts been but the shadow of declining faith in an unseen reality? (*Ex*, pp. 169–70)

As in the turn-of-the-century essays, Yeats connects art and religion, and implies that the religious impulse, the "faith in an unseen reality," has kept the arts alive in the past. This conviction is responsible for the form his own drama takes, and for his cultivation of myth as a way through, or back, to universal thought, anima mundi. "Reality" for the "believer" (the artist, in this case) is "in the soul" and attains its perfect aesthetic expression in tragedy, "when the world has slipped away in death."

But for the first time, Yeats begins to confront the theoretical aesthetic implications of his position on tragedy. If perfect "reality" resides in death, or in the soul jettisoned by passion out of nature into an ecstasy resembling death, how does a playwright represent this kind of reality? At this point, Yeats's theory of the mask as he is beginning to articulate it intersects with his idea of tragedy. Since "we . . . believers" can see reality only in the soul, he says, "we cannot do other than rejoice in every energy, whether of gesture, or of action, or of speech, coming out of the personality, the soul's image, *even though* the very laws of Nature seem . . . unimportant in comparison" [italics mine]. Energy—gesture, action, speech—not only partakes of the "laws of Nature"; energy is the first law of nature, a fact Yeats acknowledges. In comparison with the soul, however, the laws of nature seem unimportant—an idea that exactly replicates the pro-Shelley bias of the Morris essay. As in the vacillation of that essay, Yeats here shows that *even though* he must consider nature less important than the individual soul, it may have its uses all the same. The soul expresses itself through its "image," the energy of personality. It expresses itself through nature, in fact; through its opposite, the self.

The significance of his recourse to "the soul's image" lies in Yeats's growing awareness that the purities of passion, which pull the soul toward death in tragedy, are meaningless without the contrary pull of nature. He is hearing from Nietzsche that all states are mixed, all are in the process of "becoming." Yeats cannot have forgotten the ideas behind his self-soul diagram in the Common anthology—the reciprocity between day-power-self and night-knowledge-soul. Because he is discussing the "perfectness of tragedy," his bias has switched back to night and soul, but he admits that soul needs the personality, its "image" when it seeks life—or when it seeks artistic representation.

The phrases *tragic joy* and *the perfectness of tragedy* are also new in this essay. Though he has associated tragedy and the "perfect joy" of death (specifically in *Where There Is Nothing*), he has not talked about the "perfectness" of tragedy itself, preferring to describe the "measureless eternal life" (Paul Ruttledge's object of desire) as perfect, and material forms, even artistic ones, as comparatively "unimportant." Now he calls an artistic form "perfect," and it happens to be the artistic form most compellingly espoused by Nietzsche.

In *The Twilight of the Idols,* Nietzsche addresses the issue of "perfectness" in art: "This constraint to transform into the perfect is—art. Everything that he is not, nevertheless becomes for him a delight in himself; in art man enjoys himself as perfection" (*CW,* p. 172). If art in general is capable of this kind of psychological sustenance, tragedy is capable of it at its finest. In *The Dawn of Day,* Nietzsche defends the freedom of tragic poets from moral constraints, simultaneously justifying their work. Ellis quoted from the passage in his *Savoy* series, and there is no doubt that Yeats drew inspiration from it, if not in 1896, then certainly when he read *The Dawn* in 1903:

Stage-morality. He who believes that Shakespeare's stage has a moral effect and that the sight of Macbeth irresistibly detracts from evil ambition is mistaken. And he is again mistaken if he believes that Shakespeare himself was of this opinion. Any man who is really possessed by mad ambition will watch this, his emblem, with delight; and the very fact that the hero perishes in his passion is the strongest charm in the hot cup of delight. Were the poet's feelings different to these? How royally and not in the least knavishly his ambitious hero runs his course from the hour of his great crime! Only then he grows "demoniacally" attractive and encourages similar natures to imitation—demoniacal means here: in defiance of advantage and life, in favour of an idea and craving. Do you imagine that Tristan and Isolde give a warning example of adultery through its being the cause of their death? This would be turning the poets upside down: for they, and Shakespeare above all, are in love with the passions themselves, and no less with their yearnings for death—when the heart does not cling to life more firmly than the drop of water does to the glass. It is not so much guilt and its evil consequences which they—Shakespeare as well as Sophocles (in Ajax, Philoctetes, Oedipus)—wish to portray; however easy it might have been in the aforesaid cases to make guilt the lever of the play, they carefully refrained from so doing. Neither is it the wish of the tragic poet to prejudice us against life by means of his representations of life. Nay, he exclaims: "It is the charm of charms, this exciting, variable, hazardous, gloomy and often sun-steeped existence! It is an adventure to live!" (*Dawn,* pp. 231–32)

In the 1904 *Samhain* essays, Yeats writes a similar passage, expressing thoughts he will return to again and again. Echoing Nietzsche, he asks:

Has art nothing to do with moral judgments? Surely it has, and its judgments are those from which there is no appeal. . . . This character who delights us may commit murder like Macbeth, or fly the battle for his sweetheart, as did Antony, or betray his country like Coriolanus, and yet we will rejoice in every happiness that comes to him and sorrow at his death as if is were our own. . . . we are caught up into another code, we are in the presence of a higher court. . . . If the poet's hand had slipped, if Antony had railed at Cleopatra in the monument, if Coriolanus had abated that high pride of his in the presence of death, we might have gone away muttering the Ten Commandments. . . . If we were not certain of law we would not feel the struggle, the drama, but the subject of art is not law, which is a kind of death, but the praise of life, and it has no commandments that are not positive. (*Ex*, p. 154)

When Yeats talks about "law, which is a kind of death," he means the laws of nature as well as those of society. He is taking the part of Nietzsche's tragic poets, "in love with the passions themselves, and no less with their yearnings for death."

In the passage from *The Dawn of Day*, Nietzsche identifies the yearnings for death at the height of passion as the "demoniacal." Only after he commits "his great crime" does Macbeth grow "demoniacally attractive . . . —demoniacal means here: in defiance of advantage and life, in favour of an idea and craving."[3] In *Thus Spake Zarathustra* Nietzsche further identifies this craving as a manifestation of the will to power: "Only where there is life, there is will; but not will unto life, but—thus I teach thee—will unto power! Many things are valued higher by living things than life itself" (*Z*, p. 162). The willingness to risk or sacrifice life for power is at the root of Nietzsche's theory of tragedy, which relies on the intuition that power affirms, and that therefore the sacrifice of life for power is affirmative, and so life-furthering.

It is precisely on the discovery of affirmation as the basis of tragic psychology that Nietzsche grounds his claim to be considered "the first *tragic philosopher*—that is, the most extreme opposite and antipode of a pessimistic philosopher."[4] In *The Twilight of the Idols* he provides a definition of this psychology, which finds it origins historically in fertility ritual. So he arrives at the paradoxical conclusion that the sexual instinct is at the heart of tragedy:

In order that the eternal delight of creating may exist, that the will to life may assert itself eternally, there *must* also exist eternally the "pains of travail." All this is implied by the word Dionysos: I know of no higher symbolism than this Greek symbolism of *Dionysia*. In them the deepest instinct of life, the instinct of the future of life, for the eternity of life, is felt religiously—the way of life, procreation, is recognised as the *sacred* way. . . .

The psychology of orgiasm [*sic*], as an exuberant feeling of life and energy, in which pain even operates as a stimulus, gave me the key to the concept of *tragic* feeling. . . . The affirmation of life, even in its most unfamiliar and most severe problems, the will to live, enjoying its own inexhaustibility in the *sacrifice* of its highest types,—that is what I called Dionysian, *that* is what I divined as the bridge to the psychology of the tragic poet. *Not* in order to get rid of terror and pity, not to purify from a dangerous passion by its vehement discharge (it was thus that Aristotle understood it); but, beyond terror and pity, *to realise the fact* the eternal delight of becoming,—the delight which even involves in itself the *joy of annihilating.* (*CW,* pp. 230–31)

These two long passages, from *The Dawn of Day* and *The Twilight of the Idols,* put Nietzsche's case for tragedy and the psychology of the tragic poet more forcefully and radically than does *The Birth of Tragedy,* which announces that the purpose of art is to mask the insupportable "truth" of existence with its beautiful illusions. Nietzsche later accuses himself of committing the crimes of the age, pessimism and romanticism, in *The Birth of Tragedy:* "What?" he expostulates with himself in the 1886 Preface to that book, "is not your pessimist book itself a piece of anti-Hellenism, an example of Romanticism, something equally intoxicating and stupefying, a narcotic at all events, aye, a piece of music, of German music?" (*BT,* p. 13). Yeats did not have a chance to yield to the intoxication of *The Birth of Tragedy* except at second hand until he had fully taken in draughts of the later works, which are, in their uncompromising acceptance of reality, much headier.

Nietzsche's view of tragedy in the later works is closely related to his ideas of will to power and Eternal Return. While the former may have some ties to classical Greek tragedy, the latter, Eternal Return, is related to primitive ritual and the concept of time's circularity. He explains his sense of the "tragic" as antithetical to the "Christian" philosophy in a late note (1888), published as part of *The Will to Power* by Nietzsche's executors:[5]

Dionysus versus "The Crucified One": there you have the contrast. It is not martyrdom that constitutes the difference—only here it has two different senses. Life itself, its eternal fruitfulness and recurrence, involves agony, destruction, the will to annihilation. In the other case, suffering—"the Crucified One as the Innocent One"—is considered an objection to this life, as the formula of its condemnation. Clearly, the problem is that of the meaning of suffering: whether a Christian meaning or a tragic meaning. In the first case, it is supposed to be the path to a sacred existence; in the second case, *existence is considered sacred enough* to justify even a tremendous amount of suffering. . . . The God on the cross is a curse on life, a pointer to seek redemption from it; Dionysus cut to pieces is a *promise* of life: it is eternally reborn and comes back from destruction.[6]

Christ and Dionysus are both martyrs. It is the interpretation placed on their deaths, rather than the deaths themselves, that matters for Nietzsche. The Christian interpreted suffering as an objection to life and an affirmation of eternal life elsewhere; the ancient Greek worshipper of Dionysus interpreted suffering as a promise of renewal here, eternally—life being its own justification. This second interpretation Nietzsche names "tragic." Christianity's refusal to accept death, in effect, negates or "denies" life, Nietzsche says, whereas tragic acceptance of death affirms life.

The very laws of nature, including physical human life, which Yeats finds unworthy of comparison with the "reality" of the soul, are for Nietzsche the only reality. If living now (in a post-Christian culture) means "*realising in fact*" the eternal delight of becoming, then process is all, and tragedy may again be born. Humans may again, as in ancient times, Nietzsche implies, assert their individual power, their will to power or self-overcoming, against chaos and death (and for meaning and life). With no hope of heaven, post-Christians must rely, like the ancients, on courage, endurance, and their own native wit—the power to create new illusions, "saving fictions." Tragedy has always depended, in all definitions, on a human acknowledgment of the finality of death for the individual. As George Steiner puts it in *The Death of Tragedy,* "In the norm of tragedy, there can be no compensation." Steiner argues, however, that the death of God means the death of tragedy and that these deaths began after the late seventeenth century: "It is the triumph of rationalism and secular metaphysics which marks the point of no return," he says.[7] Nietzsche would argue, I think, that the triumph of rationalism and the dissolution of long-held metaphysical certainties of Western culture create the conditions for tragedy. He makes it clear that the death of God means the birth (or rebirth) of tragedy.

Nietzsche's psychology of tragedy originated, he says, with his intuition about sexuality, "an exuberant feeling of life and energy" overcoming pain and, by extension, guilt and death—literally, the death of sexual desire in orgasm, engendering birth. Yeats comes to understand this complicated, layered, "tragic" concept, and embodies it in "Leda and the Swan":

A shudder in the loins engenders there
The broken wall, the burning roof and tower
And Agamemnon dead.

(*VP*, p. 441)

Nietzsche finds that the feeling of exuberance, or power, in the engendering of new life—itself doomed to die—is vital enough to take on even the burden of human guilt. The very deep-rootedness of guilt in human nature is one of Nietzsche's most persistent themes; the eradication of guilt perhaps his most ambitious project.[8] In *The Birth of Tragedy,* he retells the ancient story of King Midas, hunting in the forest for wise Silenus, Dionysus's companion. When Midas finally catches him, he asks him what he considers humanity's greatest good. Silenus refuses to answer until Midas forces him, upon which he says: " 'Oh, wretched race of a day, children of chance and misery, why do ye compel me to say to you what it were most expedient for you not to hear? What is best of all is forever beyond your reach: not to be born, not to *be,* to be *nothing*. The second best for you, however, is soon to die' " (*BT*, p. 34). This story is part of early Greek folk wisdom, Nietzsche tells us. He derives from it, and from the pre-Socratic Anaximander—according to whom the death of beings represents "castigation for their mistake of having been born"[9]—his theory about the origin of guilt as coincident with the origin of thought. His separate and opposed ideas about guilt and tragedy—one negative, one positive—were partially borne out by the studies of Cambridge anthropologists Harrison, Cornford, and Murray, in the early twentieth century. In *The Classical Tradition of Poetry,* Gilbert Murray suggests the provenance of tragic or Dionysian ritual: "We know from Herodotus that tragedy represented the sufferings of Dionysus, and that these were, except for certain details, identical with those of Osiris. And Osiris, we know, was slain by his enemy, the Burning Set; torn in pieces as a corn sheaf is torn and scattered over the fields; bewailed and sought for in vain during many months, and rediscovered in fresh life when the new corn began to shoot in the spring." Eventually this primal mythical event split into two celebrations, the fertility ritual and the expulsion ritual—and it is from the latter, Murray says, that tragedy in its classical form derives. "The death-celebration was the expulsion of evil from the community, the casting-out of the Old Year with its burden of decay, of the polluted, the Scapegoat, the Sinbearer."[10] It seems to me that Nietzsche, who had not read Gilbert Murray but who had read Herodotus, is trying to mend an ancient or primitive cleavage between death and birth, in his insistence on "the eternal delight of becoming" as "tragic." In *A Genealogy of Morals,* he argues that human loss of a sense of instinctual reality is the cause of guilt, disillusion, and finally nihilism. Freud soon afterward bases his entire theoretical framework on the hypothesis of instinctual repression. His pessimistic conclusion in *Civilization and Its Discontents,* that accumulated guilt will simply override and submerge the human psyche collectively, was anticipated by Nietzsche, whose solution is "the eternal delight of becoming"—confronting the ironies of existence and overcoming them in the joy of the battle with them. There is never a sense, in Nietzsche, that the battle will be anything but tragic for the individuals who undertake it; they will lose. But in the traditional and archaic tragic sense, their loss will be life's gain. Their "sacrifice" will ensure that life goes on.

Nietzsche says that his particular version of tragedy does not depend on, or seek, Aristotelian catharsis: "*Not* to purify from a dangerous passion by its vehement discharge . . . but, beyond terror and pity, *to realise in fact* the eternal delight of becoming." Here Nietzsche separates himself explicitly from the idea of tragedy as purgation of guilt. To go "beyond terror and pity" is to go *before* Aristotle to earlier times, when the cruelty of sacrifice was positively enjoyed as part of the Dionysian fertility celebration, when pain and pleasure were one, when life itself was "sacred." Nietzsche's birth of tragedy may be a kind of rebirth, the closing of an ancient circle, or will to resurrection of the archetypal models of "primeval times." In *A Genealogy of Morals* he says parenthetically, of these early times, "which primeval times, by the bye, are at all times either present or again possible" (*GM,* p. 81).

In 1904, Nietzsche seems to be suggesting that Yeats write something like Heraclitian Greek tragedy with a leaning toward ritual drama, and Yeats, having read Frazer and Celtic mythology as well as Nietzsche, eventually tries to do that. In his 1904 *Samhain* series, where he discusses the "perfectness of tragedy" in its total withdrawal from life, he also talks with approval about ritual drama: "The arts have always lost something of their sap when they have been cut off from the people as a whole. . . . It was not merely because of its position in the play that the Greek chorus represented the people. . . . Ritual, the most powerful form of drama, differs from the ordinary form, because everyone who hears it is also a player" (*Ex,* p. 129). Ideally, Yeats would re-create a world so culturally unified that ritual drama could again function in a pure form. Practically, he knows he must work in "our modern theatre, with the seats always growing more expensive, and its dramatic art drifting always from the living impulse of life" (*Ex,* p. 129). But the ritual idea, the notion of appealing to audiences through their identification with the passions represented on stage in order to create community, has taken hold for Yeats. He has equated power and passion, power and ritual, and will seek a form to embody his thought.

In the world of the theater, the mechanics of realism in stage production stand for nature as superfluous to, or unimportant compared with, soul or passion. One way to create passion on stage, Yeats tells his *Samhain* readers, is through extravagance, "an emphasis far greater than that of life as we observe it." He is in the process of distinguishing between observation and "experience," which is like the mirror-lamp distinction, or the memory-imagination distinction of Blake. Observation (like stage machinery) is mechanical, lifeless, or merely rational; "experience" touches the whole being and is synthetic. To create unity in the theater, to make the audience "one people," the dramatist must leave the world of observation and the everyday. Yeats explains: "The greatest art symbolizes not those things that we have observed so much as those things that we have experienced, and when the imaginary saint or lover or hero moves us most deeply, it is in the moment when he awakens within us for an instant our own heroism, our own sanctity, our own desire. We possess these things . . . not at all moderately, but to an infinite extent. . . . How can any dramatic art, moderate in expression, be a true image of Hell or Heaven or the wilderness?" (*Ex,* p. 197). This line of thought continues the argument for a "stage morality" different from conventional morality, based on passion and the audience's identification with that passion. The passion is "infinite," and so beyond good and evil. The Hell or Heaven or wilderness presented on stage are "images" of extremities, the limits of the human imagination of passion. This "passion" is very like the condition Nietzsche names

"Dionysian" in *The Birth of Tragedy,* or "instinct" in *A Genealogy of Morals*—dynamic, orgiastic; naked energy, pure power. To represent such forces on stage, the dramatists will have to choose extreme types and "immoral" subjects, Yeats argues. But the end result of such representation, where the audience is in the presence of a "higher court," is basically and radically moral, in the extramoral Nietzschean sense. Its purpose is not edification, but life. Yeats concludes: "The misrepresentation of the average life of a nation that follows of necessity from an imaginative delight in energetic characters and extreme types, enlarges the energy of a people by the spectacle of energy" (*Ex,* p. 191). The result of witnessing a tragedy as Yeats describes it is not at all like Aristotelian catharsis; it moves beyond terror and pity to Nietzsche's "delight of becoming," a delight that repudiates pessimism and decadence in enlarging the energy of a people, a delight that Nietzsche calls "eternal," because its source, will to power or the energy of the life-force itself, is limitless. An audience that identifies its own "experience" with that of the hero participates in the power of that experience and is thereby "enlarged." In *The Life of the Drama,* Eric Bentley echoes this idea of Nietzsche's and Yeats's: "In art, recognition is preferable to cognition," and he adds: "This is where ritual comes in—ritual *is* re-enactment."[11]

In his effort to create a drama with roots in eternal passions, Yeats speaks often in the essays of this period of "going back" to an earlier art form: "In every art, when we consider that it has need of a renewing of life, we go backward till we light upon a time when it was nearer to human life and instinct, before it had gathered about it so many mechanical specialisations and traditions" (*Ex,* p. 210). Or, a bit further on in the same (1906 *Samhain*) essay: "[To learn about recitation] we must go back hundreds of years. . . . In this, as in all other arts, one finds its laws and its true purpose when one is near the source" (*Ex,* p. 214). Both these passages repeat Nietzsche's thought in *A Genealogy of Morals,* which echoes the nineteenth-century fascination with origins, that "life and instinct" are to be found in pure form nearest the source.[12] In the twentieth century, the fascination with origins takes on therapeutic value for individuals in Freud and psychoanalysis and at the same time comes to light in anthropology, ethnology, and orientalism as intrinsic to ancient world religions.

Mircea Eliade talks about the practice of tracing time backwards to its point of departure as common to Buddhistic, Platonic, and archaic thought.[13] As forerunner to twentieth-century thought, Nietzsche also aims at therapy, individual and cultural; his doctors are artists, who will furnish the "stimulus to life." Yeats's "going back" is an effort to arrive at a form that will provide that stimulus.

The age where Yeats alights on his journey backward is that "of Shakespeare and of Corneille"—a designation so broad as to indicate more a state of mind than a specific historical period. Both are tragedians, and both rely primarily on language for their effect. "We have looked for the centre of our art," Yeats says, "where the players of the time of Shakespeare and of Corneille found theirs—in speech" (*Ex,* p. 211). To a poet for whom, very early, "words alone are certain good," this is a natural choice of "centre." In those Golden Days, Yeats says, "before men read, the ear and the tongue were subtle, and delighted one another with the little tunes that were in words" (*Ex,* p. 212). Finding little tunes in words is discovering the sound beneath the sense, the Dionysian impulse to rhythm and the instinctual beneath the Apollonian structure of rational meaning. Yeats put the dichotomy more plainly in another *Samhain* essay: "What the ever-moving, delicately moulded flesh is to human beauty, vivid musical words are to passion" (*Ex,* p. 167). Language contains the antinomies that, when adjusted in the right proportion, can reproduce the extraordinary state of passion.

Another property that Yeats implies is present in language—through his impulse to return to the "source" of the arts and of recitation in particular—is universality. Language itself looks back, because it carries the past within it. It is thus a mode of apprehension ideally suited to take on the therapeutic task of remembering, and it is diametrically opposed to the mode of mathematics, whose symbols do not carry that psychic and cultural weight. Yeats says: "Somebody has said that every nation begins with poetry and ends with algebra, and passion has always refused to express itself in algebraic terms" (*Ex,* pp. 167–68). Poetry and passion, versus algebra and knowledge; Yeats stands at the point of cleavage, sides with poetry (the cultural underdog), and associates his side with "life," in an effort to turn the movement toward algebra around. Language—vivid, musical language—and extravagance or "recklessness" of character and situation, will help put passion back on the stage, with the hope of creating ritual power and, thereby, restorative energy.

A final idea in the *Samhain* essays shows Yeats working with the oppositions of form and content, with speculations about the "antithetical" in art derived from Nietzsche's *Case of Wagner* studies. Nietzsche theorizes about how tragic emotion should be created in art: through its opposite, through order, measure, and control; reason; discipline. Praising Bizet's *Carmen* at Wagner's expense, he says: "This music seems to me to be perfect. It approaches lightly, nimbly, and with courtesy. . . . It is rich. It is precise. It builds, it organizes, it completes. . . . Have more painful, tragic accents ever been heard on the stage? And how are they obtained? Without grimace! Without counterfeit coinage! Without the *imposture* of the grand style!" (*CW,* pp. 5–6). And again, opposing the chaotic formlessness of Wagner's "infinite melody" that diffuses intensity, Nietzsche offers an alternative: "In older music, in an elegant, or solemn, or passionate to-and-fro, faster and slower, one had to do something quite different, namely, to *dance.* The proportion necessary thereto, the observance of definite balance in measure of time and intensity, extorted from the soul of the hearer a continuous consideration" (*CW,* p. 70). Yeats, too, is theorizing about the representation of passion and power on the stage, still looking back to a time when language dominated: "As long as drama was full of poetical beauty, full of description, full of philosophy, as long as its words were the very vesture of sorrow and laughter, the players understood that their art was essentially conventional, artificial, ceremonious" (*Ex,* p. 172). He calls words the "vesture" of passion again, but he suddenly widens the concept from a single speech to an entire "art," whose three attributes—convention, artifice, ceremony—recall his description of the order, tradition, and labor of the poet and lover in "Adam's Curse." To express an intensity of passion, an intensity of its opposite is required; Dionysus demands Apollo, face demands mask, the "real" demands the artificial, the unique demands the conventional.

Whether or not the "players" of poetical drama "understood that their art was essentially conventional, artificial, ceremonious," the fact is that Yeats understands it. In this 1904 passage, he expresses the basic aesthetic idea behind his mask theory. It follows the one he made imaginatively in "Adam's Curse," and foreshadows others he is to make discursively in *Discoveries* (1906) and in his Journal (1909), about the power of oppositions—"antithetical optics," as Nietzsche says—in creating poetry of power. Yet the very next sentence of the essay shows that Yeats still considers the purpose of the power so generated to be "escape." Speaking of drama in the seventeenth century, he says: "The stage itself was differently shaped, being more a platform than a stage, for they did not desire to picture the surface of life, but to escape from it. But realism came in, and every change towards realism coincided with a decline in dramatic energy" (*Ex,* p. 172). Escape from the surface of life to its substance somewhere else, to the "reality" beneath or above or beyond the surface, is what Yeats in the 1890s identified as the function of "ideal thought" in the theater. His dualism between this world and the other world—seductive and dangerous, according to Nietzsche—puts the energy and passion in the "cry that calls beyond the limits of the world"; Yeats is seduced into choosing "escape" to the other world, always in the nineties, and always in the next decade when he speaks explicitly of tragedy. But he is not consistent in this choice when he speaks of art in general; in the 1904 essays I have been looking at, he vacillates, almost from sentence to sentence, between endorsing the metaphysics of symbolic art on the one hand and the oppositions of "becoming" on the other. Endorsing opposition involves "energy of the will," as he puts it in a letter to Russell of this period; endorsing metaphysics, "energy of the spirit" (see chapter 4, above). The former produces "joy" and the theory of the mask, based on will; the latter produces "ecstasy" and tragedy, based on spirit.

Romantic ecstasy, spirit freed from flesh, as Yeats says in the Morris essay, in "that extremity of life in which life seems to pass away like the phoenix in the flame of its own lighting," is a slippery concept in Yeats's writing of these years. Interestingly, whenever he speaks of practical aesthetic technique, his categorical imperatives tend to collapse, and the absolutes of tragic ecstasy give way to the realities, and relativities, of creative joy. Thus, in that compendium of ambivalence, the 1904 *Samhain* essays, as he discusses the actual presentation of symbolic ideas on stage in material form, he has this to say about "immortality" and "passion": "when one wishes to make the voice immortal and passionless, as in the Angel's part in my *Hour-Glass,* one finds it desirable for the player to speak always upon pure musical notes, written out beforehand and carefully rehearsed. On the one occasion when I heard the Angel's part spoken in this way with entire success, the contrast between the crystalline quality of the pure notes and the more confused and passionate speaking of the Wise Man was a new dramatic effect of great value" (*Ex,* p. 174). Yeats has, up to now, put "passion" on the side of immortality when talking about his own plays. He now reverses this practice, and makes the Angel "immortal and passionless" and the mortal wise man confused and passionate, and he values the "dramatic effect" of the contrast.

The Shadowy Waters

In 1906, in *Poems, 1899–1905,* Yeats published three plays: *The Shadowy Waters, The King's Threshold,* and *On Baile's Strand. The Shadowy Waters* occupied him longest, for he began it in 1885, worked on it during the 1890s, published it for the first time in the *North American Review* in 1900, and revised and republished it in different versions in 1904, 1906, 1907, and 1911. It thus stands as a witness to and a product of Yeats's self-remaking; it stands as the single best example, outside the prose essays of *Samhain,* of the conflict between his nineties ideal of tragedy, and his developing concept of the mask.

A program note in Yeats's hand, written for the performance of the play at the Abbey on July 9, 1905, illustrates the terms of the conflict: "The main story expresses the desire for a perfect and eternal union that comes to all lovers, the desire for love to 'drown in its own shadow.' But it also has other meanings. Forgael seeks Death; Dectora has always sought life; and in some way the uniting of her vivid force with his abyss-seeking desire for the waters of Death makes a perfect humanity."[14] The main story's purpose takes the lovers out of the world, following Yeats's nineties formula for tragedy that attaining perfection or an ideal ("a perfect and eternal union") means rejecting nature. It is the l'Isle d'Adam formula of *Axel,* a play Yeats admired, in which the lovers take their own lives rather than face the contradictions and complexities of living. In his book on the revisions of Yeats's verse plays from 1900 to 1910, S. B. Bushrui calls the 1900 version of *The Shadowy Waters* "the culminating point in Yeats's nostalgia for a dream-world."[15] Through all revisions, the main story remains central. In a note on the play written in 1906, Yeats describes the plot as a "fairy-tale." Forgael, "a Sea-king of ancient Ireland," is lured to sea in search of "love of a supernatural intensity and happiness." His friend Aibric and his sailors think him mad; they capture a ship and seize one of its passengers, a beautiful woman, Dectora, whom Forgael subdues by the sound of his magic harp. The sailors flee on the other ship, and Forgael and Dectora drift on alone, "awaiting death and what comes after, or some mysterious transformation of the flesh, an embodiment of every lover's dream" (*VPl*, p. 340). In the early versions—as in *Where There Is Nothing*—the questers after the ideal meet with little resistance. They simply cut the rope and, speaking much occult-laden, symbolic verse, drift away.

The second half of Yeats's program note, indicating "other meanings," suggests the kind of change Yeats's revisions tried to effect. He must have realized as he reworked the play in 1902 and 1903 that the second half of the orange was badly underrepresented in the early versions. The note shows that Yeats has in mind a balancing of the forces of life and death, to make a "perfect humanity." The plot of the play locates the perfection of the main story outside nature, but the "other meanings" locate it in a perfect humanity, composed of a union of opposites within nature. Yeats uses the word *seek* ("Forgael seeks Death, Dectora has always sought life") as Nietzsche uses it in the important passage from *Nietzsche contra Wagner* in which sufferers "seek" an art or philosophy as medicine for their "advancing or decaying life." He also echoes his own use of the word in the night-day diagram from the Common anthology, where self and soul seek their opposites, knowledge and life. Yeats has his mask theory in mind as he writes this program note; it is behind his revisions to the main story, and in conflict with it.

As he revises the play, Yeats works toward a marriage of sun and moon, day and night. All the revisions add weight to the side of "sun"—of energy, will, joy, "life." They show a clear classicizing tendency—a shift from abstract to concrete diction, hazy to definite images, increasing simplicty or severity involving much verbal exfoliation. Of his revisions to all the plays, Yeats comments in a 1906 *Samhain* essay that "every rewriting that has succeeded upon the stage has been an addition to the masculine element, an increase of strength in the bony structure" (*Ex,* p. 220). This statement seems to me proof positive that Yeats is incorporating Nietzsche's strictures about masculine strength into his own aesthetics. In *The Shadowy Waters,* the bony structure is strengthened by creating conflict. As Bushrui points out, the sailors on Forgael's ship are given more importance, and their speech is pared, purged, and made idiomatic in an effort to offset by their earthiness the otherworldliness of Forgael's romantic quest.[16] The concept of love itself has been amended; ideal in the 1900 version, in 1906 its meaning involves opposition. "For love is war, and there is hatred in it," says Forgael (*VPl,* p. 334). Yeats labors, in the way of "Adam's Curse," to establish a contrast between natural and ideal love. Bushrui says that in the 1906 version, the character of Aibric, Forgael's right-hand man, has been greatly expanded; a shadow of Forgael in the earlier version, in 1906 he "represents the practical man, who bases his life on reasoning and the laws of cause and effect."[17] He becomes, with the sailors and Dectora herself, an advocate of "natural love," who urges Forgael to "drive impossible dreams away" (*VPl,* p. 231). So begins a debate between the positions of ideal and natural love, like the positions represented by Shelley and Morris in the Morris essay. Forgael protests that to love beautiful women in the way of the world is highly unsatisfactory:

> *Forgael.* But he that gets their love after the fashion
> Loves in brief longing and deceiving hope
> And bodily tenderness, and finds that even
> The bed of love, that in the imagination
> Had seemed to be the giver of all peace,
> Is no more than a wine-cup in the tasting,
> And as soon finished.
>
> *Aibric.* All that ever loved
> Have loved that way—there is no other way.
>
> *Forgael.* Yet never have two lovers kissed but they
> Believed there was some other near at hand,
> And almost wept because they could not find it.
>
> *Aibric.* When they have twenty years; in middle life
> They take a kiss for what a kiss is worth,
> And let the dream go by.

Forgael. It's not a dream,
But the reality that makes our passion
As a lamp shadow—no—no lamp, the sun.
What the world's million lips are thirsting for
Must be substantial somewhere.
(*VPl,* pp. 321–22)

Forgael then disappears, in the 1906 version, into a long speech about dreams, trance, and the place where dream is reality, but emerges again on a heroic note: "I only of all living men shall find it." Embedded in his argument that true lovers never want to "linger wretched/ Among substantial things" is the passionate contradiction:

It's not a dream,
But the reality that makes our passion
As a lamp shadow—no—no lamp, the sun.

These lines seem to burst out of Yeats's new consciousness. They come from his recent alignment—exemplified in the night-day diagram in the Common anthology—of day with action and power. It's not a dream (the night), but physical reality (the day) that makes our passion, he has Forgael say, in a significant concession to the natural, material world. But he is not happy to have passion natural and ephemeral.

The play therefore retains its main story and ends with the lovers forsaking the world. Dectora's last lines remain the same in all versions:

Bend lower, that I may cover you with my hair,
For we will gaze upon this world no longer.
(*VPl,* p. 339; *VP,* p. 769)

The successive changes to the play add strength to the "masculine element" and the "bony structure" by providing conflict, realistic opposition to Forgael's romantic idealism. Ironically, the changes make the ending more absurd than it seems in the ornamental, symbolic version of 1900, where nothing is very real but Forgael's quest for a perfect and eternal union in love. By 1906, the pull toward life is strong enough to swing the balance to Dectora. I sympathize with her when, toward the end of the play, she says to Forgael:

Carry me
To some sure country, some familiar place.

Have we not everything that life can give
In having one another?

(*VPl,* p. 337)

Rather than rejoicing in Forgael's heroism—

Our love shall be like theirs [the birds']
When we have put their changeless image on—

I find it irritating. The real hero is Dectora, who chooses to follow her obsessed lover to death, because she loves him. It is perhaps worth noting that in a letter to Margot Ruddock written in 1935, Yeats calls *The Shadowy Waters* "hot lobster," which he defines as a style romantic and overwritten.[18] Still, the final version's elementary conflict between the ideal or supernatural and the real or natural pursues Yeats all his life. Or the other way around: Yeats pursues the conflict.

The King's Threshold

What he finds in the making and remaking of his plays between 1903 and 1906 is that dramatic form insists on objectivity—that emotion as such is not dramatic. And as emotion as such is not dramatic, the lyric poet as he appears in Yeats's nineties poetry is not heroic. In *The King's Threshold,* written in 1903, the poet appears transformed, objectified. Seanchan picks up the energy of heroic will where the "poet" in "Adam's Curse" loses it, and carries it confidently through the play. Yeats wrote the play during the spring and summer in a burst of his initial enthusiasm for Nietzsche. This enthusiasm inspires most of the play; one finds it in specific "Nietzscheanisms" in the lines, in the central theme and plot, and in the use of opposition or mask in creating both "the bony structure" of contrasting characters and the flesh of individual poetic speeches.

The 1903 version of the play ends happily, as do all versions thereafter until 1922, when Yeats wrote the "tragic" ending he had, he tells us, originally intended. The story, based on an "Old Irish Prose Romance" (*VPl,* p. 314), is about an Irish bard, Seanchan, who has been dismissed from the king's council because the king, and the "Bishops, Soldiers, and Makers of the Law," are no longer willing to share their authority with "a mere man of words" (*VPl,* p. 259).

When the play opens, Seanchan is on hunger strike for the ancient right of poets. The action consists of a procession of representatives of various social institutions and classes, all of whom try to persuade Seanchan to abandon his cause and live. Seanchan remains unmoved; like Paul Ruttledge and Forgael, he is "whole-souled." In the early versions of the play, the king capitulates in the end. In the 1922 version, he does not, and Seanchan dies.

Yeats published the new ending in *Seven Poems and a Fragment* (1922), explaining the Fragment: "I had originally intended to end the play tragically and would have done so but for a friend who used to say, 'O do write comedy & have a few happy moments in the Theatre.' My unhappy moments were because a tragic effect is very fragile and a wrong intonation, or even a wrong light or costume will spoil it all. However the play remained always of the nature of tragedy and so subject to vicissitude" (*VPl,* p. 316). In *Yeats the Playwright,* Peter Ure agrees that the play always remained tragic by nature, and that Yeats's final revision corrects his mistaken earlier judgment; in *Yeats,* Harold Bloom disagrees.[19] That Yeats was originally of two minds about the ending indicates that if tragedy is by nature subject to vicissitude, so is the poet. For Yeats in 1903, the vicissitude takes the form of ambivalent or vacillating loyalty, as we have seen, between halves of the orange. He seems to have linked tragedy firmly to the first half; his "tragic" plots of roughly the same period, of *The Shadowy Waters* and *Where There Is Nothing,* convey their heroes out of the world to the "perfect joy" of changeless death. His essays as well make clear that as far as he is concerned, a tragic hero by nature seeks escape from the natural world.

Seanchan is in fact seeking just that; he would seem therefore to fill the bill of tragic hero. But he cannot be a tragic hero as Yeats conceived tragedy in 1903 (by 1922, he can) because Yeats has been infected with Nietzsche's sense of life as affirmation and "becoming," and with his sense of the importance of art as joyous and life-furthering, he cannot—so infected yet still holding his convictions about tragedy—let Seanchan die.

For the 1903 version of the play Yeats wrote a Prologue, to be spoken by an old man with a red dressing gown, red slippers, and red nightcap, holding a brass candlestick with a guttering candle in it. He is shuffling and rheumatic—the prototype of the Old Man Prologue in *The Death of Cuchulain*—and he functions ironically, like his successor, as counterpart or countertruth to the "fiction" of the play. He is an innovation for Yeats, a break with conventional stage decorum and certainly with the fragility Yeats associated with tragedy. In the norm of dramatic convention he is antirealistic, but he represents the real. He says in front of the curtain: "After a while the stage there will be filled up with great ladies and great gentlemen, and poets, and a king with a crown on him, and all of them as high up in themselves with the pride of their youth and their strength and their fine clothes as if there was no such thing in the world as cold in the shoulders, and speckled shins, and pains in the bones and the stiffness in the joints that make an old man that has the whole load of the world on him ready for his bed" (*VPl,* pp. 313–14). Yeats's irony here is both structural and thematic. His old man comments on the nature of art's illusion and on the reality of speckled shins, inviting the audience to consider the difference between art and nature by drawing a clear distinction between them. He creates an ironic distance between the audience and the play they are about to see; he is the play's anti-self. He thus introduces, before the curtain even goes up, the concept of antithesis; the oppositions of *The King's Threshold* are not added later (as in *The Shadowy Waters*) but are integral to its bony structure from the start.

The old man of the Prologue is of course part of the play and so part of the illusion. His appearance is hardly one of unmixed realism. He speaks of his pains and his wish to be in bed, but on the other hand, he is dressed, unnaturally, completely in red. As a parody of the Red Man of Ulster, his costume links him with the characters of Irish legendry whom he introduces. His own mixed state—part hero, part fool; or part "unnatural," part "natural"—also introduces the possibility of the union of opposites, as the theme of the play itself, working within the limits of the contrast the old man sets up between art and nature, works toward a mending of that split.

More clearly than Yeats's statement of 1922, the Prologue gives the reason for his choice of ending: "Some think it would be a finer tale if Seanchan had died at the end of it, and the king had the guilt at his door, for that might have served the poet's cause better in the end. But that is not true, for if he that is in the story but a shadow and an image of poetry had not risen up from the death that threatened him, the ending would not have been true and joyful enough to be put into the voices of players and proclaimed in the mouths of trumpets, and poetry would have been badly served" (*VPl,* p. 313). Yeats has the Prologue explain that Seanchan is "but a shadow and an image of poetry"—a symbolic character, in other words; since he symbolizes immortal poetry, he cannot die. In this "apology," we see Yeats's symbolist side, desirous of essence and stasis, taking precedence over his dialectical side, espouser of permanent conflict. Yet with the exception of the ending, *The King's Threshold* is based on dialectic—the joyful and creative Apollonic will, working itself out through oppositions, in the service of life, through art, the "great stimulus to life," as Nietzsche says. Perhaps to compensate for the cessation of conflict in the ending, Yeats emphasizes its tone of "joy" rather too insistently. The final speech is accompanied by "a trumpet blast," a veritable call to resurrection, as Seanchan "rises up from death that threatened him" and speaks prophetic words:

> O silver trumpets! Be you lifted up
> And cry to the great race that is to come.
> Long-throated swans amid the waves of Time,
> Sing loudly, for beyond the wall of the world
> The race may hear our music and awake.
>
> (*VPl,* pp. 311–12)[20]

This speech includes one of the obvious "Nietzscheanisms," the idea that Zarathustra's superman symbolizes a future race of heroes. Yeats repeats the idea in his New York speech the next year, in which he alludes to Nietzsche and concludes his peroration by saying, "It may be that it depends upon us to call up into life the phantom armies of the future."[21] Harold Bloom believes that Seanchan's concern with "futurity" derives from Shelley's *Defence of Poetry*—that the play's final trumpets are Shelley's trumpets that "sing to battle" and "feel not what they inspire."[22] He is probably right about the trumpets, but the "great race that is to come" is a Nietzschean prophecy.[23] Another *King's Threshold* speech arising from Yeats's reading of Nietzsche is Seanchan's defense of poetry:

> And I would have all know that when all falls
> In ruin, poetry calls out in joy,
> Being the scattering hand, the bursting pod,
> The victim's joy among the holy flame,
> God's laughter at the shattering of the world.
> And now that joy laughs out, and weeps and burns
> On these bare steps.
>
> (*VPl,* pp. 266–67)

Simultaneous laughter and weeping, creation amid destruction is the kind of fertile chaos Zarathustra says is needed before one can "give birth to a dancing star." Yeats is also alluding to the passage on tragedy in *The Twilight of the Idols,* already much quoted in this study: tragedy goes "beyond terror and pity, to *realise in fact* the eternal delight of becoming—that delight that even involves in itself the joy of annihilating" (*CW,* p. 231).

In the same book, Nietzsche names the prerequisite for art: "To the existence of art, to the existence of any aesthetic activity or perception whatsoever, a preliminary psychological condition is indispensable, namely, *ecstasy*. Ecstasy must first have intensified the sensitiveness of the whole mechanism; until this takes place, art is not realised. . . . The essential thing in ecstasy is the feeling of increased power and profusion" (*CW,* p. 170). Seanchan, as the "shadow and image" of poetry, is presented in a state of ecstasy, especially in these proto-Nietzschean speeches.[24] His ecstasy is pronounced delirium by the bystanders, as he tells of the coming of Nietzsche's master race:

> The stars had come so near me that I caught
> Their singing. It was praise of that great race
> That would be haughty, mirthful, and white-bodied,
> With a high head, and open hand, and how,
> Laughing, it would take mastery of the world.
>
> (*VPl,* p. 301)

Another manifestation of the visionary madness of art comes as Seanchan links contagion or leprosy with the moon. His stand must be taken as antithetical to Yeats's own position of the nineties, and in accordance with Nietzsche's anti-moon position in *Thus Spake Zarathustra.*[25] Seanchan curses the Princesses who offer him food and drink, calling them "lepers." He has been lying down throughout the play to this point. His rising to his feet to fling the wine in the Princesses' faces, and staggering stage center as they withdraw in horror, underscores his words dramatically, as he says:

> Where did I say the leprosy had come from?
> I said it came out of a leper's hand,
> And that he walked the highway. But that's folly,
> For he was walking up there in the sky.
> And there he is even now, with his white hand
> Thrust out of the blue air, and blessing them

With leprosy. . . .
He's holding up his hand above them all—
King, noblemen, princesses—blessing all.
Who could imagine he'd have so much patience?
(*VPl,* pp. 297–98)

Yeats amplifies, and clarifies, his allusion to the moon's patient blessing in the new ending of 1922 in Seanchan's last speech before his death:

O, look upon the moon that's standing there
In the blue daylight—take note of the complexion,
Because it is the white of leprosy
And the contagion that afflicts mankind
Falls from the moon.
(*VPl,* p. 309)

Nietzsche speaks of the sneaking "monk in the moon"—of the moon's era as the two-thousand year period of Christian domination, and of the contagion, the sickness-unto-death, of civilization divorced from instinct that has been the result of the moon's reign. Seanchan sees the moon as "blessing" the status quo with leprosy—not as cause of the affliction but, as in *Thus Spake Zarathustra,* as symbol of it.

Seanchan is assumed to be mad, deranged by hunger. It is only when his pupils, the artists-to-be, pronounce themselves ready to die for his cause that the dramatic reversal occurs. The King asks the pupils to kneel and beg for their lives, and they answer in turn, from oldest to youngest, "Die, Seanchan, and proclaim the right of the poets" (*VPl,* p. 308). The King then capitulates (in all versions before 1922), kneels before Seanchan, and says:

Kneel down kneel down; he has the greater power.
There is no power but has its roots in his—
I understand it now. There is no power
But his that can withhold the crown or give it,
Or make it reverent in the eyes of men.
(*VPl,* p. 308)

The power struggle Yeats has dramatized in *The King's Threshold* is a poetic Investiture Struggle (the great medieval conflict between Church and State). In Yeats's version, the poet holds the position of

Church, and uses many of the same arguments against the King that Holy Church used. Seanchan's central argument is that life depends absolutely on art to provide its models (as life eternal depended on Christ as the Way) for its very continuance. Oscar Wilde had said that "life imitates art," and Nietzsche also makes this argument, cogently and in detail, in a series of connected passages in *The Twilight of the Idols*.

Under the heading "Beautiful and Ugly," Nietzsche talks of the relativity of beauty. In the next section, he hypothesizes about the psychological foundation of human horror at ugliness:

> Nothing is beautiful, except man: all aesthetics rest on this *naiveté,* it is their *first* truth. Let us straightway add the second: nothing is ugly, except *degenerating* man;—the domain of aesthetic judgment is thereby limited.—Re-examined physiologically, all that is ugly weakens and afflicts man. It reminds him of deterioration, of danger, and of impotence; he actually suffers a loss of power by it. . . . Whom does man hate? There can be no doubt: *the decline of his type.* The hatred is inspired by the most profound instinct of the species; there is horror, foresight, profundity, and far-reaching vision in it. . . . On account of it, art is *profound.* (*CW,* pp. 182–83)

In the next four sections, he gives reasons. First he repudiates Schopenhauer's claim that art results from negation of the "will," calling this claim "the most spurious psychological mintage, Christianity excepted, which history records." He brings another philosopher to his aid: "No less an authority than the divine Plato (Schopenhauer himself calls him divine) maintains another thesis: that all beauty incites to procreation." In the next section, Nietzsche continues: "Plato goes further. He says, with an innocence for which one must be Greek and not 'Christian,' that there would be no Platonic philosophy at all, were there not such handsome youths in Athens; it was only the sight of them which put the soul of the philosopher into an erotic ecstasy, and gave it no rest until it had implanted the seed of all high things in such fine soil" (*CW,* pp. 183–85). Niezsche's argument reaches a climax—and he'd be the first to put a sexual interpretation on the word—in the next section, called *L'art pour l'art.* He begins by berating "art's subordination to morality," and continues:

> When the end of the ethical preacher and improver of mankind has been excluded from art, it does not at all follow that art in itself is without an end, without a goal, meaningless; in short, *l'art pour l'art*—a serpent which bites

its own tail. "No end at all, rather than a moral end!"—thus speaks pure passion. A psychologist, on the other hand, asks, what does all art do? does it not praise? does it not glorify? does it not select? does it not bring into prominence? In each of these cases it *strengthens or weakens* certain valuations . . . is this only a contingent matter? an accident? something with which the instinct of the artist would not at all be concerned? Or rather, is it not the prerequisite which *enables* the artist to do something? Is his fundamental instinct directed towards art? or is it not rather directed towards the sense of art, namely, *life?* towards a *desirableness of life?*—Art is the great stimulus of life. (*CW*, p. 186)

Art belongs, in short, to the Eternal Return, and directs or recycles human energy back into life at every point.

This argument is the central theme and subject of Yeats's play. The trumpet call to "the great race that is to come" is one of its more literal and rhetorical expressions. In other places, Yeats emphasizes the value of art to human procreation. Catechizing his pupils, Seanchan makes them repeat their lesson; the Oldest Pupil responds:

I said the poets hung
Images of the life that was in Eden
About the child-bed of the world, that it,
Looking upon those images, might bear
Triumphant children.

Seanchan. Tell on . . .
What evil thing will come upon the world
If the Arts perish?

Oldest Pupil. If the Arts should perish,
The world that lacked them would be like a woman
That, looking on the cloven lips of a hare,
Brings forth a hare-lipped child.

(*VPl*, pp. 264–65)

These and other speeches—especially those by the cripples, who represent the voice of "folk wisdom" ("A poet has power from beyond the world") (*VPl*, p. 270)—prepare the way for the King's final capitulation.

The King's opening speech also prepares the way for the "happy" ending. He does not appear opposed to poetry; on the contrary, his speech describes the kind of harmony, and of power, poetry commands. In it Yeats uses what he has learned from Nietzsche in a less polemical way—aesthetically, as a balance of opposites. The King enters from his palace, stands at the top of the steps, and greets Seanchan's pupils, whom he has summoned to "save the life" of Seanchan:

> I welcome you that have the mastery
> Of the two kinds of Music: the one kind
> Being like a woman, the other like a man.
> Both you that understand stringed instruments,
> And how to mingle words and notes together
> So artfully, that all the Art's but Speech
> Delighted with its own music; and you that carry
> The long twisted horn, and understand
> The heady notes that, being without words,
> Can hurry beyond Time and Fate and Change.
> For the high angels that drive the horse of Time—
> The golden one by Day, by Night the silver—
> Are not more welcome to one that loves the world
> For some fair woman's sake.
>
> (*VPl,* pp. 257–58)

Whereas it is later made explicit, the concept of art's connection with time and procreation—the natural cycle of life—is announced in this opening. So too are Yeats's "halves of the orange," in his Nietzschean interpretation of the dichotomy between "Apollonic" and "Dionysiac." He is thinking about the marriage of sun and moon, male and female principles, and working with his dichotomies between the individual mind and the universal mind, immanence and transcendence, the "joyful and self-sufficient" and the "sad and desirous," in the context of art. "Music" is a metaphor for poetry, and consists of two "kinds." One kind understands "how to mingle words and notes together"; it "artfully" accomplishes the synthesis of sound and sense, emotion and reason, and is "delighted" at the resulting union. It is an art joyfully rooted in conflict and the "desire to create forms"—a Nietzschean art, "Apollonic," as Yeats understands the word. It represents the second half of the orange. By extension, as poetry, it is dramatic. The other kind of music, the type of the twisted horn, "understands" the "heady notes" that escape the temporal—time, fate, and change—because it is without words. This art is Yeats's first half of the orange, the "desire to transcend forms." It represents essentially the tragic impulse, as Yeats conceives it: pure passion, refusing limitation, reason, individuation.

Both kinds of art, however, are "driven" or bound by time (the twisted horn only "understands" the notes that hurry beyond time). They become symbolically equated with the golden and silver horses of time, sun and moon. The stringed music of self-delight sounds like various of Yeats's descriptions of the sun's symbolism, and that of the horn's like the moon's. But there is a problem with the moon's symbolizing escape from time and change, as Yeats also interprets the moon as "the symbol of change" (*E&I,* p. 91). He leaves the problem unresolved, as he leaves the gender of each type of music ambiguous. One is male, one female, but which is which we do not know. Yeats's unwillingness or inability to align his characteristics clearly under the categorical headings shows that for him the divisions are not that simple anymore. The moon, as night, has represented the transcendent half of the orange; the sun, as day, the immanent. Yet this division denies the moon's affinities with natural cycles, and the sun's with gold-wrought "eternal" artifice. Each contains something of the other; purities are impossible. The fact that Yeats circumscribes both "kinds of music" by time is a giant step in the direction of his acknowledging Nietzsche's concept of "becoming."

In the final lines of the opening speech, Yeats returns to the idea of sexual union (loving the world for some fair woman's sake), whose procreative power extends by implication to that of the union of the "two kinds of Music." That union might also bring forth "children"—works of art whose energy, combining characteristics of both parents, might bind the temporal and the eternal. The moving idea behind the union is Nietzsche's Eternal Return, which yokes the temporal and the eternal in a paradox that eliminates both "parents" as separate concepts, and produces the "third metamorphosis of the spirit," the "child": affirmation, innocence, creativity.

Formally, the king's opening speech picks up the ironies of the Prologue and carries them out on another level. Like the Prologue, it introduces the action but does not partake of it; it introduces the themes of art, procreation, time, and finally death (when Seanchan is mentioned). Strangely, the King addresses the pupils, apprentice poets, as musicians—an incongruity like the Old Man's red costume. As Yeats will soon afterward in *Deirdre* (which he begins the next year) inaugurate his convention of opening his plays with "musicians," this speech may be seen as a trial run—an experiment pointing toward the development of the idea. As with the Prologue, the impetus of the speech derives from Yeats's need to break with the decorum of realism. The Prologue itself accomplishes the break, and the opening speech goes further, by changing the mood or tone. Yeats wants to establish a "ritual" form of drama—something like Greek tragedy, in which the chorus acted as a link between audience and play, and through its chanting and dancing represented the collective Dionysian spirit of music against which the individual Apollonian conflict could be played out. In a letter to Frank Fay written on August 8, 1903, Yeats says, "I am sending your brother Seanchan today. . . . It is quite a long elaborate play, and it is constructed rather like a Greek play. I think it is the best thing I have ever done" (*L,* p. 409). The King's speech to the musicians suggests something "rather like" an address to the Greek chorus; it frames the action with the music of its lines on music, and so establishes not only distance, but a new state of mind, both reflective and receptive.

Nietzsche makes repeated references to music as the Dionysian art—at greatest length in *The Birth of Tragedy,* which I am still wary of using as a source for Yeats, because his notions of it are secondhand until 1909. In discussing the "Dionysian condition" in *The Twilight of the Idols,* Nietzsche describes the Dionysian man as a kind of Proteus: "He assumes every external appearance, every motion; he changes himself continually." Music, he says, enables people to experience this protean sympathy with all things: "Music, as we understand it at present, is also a collective excitement and collective discharge of the emotions; nevertheless it is only the survival of a much wider world of emotional expressions, a mere *residuum* of Dionysian histrionism" (*CW,* pp. 173–74). Nietzsche himself suggests the connection between music and ritual, and Yeats takes it up, tentatively, in his emphasis on music in the opening speech of his play.

The play contains other ritual touches, slight but significant. The cripples and the serving man join in a "rhythmical chant" toward the middle of the play, calling a curse upon the King if Seanchan dies. The five stanzas, chanted or sung, provide another choric effect, stronger than the first because they are in fact choral. The final stanza runs:

And nobody will sing for him,
And nobody will hunt for him,
And nobody will fish for him,
And nobody will pray for him,
But ever and always curse him and abuse him.

(*VPl,* p. 281)

The chant's content underlines the "folk wisdom" that the death of poetry will bring a curse upon the land. Its form provides a sense of the supernormal through its quality of incantation, suggestive of rite, magic, the primitive.

Finally, on quite another limb of the same ritual tree, Seanchan provokes the Monk by calling the Monk's God a bird:

A little God,
With comfortable feathers, and bright eyes.

(*VPl,* p. 293)

He asks the Monk:

Has that wild God of yours, that was so wild
When you'd but lately taken the King's pay,
Grown any tamer? . . .
Have you persuaded him
To chirp between two dishes when the King
Sits down to table?

(*VPl,* p. 292)

The phrase "that wild God" echoes Yeats's use of it, in the letter to Quinn a couple of months earlier, announcing his change of sympathy from the first to the second half of the orange: "I think I have to some extent got weary of that wild God Dionysus and I am hoping that the Far-Darter will come in his place" (*L,* p. 403). As a reader of *The Golden Bough,* Yeats knew that the spirit of the Egyptian god Osiris became a bird;[26] the Irish gods, too, often underwent metamorphoses into birds. In these speeches to the Monk, under the guise of madness, Seanchan fuses pagan beliefs and Christian practices. The Monk will "tame" the "wild God," as Christianity (according to Nietzsche) tamed the spirit of humanity. Osiris became Dionysus; Dionysus became Christ, and Christ eventually lost the Investiture Struggle and became, like the bird with comfortable feathers, serviceable to the King. Seanchan's reference to God as a bird functions on the literal level to prove him mad. On the thematic level, it illuminates poetry's connection with religious beliefs in all ages and suggests a veiled prophecy of a future dispensation when gods may again be "wild," their spirits birds, the wheel come round again.

The address to the musicians at the start of the play, the folk chants suggestive of witchcraft and spells, the allusion to the bird god, and, I think, Seanchan's madness and ecstatic prophecies, all help Yeats create a Dionysian counterpoint to the main action, an opposite "mood." He will theorize about mood later in connection with "tragic effect." In the Preface to *Poems, 1899–1905* he discusses the complexity involved in writing drama in verse, as we saw at the end of the last chapter; he begins to articulate the theory of what he has been doing in practice for several years. In dramatic prose, he says, "one has to prepare principally for actions, and for the thoughts or emotions" that accompany them, "but in verse one has to do all this and to follow as well a more subtle sequence of cause and effect, that moves through vast sentiments and intricate thoughts that accompany action, but are not necessary to it." This "more subtle sequence," he says a few sentences later, uncovers "that high, intellectual, delicately organised soul of men and of an action" (*VPl,* p. 849). This uncovering of the soul behind the action is Yeats's music of the twisted horn, and his "ritual" effects in *The King's Threshold* supply that music. If Seanchan's action can be seen as both temporal and individual on the one hand, and "eternal" and universal on the other, then Yeats has managed the synthesis, consummated the marriage, and earned the right to consider the play "the best thing" he has ever done.

Seanchan's connection to "eternity" is clearly, throughout, an eternity within or through time. There is no sense in this play of a place where conflict ceases (except in the opening reference to the "notes . . . that can hurry beyond Time"—but they too are bound). The play was exciting for Yeats to write; he revised it less than *On Baile's Strand* and *The Shadowy Waters,* because he began both before he read Nietzsche, who offered him the challenge and the method to remake himself. *The King's Threshold* was written on a rush of inspiration. The revised ending of 1922, emphasizing the moon's responsibility for mankind's affliction and including Seanchan's laughing death, only reinforces the original Nietzschean impetus. The ironic structural oppositions—Prologue vs. play, minor characters vs. Seanchan, ritual devices vs. realistic ones—assist the principal thematic opposition, art vs. life. In overcoming this principal opposition at the end, in the King's acknowledgment that he ("life") is less powerful than art, Yeats's grip on the second half of the orange falters. Seanchan remains heroic and sounds the trumpet call of prophecy at the end, but the balance of opposites is lost, the ritual circle is broken. For the curse to be defeated, the cycle renewed, the poet must die, as Yeats comes to understand.

On Baile's Strand

Just after he finishes *The King's Threshold,* Yeats begins revising *On Baile's Strand.* The play is the first of his Cuchulain plays, but it sets the hero beyond his youth in middle age, at a time in his life parallel to the historic time of the play, when the Heroic Age is giving way to more settled domestic order. The action revolves around the "binding" of Cuchulain to the will of the king, Conchubar, by means of an oath of obedience. Once bound, Cuchulain fights and kills an unknown young challenger, who proves to be his son. In high heroic passion at this revelation, Cuchulain fights with the sea and is overpowered. The Fool and the Blind Man, meant as symbolic externalizations of Cuchulain and Conchubar, contribute an antiheroic subplot. In the revisions, Yeats works out the ironies of antithesis in an unbroken cycle that incorporates tragedy in Nietzsche's sense into its structure. It creates its affirmation, or tragic joy, from the energy of the conflict of opposites; it has no need to proclaim the affirmation with trumpets, and it does not. In *Yeats the Playwright,* Peter Ure gives a lucid and inclusive account of the play's "continuous interplay of ironic meanings," and says, of Yeats's concept of tragedy: "His point of view entails a generous recognition of the value of heroic revolt, courage, and love; but they are placed in a context which proves tragic because of some element which is thwarting and contradictory in the nature of the heroic acts, the man who performs them, the spirit which inspires them, or the world in which they are done."[27] The thwarting and contradictory nature of action, character, and place is explained by Yeats's concept of mask, which he works out in practice as he remakes *On Baile's Strand*.

In his book on Yeats's revisions to his verse plays, S. B. Bushrui says that rewriting *On Baile's Strand* "took up almost the whole of 1905."[28] This was Yeats's second revision since the play's Abbey performance in December 1904, but he began writing it in 1902 and "changed it much" before its original publication in August 1903. As with *The Shadowy Waters* and *The King's Threshold,* the revisions to *On Baile's Strand* coincide exactly with Yeats's reading of Nietzsche and his developing concept of the mask. A letter he writes Frank Fay from Chicago during his tour of America in January 1904, establishes the coincidence nicely. He says he is sending some new "Cuchullain" dialogue, which he has just written; presumably he is also reading, or has read, or is about to read, Common's anthology of selections from Nietzsche. At any rate, his mind has begun "drifting vaguely towards that doctrine of 'the mask,' " as he put it in his *Autobiography* (*AU,* p. 93); the letter to Fay shows that he puts it exactly.

Speaking of Cuchulain's character, he speculates that his hero possesses the weakness inherent in his strength:

> Probably his very strength of character made him put off illusions and dreams . . . and made him become quite early in life a deliberate lover, a man of pleasure who can never really surrender himself. He is a little hard, and leaves the people around him a little repelled—perhaps this young man's affection is the thing he had most need of. Without this thought the play had not any deep tragedy. . . . He is the fool—wandering passive, houseless, and almost loveless. Conobhar is reason that is blind because it can only reason because it is cold. Are they not the cold moon and the hot sun? (*L,* pp. 424–25)

The psychologizing in the earlier part of this quotation appears to be at odds with the symbolizing at the end, both as description and as analytic method. But "that doctrine of the mask," vaguely drifting as it is, explains the discrepancies. The psychological analysis makes Cuchulain strong and self-sufficient to a fault. His strength becomes hardness; he "can never really surrender himself." He needs ("seeks"?) the young man's affection, as "self" in day—to return to the Common anthology's night-day diagram again—needs (seeks) "soul." Yeats has associated night or moon with self-surrender, and his use of "surrender" to describe Cuchulain's lack or need indicates that the early mask theory is behind his psychologizing of Cuchulain's character. Nietzsche provides many examples of this kind of analysis through antithesis: it is his principal means of discovery.

A few lines before the symbolic analysis, however, Yeats disparages character analysis, saying that his drawing of Cuchulain had proceeded on "instinct" and that too much rationalizing might kill the character: "The less one reasons the more living the character." Nietzsche is present in this thought too, in his bias toward instinct (power) as opposed to reason (knowledge). But Nietzsche's own contradictions are faithfully reflected in Yeats's letter, for the next statement's purpose is intellectual, rational. In it Yeats is trying to make sense of the oppositions he has presented in the play (while creating others in the letter); he is trying to link his developing characters and his developing "system." Here "that doctrine of the mask" is at its vaguest. Yeats almost stammers: "he is the fool—wandering passive, houseless and almost loveless. Conobhar is reason that is blind because it can only reason because it is cold. Are they not the cold moon and the hot sun?" He has already created the parallels between Cuchulain and Fool, Conchubar and Blind Man, in his early version of the play. Now he connects the characters to the symbols sun and moon; yet to call Cuchulain "passive" seems inappropriate, given his "strength of character" and his deliberateness as a lover. In the earlier description Yeats has also called Cuchulain "a little hard," a little repellent, a little loveless—all, surely, attributes of "coldness." In fact the description of Cuchulain as "wandering passive, houseless and almost loveless" would seem to be better symbolized by the cold moon than the hot sun. But Conchubar is defined as "cold" in Yeats's wonderful circular sentence: "Conobhar is reason that is blind because it can only reason because it is cold."

This sentence only makes sense in the context of other associations we know Yeats was making at about the same time. In the Preface to *Gods and Fighting Men,* he speaks of the "cold cup of the moon's intoxication," and in the night-day diagram of Common's anthology he equates night and knowledge, or "reason." Blindness he has much earlier, in "At Stratford on Avon" (1901), associated with wisdom (he speaks of "a wise man who was blind from very wisdom" [*E&I,* p. 107]). Coldness, reason, blindness, and the moon are associated with "the first half of the orange," transcendence (or surrender) of self, "self turned toward soul, seeking knowledge," as Yeats scribbled in the anthology's margin. As that marginal note makes clear, and as the contradictions in this letter imply, the nature of the "given" quality (cold, moon, reason) makes it "seek" its complement (hot, sun, power). Furthermore, by nature, the one quality bears a close relation to the other, in the sense that it contains or implies or depends on the other, as day by definition depends on and implies night. The psychological description of Cuchulain shows him to be both strong and weak; the symbolical description in its contradictions (he is both "wandering passive" and "hot sun") also, unintentionally, reveals his "mixed" character. When Yeats takes up "almost the whole of 1905" rewriting *On Baile's Strand,* he strengthens the sense of antithesis he begins to develop in this letter to show how, although Cuchulain and Conchubar are sun and moon and so opposites, they each contain the other. Therein lie the seeds of the tragedy.

I shall use the version of the play published in 1906, for it contains the revisions Bushrui has studied in detail. I am content to note that as he says, the revisions make the play "more forceful"; that both Cuchulain and Conchubar become "more arrogant" and "boastful"; that "it is a masculine arrogance, coarse and harsh."[29] I am also content to note that the kings are made "the docile section of any community," the "mediocre"; and that the Singing Women are added and "bring in an element of ritual and supernatural."[30] The revisions work toward clarity of outline, the same forcefulness that characterizes all of Yeats's revisions after he is himself strengthened by Nietzsche. Cuchulain and Conchubar are counterparts, themselves counterbalanced by the Fool and the Blind Man. They are sun and moon or day and night at war yet mutually dependent, their opposition striking sparks that powers the action and creates the tragedy. If Yeats clarifies this central conflict in his revisions, he also adds weight to the undersong, the Dionysian element, the "soul" of the action. The group of minor kings, the Singing Women, and the binding oath all strengthen the de-individuating principle, which is already present in the early versions in Cuchulain's apparent "enchantment" by witchcraft as he refuses to fight the young challenger, and in its chief representative, the sea.

Jeffares has said that Cuchulain is "an heroic great man," drawn probably out of an admiration of Nietzsche's theories;[31] and both Keane and Bohlmann, in their studies of Yeats and Nietzsche, maintain that Nietzsche's influence is responsible for Yeats's drawing of the principal contrast in the play between Cuchulain and Conchubar. Keane says: "Cuchulain is, in fact, precisely Nietzsche's 'noble type of man': Conchubar is the leader of 'the herd.' Indeed, the play is nothing so much as an embodiment of Nietzsche's distinction between the noble man and the herd man, master morality and slave morality."[32] This allegation is borne out by much of the dialogue of the first half of the play—the half most extensively revised. Cuchulain resists being "bound" by Conchubar, considering it a sign of weakness and even of degeneracy of the race. He says, for example:

> Conchubar,
> I do not like your children. They have no pith,
> No marrow in their bones, and will lie soft
> Where you and I lie hard.
>
> (*VPl*, p. 481)

Cuchulain the self-sufficient hero separates himself deliberately from the crowd and, secure of his fame, declares he has no need of children. Conchubar tells him that all men are "miserable" knowing that without heirs their family lands will "pass into a stranger's keeping" and Cuchulain replies:

> The most of men feel that,
> But you and I leave names upon the harp.
>
> (*VPl*, p. 483)

A passage in *A Genealogy of Morals* describes the psychology of herd mentality and its opposite. It fits the Cuchulain-Conchubar situation, and the page on which it appears is dog-eared in Yeats's copy. Nietzsche has been describing the "formation of herds":

> It is law universal for the strong to strive *away* from one another, as for the weak to strive *towards* one another. Whenever the former enter into an alliance with one another they do so (with much resistance on the part of each individual conscience) solely for the purpose of joint action and aggression, and with the prospect of an aggressive joint-action and a joint-indulgence of their will to power. The weak, on the other hand, will gather together, just taking *delight* in the gathering. In so doing their instinct is appeased, to the

same degree as the instinct of the born "masters" [i.e., the solitary beast-of-prey species of man] is by organisation provoked and alarmed from the bottom. (*GM*, p. 185)

In *A Genealogy of Morals, Beyond Good and Evil,* and in fact everything of Nietzsche we know Yeats read, the distinction between "master" and "slave" morality presupposes the historical distinction between classical and Christian, and takes on other connotations, which Yeats begins to attribute to qualities belonging to sun and moon, as we have seen. "Master" morality (the sun) affirms and creates; "slave" morality (the moon) involves "passive acceptance of a code." Since Conchubar is seeking to "bind" Cuchulain with an oath, for the future security of "threshold and hearthstone" and all "settled" virtues, he seems, indeed, representative of slave morality; and Cuchulain, in turn, is "provoked and alarmed from the bottom."

Conchubar also represents "wisdom" as opposed to Cuchulain's strength or power, a point made several times by Conchubar:

> I need your might of hand and burning heart,
> And you my wisdom. (*VPl,* p. 491)

And again, as Cuchulain takes the oath: "I give my wisdom, and I take your strength" (*VPl,* p. 499). So Conchubar and Cuchulain also represent the knowledge-power dichotomy, and the valuation given these qualities is Nietzsche's: the bias is toward power and the heroic. For although Concubar actively seeks Cuchulain's strength, Cuchulain does not, in turn, seek Conchubar's wisdom. Rather, he submits.

The reason given for his submission is simply historical. The tide of time has turned against his way of life, and he accepts the fact. When as a last resort he turns to his own band of young warriors and says, "we'll out of this/And sail upon the wind once more" (*VPl,* p. 491), a young king answers:

> Cuchulain, take the oath.
> There is none here that would not have you take it.
> *Cuchulain.* You'd have me take it? Are you of one mind?
> *The Kings.* All, all, all, all.
>
> (*VPl,* p. 493)

In this dialogue with its choral response, the one becomes the all, individuality is submerged in universality. "Self" has turned into "soul" on a social or historical level, as aristocracy gives way to democracy or socialism. As Cuchulain admits, "all's changed":

> Are you so changed?
> Or have I grown more dangerous of late?
> But that's not it. I understand it all.
> It's you that have changed. You've wives and children now. . . .
> It's time the years put water in my blood
> And drowned the wildness of it, for all's changed
> But that unchanged.—I'll take what oath you will.
>
> (*VPl,* p. 493)

All's changed, that is, "but that unchanged." Cuchulain's "blood" is still wild, still passionate, and constant or changeless in its passion. The oath he agrees to take is meant to "bind" or limit this wildness; at the same time, it is meant to bar the "Shape-Changers," or "witches," wild spirits of flux or fate, from Conchubar's threshold. Ironically the Shape-Changers represent the changeless, as Zarathustra's mistress Life is "changeable only," and permanent only in change. In this, they and Cuchulain's wild blood are linked: "All's changed / But that unchanged," which, like the sea itself, represents power and energy, Dionysian inexhaustibility.

The harder Conchubar tries to exclude the Shape-Changers, the closer they press around him. He prepares for the oath-taking by admonishments to customary ritual:

> The holders of the fire
> Shall purify the thresholds of the house
> With waving fire, and shut the outer door,
> According to custom; and sing rhyme
> That has come down from the old law-makers
> To blow the witches out.
>
> (*VPl,* p. 493)

"The witches" cannot be oath-bound, however; they, like the "passion" Yeats talks about in the definitions of tragedy that occur in his essays, refuse all limitation, defy all order. The women's song against the Shape-Changers as Cuchulain takes the oath is, ironically but obviously, an invocation and a prophecy:

> May this fire have driven out
> The Shape-Changers that can put
> Ruin on a great King's house
> Until all be ruinous. . . .
> They would make a prince decay
> With light images of clay
> Planted in the running wave. . . .
> Those wild hands that have embraced
> All his body can but shove
> At the burning wheel of love
> Till the side of hate comes up.
>
> (*VPl,* pp. 495, 497)

The Shape-Changers are enemies of stasis, even of stasis in love. Cuchulain's position on love is antithetical to Forgael's in *The Shadowy Waters,* and consistent with what the women sing of the Shape-Changers:

> I have never known love but as a kiss
> In the mid-battle, and a difficult truce
> Of oil and water, candles and dark night,
> Hillside and hollow, the hot-footed sun
> And the cold, sliding, slippery-footed moon—
> A brief forgiveness between opposites.
>
> (*VPl,* p. 489)

Permanence in love—the "changeless" world Forgael seeks—is impossible; conflict, the "burning wheel," is "that unchanged."

As soon as Cuchulain takes the oath, more changes occur. Cuchulain meets his son and recognizes his "like"; his friendship with the young man is not "a difficult truce of oil and water," but sun meeting sun (pun intentional). The oil and water are Cuchulain and Conchubar, whose opposition continues after the oath-taking—which could appear to mend it—by a brief but tragic reversal of characteristics. Temporarily, Cuchulain "puts on" Conchubar's "wisdom," and Conchubar Cuchulain's "wildness," and so the wheel of conflict keeps turning. Conchubar insists that a "witch" has turned Cuchulain's head, which charge Cuchulain rationally denies:

> *Conchubar.* Some witch of the air has troubled Cuchulain's mind.
>
> *Cuchulain.* No witchcraft. His head is like a woman's head
> I had a fancy for.

Conchubar. A witch of the air
Can make a leaf confound us with memories.
They run upon the wind and hurl the spells
That make us nothing. . . .

Cuchulain. No, no—there's nothing out of the common here;
The winds are innocent.

(*VPl,* pp. 508–9)

At this moment the wise Conchubar becomes prey to the very witches he has attempted to bar from his door and to a wildness he has attempted to tame in "binding" Cuchulain. Cuchulain for his part becomes reasonable and even domestic, in his willingness to be friends with the boy. Conchubar and Cuchulain have briefly revealed their mixed natures in exchanging characteristics, but as they have reversed their roles, the conflict continues unabated. If at this point, one of them, but not the other, would turn again, there would be no tragedy. As it is, both turn again, reverting to their former roles. Conchubar resumes his position as wise leader, High King, and forbids Cuchulain's friendship with the boy. Cuchulain, his heroic status challenged by the other kings, takes on his former warrior wildness and rushes into battle, killing, as Yeats says in the letter to Fay, "the thing he had most need of."

The "tragedy" in this play, as in none other by Yeats until now, is contained entirely within the structure of opposition built into character and played out in action. It is to the letter a Nietzschean kind of tragedy. The denouement of Cuchulain's fight with the waves upholds the heroic purpose, which "wills" its own power even at the cost of its own destruction. It is a "sacrifice" the hero makes, as Yeats says in his Introduction to *Fighting the Waves* (1934), "of himself to himself, almost, so little may he bargain, of the moment to the moment" (*VPl,* pp. 569–70). It is a ritual sacrifice like that of Dionysus, torn to pieces in affirmation of life's continuity; it is a sacrifice of the moment (time) to the moment (time-to-come), lived in and for its own sake.

The action of Blind Man and Fool, the mirrors of Conchubar and Cuchulain, at the end of the play suggests the return to life after tragedy. As these lesser characters have partaken of the nature of a Greek chorus, commentators on the action, their brief dialogue at the end acts as a final comment on the sacrifice. The Fool is characteristically absorbed in the tragedy still transpiring under his eyes; the Blind Man, characteristically, in material survival, and he has the last word:

Fool. The waves have mastered him.

Blind Man. Come here, I say.

Fool. What is it?

Blind Man. There will be nobody in the houses. Come this way; come quickly! The ovens will be full. We will put our hands into the ovens. (*VPl,* p. 525)

His ultimate deflation of the high tragic action in the Blind Man's wish to steal the bread out of ovens marks Yeats's recogniton of the value of that action, which must take place in a world where bestial appetite prevails. Paradoxically, however, if the ending deflates, it also inflates, for the fact is that the appetite does prevail; the world continues; life goes on. It is, after all, bread which is stolen, and its suggestion, by association, of the body of Christ is appropriate to the ritual nature of Cuchulain's tragedy. Yeats only hints at this association, which will probably not even occur to the theatergoer on a conscious level, but its implication is clear. Cuchulain's slaying of his son and impossible battle with the sea are "extravagant" actions. They may, therefore, through their "misrepresentation" of "average life," help to "enlarge the energy of a people through the spectacle of energy," as Yeats says in the 1904 *Samhain* essay (see above). They cause the audience to identify with its own "infinity" or "immoderate" capacity for passion. But then, by a return to the thought of stomachs and bread to fill them, Yeats refocuses its attention and enlarged energy on the spectacle of life's continuity, implying the connection between suffering or "sacrifice" and daily bread. Both are important parts of the whole "burning wheel," and both—he seems to say through the hinted-at association of bread and sacrifice—are sacred.

When Yeats "ennumerates old themes" in his late poem "The Circus Animals' Desertion," he chooses *On Baile's Strand* as the epitome of his own enchantment to "players and painted stage":

And when the Fool and Blind Man stole the bread
Cuchulain fought the ungovernable sea;
Heart-mysteries there, and yet when all is said
It was the dream itself enchanted me.

(*VP,* p. 630)

Ellmann and Donoghue have suggested that the heart-mysteries refer to Major MacBride's "theft" of Maud Gonne and Yeats's subsequent despair;[33] there is no doubt that the poem throughout explores the distinction and interconnection between Yeats's "heart" or real life experience and his art. But these lines also suggest that by the time he completed *On Baile's Strand,* his art had begun to absorb him altogether—to captivate or enchant his heart. "The dream itself," the working out of "masterful images," took all his love:

> Those masterful images because complete
> Grew in pure mind.
>
> (*VP,* p. 630)

The images of Fool and Blind Man, Cuchulain and Conchubar, are "complete," and their completeness—the perfect balance of oppositions—gives them mastery over that which is incomplete: "a mound of refuse or the sweepings of a street" (*VP,* p. 630), real life. That Yeats uses the word *mastery* reflects a mystery of its own. Nietzsche originates the use of the word in Yeats's vocabulary, by insisting so often that "master morality affirms"; that the "masters" or "noble" types create; that "mastery" over oneself is a form of self-overcoming or will to power expressed in control, harmony, balance. In *On Baile's Strand,* Cuchulain represents "master morality" or the heroic, but at the end of the play, the Fool repeats four times, so that the words become a choral refrain, "the waves have mastered him." The master is mastered, and by a master, for the play demonstrates the artistic control Yeats sought, and found, "in pure mind."

The seeking for control of oppositions, each with a life or opposition of its own, was an exciting, absorbing, enchanting business. The word *enchant* in "The Circus Animals' Desertion" ("It was the dream itself enchanted me") also produces an echo; Nietzsche is for Yeats "that strong enchanter." Yeats's mastery of completeness that "grew in pure mind" could happen because of his double enchantment: first to Nietzsche's definitions and examples of mastered experience, and second to his own, growing from the first. Even the ladder at the end of the poem ("I must lie down where all the ladders start") is Nietzsche's. In *Thus Spake Zarathustra,* Zarathustra commands: "And if thou now lackest all ladders, thou must know how to mount thine own head; thine own head and past thine own heart!" "Masters" create their own ladders out of their minds, becoming their own ladders. Yeats's circus animals are his ladder up, beyond his own heart. In 1906, he is, "when all is said," enchanted with his ability to produce the ladder. "The dream itself," of which Cuchulain is a part, involves a serious effort to reinstate "life" through its opposite, an art that masters life and thus "stimulates" it.

Deirdre and *Discoveries* (1906)

In the autumn of 1906 Yeats works on a new play, *Deirdre,* and at the same time, on a series of prose essays. A letter to his old friend Katherine Tynan describes his work on the "Cuchulain plays" and adds, "This dramatic work has been a great joy." He concludes the letter with the announcement, "I am doing my *Deirdre* side by side with a curious impressionist book on the work here—almost a spiritual diary" (*L,* p. 476). The curious impressionist book was published, unsigned, in three installments, in the September, October, and November 1906 issues of *Gentlemen's Magazine,* as "My Thoughts and My Second Thoughts." It was reprinted with additions by the Dun Emer Press in 1907 as *Discoveries.* In September 1906, he writes Florence Farr that he cannot get to London because "Deirdre has me tied to the table leg" (*L,* p. 480). *Deirdre* was produced at the Abbey on November 24, 1906.

In 1906, Yeats is reprimanded by his father for "dropping affection from the circle of your needs": "Is this the theory of the overman, if so, your demi-godship is after all but a doctrinaire demi-godship."[34] As well, on a lecture tour to Edinburgh in the fall of 1906, he stayed with Sir Herbert Grierson, who recalls: "I had not left the bedroom, to which I conducted him to change, before he had told me of his interest in Nietzsche as a counteractive to the spread of democratic vulgarity."[35] This is also the year in which Yeats "damns all Celtic Christmases now and forever," in a letter to Stephen Gwynn, and goes on: "What Dublin wants is some man who knows his own mind and has an intolerable tongue and a delight in enemies" (*L,* p. 474). And in this year Yeats is labeled a "Nietzschean" in print, in A. R. Orage's book *Friedrich Nietzsche: The Dionysian Spirit of the Age.* In his Introduction, Orage says, "Already half a dozen well-known English writers might be named who owe, if not half their ideas, at least half the courage of their ideas to Nietzsche." Among the authors he names is W. B. Yeats.[36]

If Yeats's aristocratic posturing and defiant gesturing express some outward and visible signs of his enchantment with Nietzsche in this year, his work expresses its inward and spiritual grace—which is to say that his more complete interpretation of Nietzsche goes into his writing. A letter to his father in July 1906, reveals something of his awareness of a new kind of aesthetic for the stage:

> Mrs. Campbell and her generation were trained in plays like *Mrs. Tanqueray,* where everything is done by a kind of magnificent hysteria. . . . This school reduces everything to an emotional least common denominator. . . . A new school of acting is now growing up under the influence of the various attempts to create an intellectual drama, and of changes deeper than that. The new school seizes upon what is distinguished, solitary, proud even. . . . I feel these things rather vaguely as one feels new things. (*L,* pp. 475–76)

Yeats's criticism of the "old school" of acting sounds much like Nietzsche's criticism of Wagner in *The Case of Wagner* and of the "modern" stage in general in *Nietzsche contra Wagner,* where he condemns the modern addiction to "naturalistic stage-playing" and to "the espressivo at any price" (*CW,* pp. 70–71). Yeats's vague feelings about "these things" become increasingly certain during the next decade, so that by 1919, in his essay "A People's Theatre," he recommends, without a hint of vagueness, an art which is "stern and solitary," and declares that he is seeking "not a theatre but the theatre's anti-self" (*Ex,* p. 257). The play *Deirdre* and the "curious impressionist book" that became *Discoveries,* written side by side in 1906, demonstrate Yeats's attempt to create an "intellectual drama," and to express his ideas about the "new things" he vaguely feels.

One would expect, given Yeats's avowals of admiration for Nietzsche's ideas in this year, that these works would show Nietzschean influence at every turn. In fact, they do; but in more subtle ways than in *Where There Is Nothing, The King's Threshold,* and the essays of *Samhain* 1903 and 1904, where Nietzsche is included intact, unassimilated. In *Deirdre* especially, the "Nietzschean element" is more diffuse than in any earlier plays, including *On Baile's Strand.* It exists precisely in what Yeats defines in the letter to his father as the attempt "now growing up to create an intellectual drama," which "seizes upon what is distinguished, solitary, proud even." The solitude Yeats is talking about here is different from—therefore "new"—the loneliness that fills his earlier poetry. There the lover is alone, remembering forgotten beauty and brooding upon "her high lonely mysteries" (*VP,* p. 156); or "The sad, the lonely, the insatiable" long for escape from "battles never done" (*VP,* p. 114); or the passing, "labouring world" is reflected by "this lonely face" (*VP,* p. 112). In *Deirdre,* the solitude remains, but as the theme and imagery of the play make clear, it has taken on distinction, pride, and passion: it has become heroic. In *On The Boiler* (1939), Yeats says of his writing for the theater, "I have aimed at tragic ecstasy. . . . I am haunted by certain moments," and lists among them, "Mrs. Patrick Campbell in my *Deirdre,* passionate and solitary" (*Ex,* pp. 415–16). In *A Vision,* and in "The Phases of the Moon," Yeats makes Nietzsche the sole human representative of Phase 12, the phase of heroes. Certainly, in his life and in his work, Nietzsche epitomizes solitary heroism. He even epitomizes the "will to" solitude, finding it preferable to life among "the masses"; he chooses it, and rejoices in it.

The myth of Deirdre and Naisi, the lovers who flee their king and kingdom, choosing voluntary exile in order to preserve their love, comes ready-made to fit the theme of passionate, willful solitude. Deirdre has been raised—in solitude: the theme reechoes—to be the bride of Conchubar; his outraged honor is at stake, as well as Deirdre's and Naisi's fealty. The artistic problem is how to make their choice of flight heroic and not merely willful. The myth also provides the solution: have them return to betrayal and death. Yet the bones of myth are not enough to create a living drama, as Yeats found watching George Russell's *Deirdre* on tour in the Irish countryside. In his first piece in *Discoveries,* Yeats says of this performance[37]: "The play professed to tell of the heroic life of ancient Ireland, but was really full of sedentary refinement and the spirituality of cities. Every emotion was made as dainty-footed and dainty-fingered as might be, and a love and pathos where passion had faded into sentiment, emotions of pensive and harmless people, drove shadowy young men through the shadows of death and battle. I watched it with growing rage" (*E&I,* P. 263). He summarizes his experience on tour and the feelings it produced at the end of the essay: "If we poets are to move the people, we must reintegrate the human spirit in our imagination" (*E&I,* p. 264). He still wants to move "the people" in 1906, and his means, reintegration of the human spirit, might be more crudely expressed as finding his audiences where they live, in their own unrefined, possibly harmful, passions and thoughts: in action, not passivity; in substance, not shadow; in the creative sun, not the reflective moon.

Yeats's *Deirdre* goes about the job of giving substance to shadow in his "new," intellectual, Nietzschean way, through opposition. If the "old school" of acting produced emotion through "magnificent hysteria," the "expressivo," the new school would operate by containment and irony. It would intensify the emotion, turning "sentiment" into "passion," through emotion's antithesis, intellect. By calling intellect to the service of emotion (as Nietzsche does throughout *The Case of Wagner*), Yeats is also serving his hope for the "reintegration of the human spirit." As in *The King's Threshold* and *On Baile's Strand,* Yeats creates an ironic distance between the audience and the central action of the plot. His tentative gestures toward a voice or voices resembling a Greek chorus in the earlier plays become clearer in his use of the Musicians in *Deirdre.* The musicians create the "soul" behind the action through their poetry, and they remind the audience through their comments that it is seeing reenacted what it already knows. Thus they serve both lyric and dramatic purposes, and link the two forms. They are not omniscient; like the Greek chorus, they are witnesses to tragedy whose events they are powerless to influence. But they are also on-the-spot reporters, conscious of their power to interpret and perpetuate the tragedy. They represent, in fact, the poet himself. At a crucial point, Deirdre asks them to "set it down in a book" (*VPl,* p. 374), and gives the First Musician her bracelet, as a token, "To show that you have Deirdre's story right" (*VPl,* p. 377).

The Musicians' last dialogue, a dramatic poem spoken after Deirdre "goes behind the curtain" to kill herself on Naisi's body, shows that they have Yeats's version of Deirdre's story right:

First Musician. They are gone, they are gone. The proud may lie by the proud.

Second Musician. Though we were bidden to sing, cry nothing loud.

First Musician. They are gone, they are gone.

Second Musician. Whispering were enough.

First Musician. Into the secret wilderness of their love.

Second Musician. A high, grey cairn. What more is to be said?

First Musician. Eagles have gone into their cloudy bed.

(*VPl,* p. 387)

These lines, which tell of pride, solitude, and distinction in death are effective precisely in inverse proportion to their volume. No "magnificent hysteria" here, no sentimentality, no loud cries; the tone is quiet, the diction simple, the event understated. The Musicians are self-conscious artists: "Though we were bidden to sing, cry nothing loud"; their sense of decorum calls attention to itself, and then its very spareness and severity overcomes itself in the last line. They seem to be improvising, as in jazz, on a series of phrases, progressing through repetition, feeling their way slowly but effortlessly toward a thought that brings all the phrases together:

> A high, grey cairn. What more is to be said?
> Eagles have gone into their cloudy bed.

These lines in their deliberate economy prefigure the more famous ones of "Nineteen Hundred and Nineteen":

> Man is in love and loves what vanishes,
> What more is there to say?

(*VP,* pp. 429–30)

The emphasis in both these poems is on the poet's acknowledgment that few words say it better than more, when "it" is of the highest importance. Form and content become antithetical, each other's "mask" or opposite, and their opposition creates the energy that gives the lines their power. The few words, however, must be the right ones. In the lines from *Deirdre,* "a high, grey cairn" calls up images of mountain heights, solitude, and coldness (*grey* suggests cold, to me)—all, incidentally, regions and states of supreme heroic virtue for Zarathustra. This is the proper element for "eagles," "the proudest animals under the sun" and the sun's symbol in *Thus Spake Zarathustra;* it is their home, their resting-place and point of departure, and the right place for Deirdre and Naisi. Naisi calls Deirdre his eagle, and the Musicians give the name as well. As far as I can tell, Yeats uses the eagle as symbol of heroic pride and aristocratic distinction for the first time in *Deirdre.*

The Musicians' lines underscore an opposition the play has demonstrated throughout. From the beginning, Yeats has defined the scene as one of "silence and loneliness," as his opening stage directions specify. The guesthouse in the wood is small, and "night" is "closing in" (*VPl,* p. 345). As night continues to close in, the sense of place as narow enclosure increases until, finally, it becomes a trap or cage. "Dark-faced men" pass before the windows, "by one and in silence" (*VPl,* p. 349). They are guarding the room, trying to confine its "immoderate" things: Deirdre's beauty, described by the Musicians as "too much" ("she'd too much beauty for good luck" [*VPl,* p. 346]), and love, "born out of immoderate thought" (*VPl,* p. 352). As Deirdre and Naisi, knowing their doom, sit down to chess, Yeats intensifies the opposition between limit and limitlessness, Apollonian structure and Dionysian energy, and yokes them in the mastered energy of game and song. The stage directions, before the chess game begins, read: "The light is almost gone from the wood, but there is a clear evening light in the sky, increasing the sense of solitude and loneliness." But as Deirdre has earlier "raddled" her cheeks in order that the pallor of her fear not show and to make herself "brave and confident" (*VPl,* p. 354), she now insists, again, on the "profundity" (as Nietzsche has it) of form or appearance, and on the need for control or balance of opposites, and on heroic gaiety:

> Make no sad music.
> What is it but a king and queen at chess?
> They need a music that can mix itself
> Into imagination, but not break
> The steady thinking that the hard game needs.
>
> (*VPl,* p. 374)

The Musicians do not give Deirdre what she requires; her demand for rigor at such a moment is more than they can fulfill (they succeed better at the end), and they sing a song about love and death, incorporating Zarathustra's laughter and joy in the moment that renews itself out of its own plenitude:

> Love is an immoderate thing
> And can never be content
> Till it dip an ageing wing
> Where some laughing element
> Leaps and Time's old lanthorn dims.
>
> (*VPl*, p. 375)

The song so mixes itself into Deirdre's imagination that it breaks the steady thinking that the hard game needs. She responds—as Yeats hopes his audience will, by identifying with it their own "immoderate" passions—by rising to kneel at Naisi's feet. Her "knowledge" at this moment is all passion:

> And I know nothing but this body, nothing
> But that old vehement, bewildering kiss.
>
> (*VPl*, p. 376)

After Conchubar has Naisi killed, however, she regains mastery over herself, plays a part, and so escapes Conchubar's net. The heroic act demands that intellect be yoked with passion, as aesthetically form must be with content, at war yet one. Deirdre's will to power enables her to overcome herself, and thus to overcome Conchubar—to value death more than life; in overcoming herself, she becomes and remains herself, a "free spirit." Her death is not a defeat but a joy and an affirmation, as Nietzsche insists tragic death should be.

Yeats's mastery of ironies gives Conchubar the last word (as he gives it to the Blind Man in *On Baile's Strand*). Conchubar recovers his pride after defeat, much as Deirdre recovers hers. Both resume their masks or wills-to-power, only whereas Deirdre's is one of self-knowledge, Conchubar's is one of self-deception:

> Howl if you will, but I, being King, did right
> In choosing her most fitting to be Queen,
> And letting no boy lover take the sway.
>
> (*VPl*, p. 388)

Thus the play ends on a note of irony that helps explain the tragedy. Conchubar is so blind, so sure of his rectitude, that even the "facts" (the "boy lover" in fact not only took but held the sway) bend to his will. The opposition here is between actual experience on the one hand, and interpretation of experience on the other. Thought, for Nietzsche, is always perspectival or relative, dependent on the thinker, and always biased; but it is less so if it is firmly rooted in the body and the body's instincts. Deirdre's base of power is her physical passion ("I know nothing but this body"); therefore her knowledge is more complete than Conchubar's, whose frustrated lust keeps his knowledge abstract, theoretical, inbred, and fantasy-ridden. There is no sense in this play, as in *On Baile's Strand,* of complementary opposition between characters; Deirdre is complete; Conchubar, partial. Deirdre knows that "power" will rest with Conchubar-the-stunted when she and Naisi die; hence, her gift of her bracelet to the Musicians, to ensure not only that they will tell her story right, but more important, that they will be believed. Her bracelet represents concrete proof of her lived experience—a kind of proof more telling than words. But if the Musicians also represent the poet, the bracelet then represents the physical or natural side of life, which Yeats is coming to understand as the base of power that poetry must embody if it is to move the audience or the reader.

The *Discoveries* pieces also illustrate Yeats's definite shift in sympathy from the first to the second half of the orange—to immanence, nature, self. Also, as in *Deirdre,* they show that the expression of this immanence in art must be "lofty and severe" to be convincing. In an important and much-quoted piece called "The Tree of Life," Yeats tries to describe his sense of the "antithetical" (though he doesn't yet use the word) as it explains his own artistic position in relation to the world and to himself. The essay is, like a good deal of Yeats's prose, complicated, figurative, and dense. It demands the kind of reading Nietzsche calls *lento* in *The Dawn of Day* and "chewing the cud" in *A Genealogy of Morals:* slow and ruminative. It is complicated not only because its subject is difficult, but because Yeats is not sure enough himself of his meaning to express it more clearly. It tries to put in aesthetic terms what the night-day diagram in the Common anthology put more generally—the interconnected relationship between "self" and "soul."

He opens with a Nietzschean idea: "We artists have taken overmuch to heart that old Commandment about seeking after the Kingdom of Heaven."[38] Nietzsche puts the same thought many different ways, all of them blunter; for example: "A Christian, who is at the same time an artist, is not to be found. . . . Raphael said yea, he did yea, consequently Raphael was no Christian" (*CW,* p. 172). Yeats's Kingdom of Heaven here is conventional, like Nietzsche's, commanding salvation through self-denial—though the reader must deduce this interpretation from what follows: "Verlaine told me that he had tried to translate *In Memoriam,* but could not because Tennyson was 'too noble,' to Anglais, and when he should have been brokenhearted had many reminiscences.' " Tennyson, in other words, sought the Kingdom of Heaven by nobly denying or hiding his broken heart. Verlaine, on the other hand, took "delight in singing his own life," Yeats says. He quotes Verlaine from "the lecture he gave at Oxford," where "he insisted that 'the poet should hide nothing of himself,' though he must speak it all with 'a care of that dignity which should manifest itself, if not in the perfection of form, at all events with an invisible, insensible, but effectual endeavour after this lofty and severe quality.' " There is a contradiction here that forms the basis for the opposition Yeats is unfolding. The poet should "hide nothing," but he should do it with loftiness and severity, an endeavor after "perfection of form." Nietzsche also expresses this idea in *The Twilight of the Idols:* "This constraint to transform into the perfect is—art. Everything that he is not, nevertheless becomes a delight in himself; in art man enjoys himself as perfection" (*CW,* p. 172). Transformation into perfection in art involves "constraint"—loftiness, severity; delight in the world mixes with delight in the self, "constrained" to perfection through form.

Yeats then says that "the generation I belong to" compared Verlaine to Villon, because of his delight in "singing himself." In Yeats's 1904 *Samhain* paragraph on "the two kinds of poetry," Villon represents the energy of "life herself" in "one of her eternal gestures." That paragraph owes its substance to Nietzsche, as does this *Discoveries* piece, Verlaine notwithstanding. When he heard Verlaine at Oxford, Yeats says he had no use for him: "I was interested in nothing but states of mind, lyrical moments, intellectual essences." He continues, "I had not learned what sweetness, what rhythmic movement, there is in those who have become the joy that is themselves." This sentence expresses the leading discovery of *Discoveries.* It makes the goal of the artist's quest, not the Kingdom of Heaven, but the kingdom of earth and at its center, the self. Nietzsche sings of joy in the becoming Self, "yea" to the moment, in the climactic passages of *Thus Spake Zarathustra*. Earlier in the book he transvalues "the three best-cursed things in the world": voluptuousness (lust), passion for power, and selfishness. Of the last, he says that his word

> blessed *selfishness,* whole, healthy selfishness that springeth from a mighty soul.
>
> The flexible, persuading body, the dancer whose likeness and summary is the self-joyful soul. (*Z,* p. 275)

Yeats's discovery of "sweetness" and "rhythmic movement" in the joy of self-expression gains depth and complexity from the knowledge that it is double-edged, a union of body and soul in the harmony, rhythm, or "dance" of becoming.

This knowledge, however, Yeats does not express directly. After he records what turns out to be his major "discovery," he backtracks to record discoveries that led up to it:

> Without knowing it, I had come to care for nothing but impersonal beauty. I had set out on life with the thought of putting my very self into poetry, and had understood this as a representation of my own visions and an attempt to cut away the non-essential, but as I imagined the visions outside myself my imagination became full of decorative landscape and of still life. I thought of myself as something unmoving and silent living in the middle of my own mind and body. . . . Then one day I understood quite suddenly, as the way is, that I was seeking something unchanging and unmixed and always outside myself, a Stone or an Elixir that was always out of reach, and that I myself was the fleeting thing that held out its hand.

Whether Yeats sees himself as still or fleeting, he sees what is external to himself as "still life." His description presupposes static art forms, separate from the contradictions of life. The diction and concepts of the last sentence echo those of Yeats's nineties reviews (particularly the 1894 review of Ibsen's *Brand,* which describes the "Stone" and "Elixir" of the alchemists as artistic metaphors for transmutation and dissolution, respectively) and stories (particularly *Rosa Alchemica,* in which the artist-narrator's quest is exactly Yeats's in this sentence—for a Stone or Elixir always out of reach). Yeats's discovery that as an artist in the nineties he was seeking an opposite is an important step on the way to his mask theory. "The more I tried to make my art deliberately beautiful," he then says, "the more did I follow the opposite of myself, for deliberate beauty is like a woman always desiring man's desire." The irony of his position is that while he thought he was putting his "very self" into poetry, he was in fact putting something outside himself. His "seeking" an opposite was probably unconscious or intuitive in, say, the "deliberately beautiful" poems of *The Wind among the Reeds* (1899); his conscious "discovery" of his method came afterwards.

It came, I would say, after reading Nietzsche. His simile of deliberate beauty "like a woman" follows Nietzsche's pattern of personifying his important abstractions as female: Truth is a woman in *Beyond Good and Evil;* Life is a woman and Wisdom is a woman in *Thus Spake Zarathustra.* The high seriousness and ardor with which poets were wont to address their Muses gives way, in Nietzsche, to playfulness with a hint of coyness and, occasionally, more than a hint of patronage. The stereotyped concept of woman "always desiring man's desire" in Yeats's version is Nietzschean, though its tone of self-deprecation is not. Principally, however, Nietzsche's descriptions of artists who unconsciously develop their antitheses in *Nietzsche contra Wagner* would have fired Yeats's discovery. The opening section of that book must be a source study for anyone interested in understanding the genesis of Yeats's mask theory. It is called "Where I Admire," and it begins: "I believe artists often do not know what they can do best: they are too conceited for that. Their attention is directed to something prouder than those little plants give promise of, which know how to grow up in actual perfection, new, rare, and beautiful, on their soil. The final excellency of their own garden and vineyard is superficially estimated by them, and their love and their insight are not of equal quality." He then describes a certain musician, whose real genius lies in the opposite direction from his inclinations. "Yes," he says at the end of a long passage on the real genius: "He is a *master* of *minutiae.* But he does not *wish* to be so; His character loves rather the large walls and the audacious wall-painting. . . . He fails to observe that his spirit has a different taste and inclination—antithetical *optics.*" It transpires, unsurprisingly, that the "musician" is Wagner, and Nietzsche concludes the piece with this thought: "I admire Wagner in everything in which he sets *himself* to music" (*CW,* pp. 65–66).

It is Nietzsche's antithetical *optics* that Yeats begins to be aware of when he discovers that he is seeking an opposite. So he stops trying for "deliberate beauty." "Presently," he says, "I found that I entered into myself and pictured myself and not some essence when I was not seeking beauty at all, but merely to lighten the mind of some burden of love or bitterness thrown upon it by events of life." He is here describing what happened in writing "Adam's Curse," when "it had all seemed happy" because he had "pictured himself": Nietzsche's "antithetical optics" had freed him from self-consciousness. Yeats continues: "We are only permitted to desire life, and all the rest should be our complaints or our praise of that exacting mistress who can awake our lips into song with her kisses. But we must not give her all, we must deceive her a little at times. . . . Our deceit will give us style, mastery, that dignity, that lofty and severe quality Verlaine spoke of." "We are only permitted to desire life"; Yeats's argument makes sense if the stress is put on *life* and not on *desire*. "We" are "we artists"; and "life" is movement, opposed to "essences," ideals, or the Kingdom of Heaven. The new commandment has momentous implications for one accustomed to conceiving his major dichotomy as between immanent and transcendent. Now, instead of seeking something "outside" himself, he will do his questing within himself and the world. The "exacting mistress," life, is straight out of *Zarathustra;* the "we must never give her all," straight out of Yeats's own "Never Give All the Heart." As in that poem, here Yeats is saying that "mastery" in art (as in love) depends on "deceit," playing a part, the pretending not to care, or not to care too much. The idea is like Eliot's "Teach us to care and not to care," and it depends on a fracturing of the self. Opposition is still present, but it is internalized, self against anti-self; the anti-self gives the appearance—the lofty and severe quality—and becomes the "Apollonian" side of the dichotomy; the self becomes the Dionysian, and gives the passion.

Yeats seems to be aware that in his talk of deceiving his mistress, life, he may have expressed himself a bit vaguely, for he tries again: "To put it otherwise, we should ascend out of the common interests, the thoughts of the newspapers, of the market-place, of the men of science, but only so far as we carry the normal, passionate, reasoning self, the personality as a whole." Now he has said it. The question is one of distance, of how "far" we artists should ascend out of the common interests. He has prefigured the question and the answer over ten years earlier, in his poem "To the Rose upon the Rood of Time," when he invokes the Rose of mystical unity with the One. "Come near, come near," he says, and then:

> —Ah, leave me still
> A little space for the rose-breath to fill!
> Lest I no more hear common things that crave.
>
> (*VP,* p. 101)

He is aware in 1893, as in 1906, that too great distance from "common things" means the death of poetry, which depends on them. But *some* distance is necessary, some "deceit"; it is now a question of degree and not, as in his work of the later 1890s, of kind. Yeats's purpose in 1906 is to explore, and present, "the normal, passionate, reasoning self, the personality as a whole." There are enough contradictions in that subject to last a lifetime.

But the short essay "The Tree of Life" is not finished yet. Having produced a fine, resonant, but prosaic explanation of his purpose, Yeats concludes: "We must find some place upon the Tree of Life for the phoenix' nest, for the passion that is exultation and the negation of the will, for the wings that are always upon fire, set high that the forked branches may keep it safe, yet low enough to be out of the little wind-tossed boughs, the quivering of the twigs" (*E&I,* p. 272). The "phoenix' nest" recalls his description, in the 1903 essay on William Morris with which this chapter began, of Shelley's desire, which seeks "in love that ecstasy which Shelley's nightingale called death, that extremity of life in which life seems to pass away like the phoenix in the flame of its own lighting." Morris, on the other hand, seeks joy in the recurrence of natural things, and is thus the "happiest of poets," but not the most passionate. As this ending of "The Tree of Life" shows, Yeats now wants to have it both ways. He is afraid that his espousal of the "normal, passionate, reasoning self" may be too far away from the intensity of desire he loves in Shelley, and too willful. So he ends by invoking the phoenix, but he places her nest securely on the Tree of Life, both high enough and low enough to light the artist's work.

Yeats never once uses the word *tragedy* in *Discoveries.* Yet in a sense, his major discovery is precisely Nietzsche's concept of tragedy as becoming and recurrence—that that is all there is, for the artist, and that it is enough. In another *Discoveries* essay, Yeats speaks of "the two kinds of asceticism," that of the saint and that of the artist.

Both identify themselves with what they believe to be "permanent," but their beliefs are diametrically opposed. "The imaginative writer," he says, "differs from the saint in that he identifies himself—to the neglect of his own soul, alas!—with the soul of the world. . . . Those things that are permanent in the soul of the world, the great passions that trouble all and have but a brief recurring life of flower and seed in any man, are indeed renounced by the saint, who seeks not an eternal art, but his own eternity." And further on: "The end of art is the ecstasy awakened by the presence before an ever-changing mind of what is permanent in the world, or by the arousing of that mind itself into the very delicate and fastidious mood habitual with it when it is seeking those permanent and recurring things" (*E&I,* pp. 286–87). And finally, in a piece called "The Serpent's Mouth": "If it be true that God is a circle whose centre is everywhere, the saint goes to the centre, the poet and artist to the ring where everything comes round again. The poet must not seek for what is still and fixed, for that has no life for him; . . . but be content to find his pleasure in all that is forever passing away that it may come again" (*E&I,* p. 287). To "be content" in the passing away of things that they may come again is the heart of ancient ritual and the heart of Nietzsche's "ring of rings," eternal recurrence. Yeats's "discovery" that the poet "must not seek for what is still and fixed" is a major reversal of his earlier position, when he says he was seeking "something unchanging and unmixed and always outside myself, a Stone or an Elixir" of the absolute or the ideal. He does not now deny the existence of the stone, but he renounces it, in favor of the living stream—as the saint renounces the living stream in favor of the stone.

His last essay in *Discoveries,* however, ends with a stunning ambiguity. The piece is called "The Holy Places" and maintains, like Cuchulain in *On Baile's Strand,* that history is responsible for his present predicament. Since "sanctity" has died out of nature, poets have sought the marvelous in "strange and faraway places." This sounds like Wordsworth's dialogue with Coleridge in *Biographia Literaria;* Yeats sides with Wordsworth: "There are moments when I cannot believe in the reality of imaginations that are not inset with the minute life of long familiar things and symbols and places" (*E&I,* p. 296). He is also echoing Nietzsche's injunction to artists to cultivate their own gardens. Yeats's concluding sentence reads: "I am orthodox and pray for the resurrection of the body, and am certain that a man should find his Holy Land where he first crept upon the floor, and that familiar woods and rivers should fade into symbol with so gradual a change that he may never discover, no, not even in ecstasy itself, that he is beyond space, and that time alone keeps him from Primum Mobile, Supernal Eden, Yellow Rose over all" (*E&I,* p. 297).

This conclusion ostensibly reverses his earlier hope that through ecstasy, a person might pass beyond space and time to mystical knowledge of Primum Mobile, God, outside nature. It adopts a position ostensibly consistent with that of the book as a whole: that the phoenix of ecstasy lives on the Tree of Life, dies, flames up and is born again with all "permanent and recurring things." But the sentence's diction, its use of the subjunctive, leaves the door open for the "discovery" it ostensibly denies. The familiar should "fade into symbol" so gradually that a man "may never discover"—not *even* in ecstasy—"that he is beyond space, and that time alone keeps him from Primum Mobile. . . ." "He"—here not only the artist, but everyone—is to remain committed to space and time and is never to "discover" that his commitment "may" be an illusion. But if "he" does not discover it, then how can it (Primum Mobile, the absolute) be said to exist? It seems to me that in this last sentence—at the very eleventh hour—Yeats is playing with both the possibility of "discovering" miracle and the possibility of not discovering it. If it is not discovered, and familiar woods and rivers "fade into symbol," then nature and life itself will again be sacred, as Nietzsche hoped. By the absorption of the sacred into the human and natural world, the old split between God and humanity would be healed. But if it (Primum Mobile) *is* discovered . . . what then? The book ends on a veiled interrogative that probably expresses Yeats's own ambivalence about the nature of God and humanity. It is interesting that he uses classical and occult euphemisms (Primum Mobile, Supernal Eden, Yellow Rose over all) for the word *God.* He suggests that there is something beyond the knowable, but does not identify it plainly. After all, the direction of his thought and work over the last three intellectually exciting years has been toward Nietzsche's denial of God, faith in the earth, and espousal of the human capacity to celebrate that faith through the ceremony of tragedy. But Yeats does not commit himself to the new faith unequivocally. If anything can be said to be "Yeatsian," it is the refusal to take a final position.

6.

The Perilous Path

Mask and Tragedy, 1907–10

In a Note to *The Player Queen* in *Plays in Prose and Verse,* 1922, Yeats writes:

> I began in, I think, 1907, a verse tragedy, but at that time the thought I have set forth in *Per Amica Silentia Lunae* was coming into my head, and I found examples of it everywhere. I wasted the best working months of several years in an attempt to write a poetical play where every character became an example of the finding or the not finding of what I have called the Antithetical Self; and because passion and not thought makes tragedy, what I made had neither simplicity nor life. I knew precisely what was wrong and yet could neither escape from the thought nor give up my play. (*VPl,* p. 761)

Yeats was indeed absorbed in theory from 1907 to 1910 and baffled in his attempt to embody that theory dramatically, as he had not been, for instance, in his attempt in *On Baile's Strand* (which has nonetheless been criticized for "too obviously schematic matching of characters"[1]). If players and painted stage took all his love in the earlier plays of the decade, now "thought" about character takes, if not his love, his creative energy and his time. These last years of the decade illustrate in his own career—more completely than the earlier years—his description of Blake's decline in "fluency of composition": "He was thinking out his symbolic system, and considering how to make it the chief matter of his art."

Yeats was aware at the time of "what was wrong"—of his overemphasis on thought that was checking the fluency of his own composition, particularly in *The Player Queen,* and more generally as well.

His creative Pegasus seemed to him, as he put it in one of the poems he managed to eke out, to

> Shiver under the lash, strain, sweat and jolt
> As though it dragged road-metal.
>
> (*VP,* p. 260)

The poem is called "The Fascination of What's Difficult," and it pronounces a curse not only on "plays / That have to be set up in fifty ways," but indirectly on the taskmaster who has set him to the labor of intellect and will, Nietzsche. There is a passage in *The Antichrist,* reproduced in the Common anthology on a page with marginal notes by Yeats, in which Nietzsche describes the task, and it stands behind not only this poem but also much of Yeats's "thought" of the time: "The most intelligent men, as being the *strongest,* find their happiness in that wherein others would find their ruin: in the labyrinth, in severity towards themselves and others, in effort; their delight is self-conquest; with them asceticism becomes nature, requirement, and instinct. The difficult task is regarded by them as a privilege; to play with burdens which crush others do death, as a *recreation.*"[2] Yeats admits in the poem that what's difficult is also fascinating, though dangerous if not fatal to the very life Nietzsche everywhere espouses—natural life:

> The fascination of what's difficult
> Has dried the sap out of my veins, and rent
> Spontaneous joy and natural content
> Out of my heart.

The poem is a complaint as much about intellectual growing pains as about "theatre business, the management of men." Nietzsche also says, "What does not kill me, strengthens me"—but this extreme asceticism is undercut ironically by the aphorism's title, "From the military school of life" (*CW,* p. 100). Yet he is serious about the human need to experience difficulty and pain; the need becomes a necessity and an "instinct" with the "most intelligent." In *Nietzsche contra Wagner* he says that taking sides *against* himself is the way *to* himself and his work—to "an imperious something for which for a long time we have had no name, until it finally proves to be our task,—this tyrant in us retaliates frightfully for every attempt which we make to shirk it or escape from it" (*CW,* pp. 83–84).

The ideas in these passages remain fascinating to Yeats. In his Journal of 1909, he says, "The Abbey Theatre will fail to do its full work because there is no accepted authority to explain why the more difficult pleasure is the nobler pleasure" (*Mem,* p. 180). The same idea becomes the burden of his song in "To a Friend Whose Work has Come to Nothing" (1904): "Be secret and exult, / Because of all things known / That is most difficult" (*VP,* p. 291), and of his thought in *Per Amica Silentia Lunae* (1916) that was "coming into his head" in 1907. Nietzsche's emphasis on the need for pain, labor, difficulty, and obstacle in finding oneself and one's task exists in many statements Yeats makes in *Per Amica* and later, when he speaks of choosing, or being led to, "whatever among works not impossible is the most difficult" (*Myth,* p. 361). The most difficult task is that which "rouses the will to its full intensity" (*AU,* p. 120). Once roused, the will becomes creative: it makes for itself a mask or, as Yeats calls it in *Per Amica,* an Antithetical Self.

He has been finding and making his mask since 1902, unconsciously perhaps in "Adam's Curse," and with conscious intention by the time he writes *Discoveries.* He has put his "mask theory" to work as an aesthetic method in the plays published in 1906. In an essay of 1907, he articulates his ideas about the outcome of that method. The essay's title, "Poetry and Tradition," places it in the critical line of Arnold and Eliot. Written after the *Playboy* riots, after his trip to northern Italy with Lady Gregory, after O'Leary's death—all of which occurred in the first half of this year—and during his initial struggles to make *The Player Queen* a tragedy, the essay mourns the passing of "romantic Ireland," now with O'Leary in the grave. Yeats puts in the past-tense qualities of "that ideal Ireland" that had been present-tense ideals in his turn-of-the-century essays. "We were to forge in Ireland," he says, "a new sword on our old traditional anvil for that great battle that must in the end reestablish the old, confident, joyous world" (*E&I,* p. 247).

O'Leary and Irish "tradition" take on, however, new qualities of strength deriving from Yeats's Nietzschean preoccupation. O'Leary himself is credited with a Zarathustran saying: "I have heard him say," Yeats says of O'Leary, " 'I have but one religion, the old Persian: to bend the bow and tell the truth' " (*E&I,* p. 247). This Zarathustran saying is from a text that could have been included among those on self-overcoming through antithesis. It is from a chapter called "Of a Thousand and One Goals," in which Zarathustra describes the plurality of values among different peoples of the earth as "the voices of their Will to Power":

> That is laudable which is reckoned hard; what is indispensable and hard is named good; and that which [is] hardest,—that is praised as holy. . . .
>
> "To speak the truth and handle bow and arrow well"—that was at once loved and reckoned hard by the people from whom my name cometh. (*Z,* pp. 76–77)

That Yeats attributes the saying to O'Leary reminds us that he is striving to identify his own new values with his old tradition.

The second half of the orange, Apollonian joy in creativity, predominates in the essay as the quality in "tradition" without which poetry and drama cease to be powerful: "Certainly we would not delight in that so courtly thing, the poetry of light love, if it were sad; for only when we are gay over a thing, and can play with it, do we show ourselves its master, and have minds clear enough for strength. . . . pure joy masters and impregnates; and so to world end, strength shall laugh and wisdom mourn." (*E&I,* pp. 252–53). While it is true that Yeats was impressed with the courts of Urbino and Ferrara, whose magnificent walled castles he visited in Italy, and with Castiglione's *The Courtier,* the "gaiety" and mastery he describes as essential to creativity derive principally from his reading in Nietzsche, no doubt reinforced by Castiglione's advice to courtiers. He again misrepresents his central debt, echoing an earlier misrepresentation, when he says: "In life courtesy and self-possession, and in the arts style, are the sensible impressions of the free mind, for both arise out of a deliberate shaping of all things, and never from being swept away, whatever the emotion, into confusion or dullness. The Japanese have numbered with heroic things courtesy at all times whatsoever" (*E&I,* p. 253). In 1903, writing the Preface to *Gods and Fighting Men,* Yeats also attributes this "heroic" virtue of Nietzsche's to the Japanese, which suggests that the idea impressed him then, that he feared its source's influence and so misrepresented it, and that both influence and fear are still operating powerfully in 1907—or that he simply remembered only what he himself had said earlier.

By this time, explicitly and in theoretical analysis, Yeats subsumes even tragedy under the "shaping joy" of "making and mastering." As in the earlier essays, he talks of Timon and Cleopatra, but now implies that our "sorrow" for them arises from the artist's "joy" in their creation: "That shaping joy has kept the sorrow pure, as it had kept it were the emotion love or hate, for the nobleness of the arts is in the mingling of contraries, the extremity of sorrow, the extremity of joy, perfection of personality, the perfection of its surrender, overflowing turbulent energy, and marmorean stillness; and its red rose opens at the meeting of the two beams of the cross, and at the trysting-place of mortal and immortal, time and eternity" (*E&I,* p. 255). To create this trysting place requires, he begins to see, utmost art. It requires the power of the mask, its "shaping joy," which makes unity between opposites possible. A final thought in the essay expresses the paradox of the artist's work. Yeats is upholding again art's freedom from politics: "we artists, who are the servants not of any cause but of mere naked life, and above all of that life in its nobler forms, where joy and sorrow are one, Artificers of the Great Moment, became as elsewhere in Europe protesting individual voices" (*E&I,* p. 260). The irony of the contemporary artists' position is expressed in Yeats's word Artificers. That artists no longer belong to a community of shared heroic values, but have become "protesting individual voices" in a Europe now "safe" for mediocrity, is the Nietzschean complaint upon which Yeats ends the essay. In a world in which art has, as Yeats puts it in *At the King's Threshold,* lost its ancient rights, artists must now "will" their power. They must become Artificers—Yeats uses the word in Nietzsche's complex positive sense—who so "mingle" their "contraries," deliberately and cunningly, that they "master" the fate of their place in time and, against or even because of the odds, create the Great Moment, Nietzsche's moment of synthesis and power: perfection.

The problem is still, for Yeats, how to do it. The contraries are unwieldy, the task is "most difficult." Between 1907 and 1910 his fascination with the difficult takes the form of at least seventeen separate drafts, some in prose and some in verse, of his "verse tragedy," *The Player Queen.* Twelve of these have been transcribed and edited by

Curtis B. Bradford in *W. B. Yeats: The Writing of The Player Queen.* In 1908, Yeats also writes a second series of *Discoveries,* and at the end of the year he begins a journal that he keeps up steadily through 1909 and into 1910, when he writes his prose essay on tragedy. In 1909, Nietzsche's *The Birth of Tragedy* is finally published in English translation, and there is little doubt that Yeats reads it in that year. Ideas from drafts of *The Player Queen,* essays, the Journal, and *The Birth of Tragedy* are all running through Yeat's mind at once. The effect on his productivity is temporarily disastrous. After the essay "Poetry and Tradition," his concepts of mask and tragedy diverge again. The divergence causes him severe problems in bestowing "shaping joy" on *The Player Queen.*

The earliest scenarios of that play contain the antagonism, which remains central through all changes to the final version of 1922, between the "Real Queen" who has given her heart up to religion, and the "Player Queen" who has given her heart up to the play. Summarizing the first scenario, which he does not print, Bradford says that the Player Queen is shown to be for her fellow players "a very difficult colleague, largely because she can never quit acting. . . . But all her fellow actors agree she is a genius. Yeats is here studying the effect of role-playing on character, the effect of the mask on the face beneath it" (*PQ,* p. 21). Yeats is also, it seems, setting up a contrast like the one he explored in *Discoveries,* 1906, between saint and artist—the saint (the Real Queen) who goes to the center of the circle, the artist (the Player Queen) to the ring where everything comes round again. The contrast adds to what might have been a study in psychological symbolism—the effect of mask on face—a historical dimension, implicit from the play's very origin, in the "Christian" preoccupation of the Real Queen, as against the "artistic" preoccupation of the players. I think it is crucial in understanding Yeat's mask theory, and his *A Vision,* to know that psychology, aesthetics, and history are interconnected in his very earliest inkling of the system: in the Common anthology's diagram, where Christ and Socrates oppose each other as night and day, soul and self, single and multitudinous influxes; in drafts of *The Player Queen;* and in the essays and Journal of this period. The interweaving of psychology, aesthetics, and history in a series of mutually dependent and multilevel oppositions grows in part, as we have seen, out of Nietzsche's insistent and repeated contrasts:

Rome vs. Judea, master (noble) vs. slave morality, actor vs. acted upon, will vs. fate.

Scenario 3 is the longest and most complete of any of the nine scenarios Bradford prints (all were written, he believes, before 1910, though they were neither numbered nor dated by Yeats). This one contains most of the complications Yeats introduces in his drafts to 1910. First, it makes the historical ironies clear. The players are to present a morality play based on Noah's flood. They are thus, in their selection of subject matter, ostensibly on the side of the Queen, who is shown to be such a religious fanatic that the townspeople are in revolt over her schedule of taxation on sin. The scenario opens with a dialogue between the Queen and her Prime Minister. The Prime Minister insists she show her face to the people, in order to subdue them with her "pomp and glory and state. . . . What have they to do with a praying Queen. . . . She must be the people's soul made greater, as they understand greatness. She answers rather pettishly that she is doing all he wants. They are about to go out the big door at the back. She looks back longingly. In a little while those players will be dancing their good pious story and doing some real good, not like her" (*PQ,* p. 23). Then the Player Queen, who has hidden herself in a large cider vat at the back of the stage, sticks her head up, singing "a sort of song of apple juice and intoxication founded on the Song of Solomon." The Friend (another female player, Nona in the final version) comes in and discovers the Player Queen: "Delight at finding her. It is almost time to begin. Where has she been? Why has she hidden herself. Player Queen tells her that she has made up her mind never again to dance Noah's wife or any other part that does not make her feel passionate, very noble, very intense. She runs over the names of various parts, mystery, epic, romance, etc., no, he [the producer] will never do that, because people don't want those parts. They must please the people. She replies no, they must please her" (*PQ,* p. 23).

In these first two outlines of dialogue Yeats establishes a parallel between the Real Queen and the Player Queen, and a parallel conflict between the "queens" and the people. The Real Queen supports the Noah play (Yeats later suggests that she might have composed it herself, to "edify her people" [PQ, p. 37]), but the people oppose the Real Queen. In "pleasing herself," the Real Queen seeks God, and seeks to impose God on her people. The Prime Minister tells her she must give the people what they want, a show of royalty. The Player Queen, on the other hand, in pleasing herself seeks passion, romance, mystery—also in opposition to the people. The Friend tells her they "don't want those parts." On stage, it becomes clear in later versions, they want realism. In draft after draft, Yeats keeps the conflict between "what will sell" on the stage—realism—and what will sell in real life—artificiality, pose. It's a lovely irony, and it encompasses the historical, for religion is out as a way of life with the same audience for whom realism in art is in. The fact that Noah's flood has been the chosen set piece, furthermore, introduces the theme of history on a more general level, suggesting the apocalyptic concept that becomes explicit in revisions after 1915. The players' play of the Deluge symbolizes an earlier apocalypse, an historical extremity, and prefigures a second that Yeats announces through the Unicorn in his final version.

Scenario 3 takes up, in a general way, the complicated interrelation between history and aesthetics, within an even more general and indirectly suggested framework of vast historical movements. It also takes up the ironies implicit in personal relationships. These are much more substantially developed in the drafts of the dialogue, but in this scenario Yeats makes a parenthetical note to himself that shows him aware of "tragic" motivation. He outlines the plot—the Player Queen's discovery of and jealousy over the Poet's (Septimus, in the final version) affection for "the Friend"; her changing roles with the Real Queen; her decision to take on the Queen's death at the hands of the outraged mob if necessary. She argues with the Prime Minister, who knows her real identity, and says to him: "You said to the Queen this morning here in this very place that she had but to smile and show herself. I will have victory today by being myself. I will show myself and if they wish then to overthrow us, so be it." A few lines later, Yeats writes: "In order to give her sufficient momentum for later parts probably her songs when she is in the cider vat should be love songs. In her conversation with the Friend she might speak first of her love and then of her refusal to play the part of Noah's wife. Perhaps she may even desire a great part in which she can express her love. She can describe herself or be described as one of those people who torture those they love" (*PQ*, p. 25). The main point about this comment is Yeat's awareness that in order to be "herself"—that is, to wear the mask of queen—the Player Queen must be given sufficient momentum by her passion. The momentum must be seen to come from her love for the Poet, through whose desertion she finds the power and courage of the "daemoniacal"—to go beyond her human fear of death, to act with heroic abandon.

Ideas like these must have been at the base of Yeat's feeling that the play must be a tragedy. In Draft 6 he reverts to themes and imagery from *Deirdre* in his attempt to push the ironies of the oppositions he has assembled through to tragedy. He makes the Player Queen's motivation to heroism clear by making explicit her moment of choice. She asks the Poet to send the Friend away; she asks him, in other words, to make an absolute choice in love. He resists, and finally, pushed, chooses the Friend: "This woman is more worthy of love than you are, and whether in this world or in the next I give her my love." The Player Queen responds, "Then it is over. What more have I to do with life?" (*PQ*, p. 52). Her "momentum" thus established, she changes dress with the Real Queen, takes a strong line against the rebels, and challenges them:

> Who is there among you that dare strike?
> Your fathers' lives, and the lives of their
> fathers before them were
> but twigs
> woven in the nest that gave the eagle birth. Who
> among you all dare face the eagle?
> Eagle begat eagle up
> through all the centuries, and in my eyes all the
> eagles look at you.
>
> (*PQ*, p. 56)

After two pages of exchanges with the Real Queen, the Poet, and the crowd, the Player Queen says: "I have come here to seek my death. I am waiting for it. What more is to be said?" In *Deirdre,* when eagles go into their cloudy bed, there is little more to say, but in *The Player Queen,* there is a great deal. Heroic death is now problematic; heroism itself is in question. The Real Queen says the Player Queen "is an angel who has been sent down from Heaven to take my place." The

Poet says, "She is my sweetheart. Can you not see she is but playing? She has reddened her face with raddle—that is why she has such courage. If you could only see her, perhaps she is very pale" (*PQ*, p. 59).

These lines call attention to the difference between the tragedy in *Deirdre* and the one Yeats is attempting in *The Player Queen*. In *Deirdre*, Deirdre in fact does raddle her cheeks to give herself courage, the Musicians and the audience know she does it, but no one else does, and she plays her part as queen through to her death. She is, of course, a real queen, and the face paint demonstrates the idea that real queens need a mask to help them be "themselves"—more than human, heroic. Yeats uses this idea in *The Player Queen*, having various characters preach it explicitly to the Real Queen, who persists, in most drafts, in remaining hostile to the concept of image. To the Prime Minister she expresses moral outrage: "You are wrong, sir, to encourage the people to think of outward, needless things. . . . What is there in this face? There are many better faces" (*PQ*, p. 45). The Prime Minister answers: "Will your Majesty permit an old man to speak plainly? It is the Queen's duty to make the people greater by what she seems. She is the image of what they would be, a symbol, an image. . . . She may sorrow over her sins, but she must always seem to be all power and haughtiness. Your state is a mask which you must wear always on your face" (*PQ*, p. 45). The Real Queen remains outraged, but the Player Queen, overhearing from the cider vat, understands, and later gives her own heart up to the mask.

She does not raddle her cheeks for courage, like Deirdre; she plays for the sake of playing. Her love for the Poet is not very convincing; her real passion is revealed in a speech to the Real Queen in Draft 6. She has changed roles with the Real Queen and has addressed the mob in her speech about eagles. Now, confronted by the Real Queen's challenge to her identity, she counters: "I remember you now. You were to have played before me this day. I have heard of her. All her life she has longed to play some great part, at whatever cost. It has crazed her at last, and so she goes about dreaming that she is a queen. Ah, could you but understand the wild blood of these artists. They thirst for all the greatness of the world and dream in their folly they could be it" (*PQ*, p. 57). The speech is meant to mask the Player Queen's real motivation, love of the Poet, but there is much self-revelation in it. The self-revelation continues, under the disguise of her "mask" as queen, when she is next confronted by the Poet, who also seeks to unveil her. The Player Queen tells the crowd:

> He and she [the Real Queen], they have planned this mummery. They are so vain, these artists—O, I know them well. They are so vain. Why I will make this man say that I was troubled, and that he [and] I loved, and that he cast me off and so now I seek death, or but to show myself fearless of it, looking at [it] as eagles at the sun but to win his praise.
>
> *Poet.* But it is true; yes, it is all true.

When the Friend joins in to corroborate the story, the Player Queen, still in role and enjoying it (the crowd is laughing at the claims of Real Queen, Poet, and Friend), says to the crowd: "Why you can see that this was all arranged beforehand. It is a play, a stage play to amuse you, that is all" (*PQ*, p. 58). By this time, Yeat's irony has turned against itself and against the possibility of tragedy. All is confusion on stage; the questions are now: What is real? Where is truth? No sufficient answers are forthcoming, and the play ends comically in this draft, with the Player Queen's return to the part of Noah's wife.

In his scenarios, Yeats has the Player Queen die in various ways—by poison, by hurling herself from a battlement—but he never writes a dramatic scene embodying these plans in any of the seventeen drafts. He becomes engrossed in, and eventually frustrated by, the complications inherent in the mask. On July 17, 1908, he writes his father:

> I am working on *The Player Queen*. . . . it is still all scenario, I think it is my most stirring thing. . . . Side by side with my play I am writing a second series of *Discoveries*. I find that my philosophical tendency spoils my playwriting if I have not a separate channel for it. There is a dramatic contrast of character in this play which can be philosophically stated. I am putting the philosophical statement into a stream of rambling thoughts suggested by impressionist pictures and a certain Italian book, and Lane's gallery in general, and the pictures I pass on the stairs at Coole. (*L*, pp. 532–33)[3]

The separate channel for Yeat's philosophical tendency, the second series of *Discoveries,* was not printed during his life; perhaps he realized that channel or no channel, the philosophical tendency did in fact prevent *The Player Queen* from assuming the form he intended for it as his "most stirring thing." He left the "stream of rambling thoughts," like the drafts of *The Player Queen,* in manuscript notebooks. "Discoveries: Second Series" was transcribed and edited by Curtis Bradford and published in the *Massachusetts Review* in 1964. Its main concern is with "Changing Canons of Form" (as one of its sections has been named) in art, and with Yeat's own relationship to the change.

The philosophical tendency, unsurprisingly, shows clear ties with Nietzsche. Yeats is going to compare his feeling for art "twenty years ago" as an art student in Dublin with his feelings in 1908, but he begins in a section titled "Pantheism" with a story about a friend in art school and his "little book full of vague Hindoo pantheism."[4] He condemns the little book's subject: "That vague Eastern pantheism, lacking some salt that goes not of [with?] it in the Western journey, has injured the manhood of a generation. It has made today's task seem nothing by setting vague immensities to frown it into littleness. Young men should have been busy making themselves perfect in some one of those trifling works."[5] The last part of this paragraph echoes Nietzsche's thought in *Nietzsche contra Wagner* that artists should perfect "those little plants" in their own garden. The earlier part expresses what will be a recurring opposition in Yeat's later verse between "Asiatic vague immensities" and Western form. The immensities of the East are treated by Nietzsche with the scorn one would expect from the philosopher of the will to power. In *A Genealogy of Morals,* he diagnoses the disease of modern Europe, nihilism, and wonders whether it is not a "roundabout way to a new Buddhism? to a European Buddhism?" (*GM,* p. 8). Yeats indicts the vague Hindoo pantheism (that so took his own imagination in the 1880s) for injuring the manhood of a generation—following Nietzsche's line that moral turpitude and egalitarianism were symptoms of an "effeminate" softening of the will undermining European civilization.

Yeats's quarrel with the Eastern vague immensities he met in his Dublin art school days is only his introduction to another quarrel, or question, that he puts to himself in the next section. Why is it, he asks, that I used to hate a picture of Manet I now no longer hate so much? He is trying to articulate the extent and meaning of the "change" he felt "in" and "around" him in 1903. He refers to one of his own earlier pronouncements on art: "I remember arguing that modern streets could not be fitting subjects for art, for even Whistler had to half lose them in mist to make them pleasant to the eye." The argument occurs in his 1901 essay "At Stratford-on-Avon," where he talks about the arts' gaining strength "in retreat" from the vulgarity of modern streets, at a time when he is hoping that his new literary theater might provide Ireland with some "ideal thought." Now, however, when he sees the Manet he once hated, he thinks, "I shall someday like that athletic spirit, and feel when I share its contemplation that I live for a moment another's stronger life." He acknowledges the painting's strength, but hesitates to embrace its implications—which become clear as the "ramblings" continue. He confesses:

> I wish to find out if I am a romantic of some kind, or only an ignorant man, puzzled at the middle of a revolution that has changed all about him. Nor is it only in painting I find myself changing. Much of my own poetry, every place where it is most traditional, is less vivid to me than it was. I find myself at moments desiring a more modern, aggressive art—an art of my own day. I am not happy in this mood unless I can see precisely how each poem or play goes to build up an image of myself, of my likes and dislikes, as a man alive today.[6]

"Athletic," "stronger life," "aggressive"—Yeats builds upon these descriptions of art in his own day in his next section. "Those pictures that now delight me most," he says, "are the least meditative, most animal, active, living, triumphant: more even than Renoir, Mancini—like the sun in his strength." This observation reinforces, again, Yeats's 1903 shift in sympathy from first to second half of the orange, a shift whose direction sunward has continued since 1903. The impressionists "seem no longer as ugly as they did even two years ago," he says, and furthermore as logical corollary, pictures "that were delightful" to him, he now finds "changed and withered"—Watts, Shannon, Moreau.[7]

The age of the Pre-Raphaelites is eclipsed for Yeats; the high Renaissance has taken its place. This substitution seems to involve some contradiction, for he has been praising "modern" art. He has been praising, not the subject matter, however, but the formal energy of modern art. When he speaks of subject matter, his opinion shifts again. "From the Renaissance onward artists have had to struggle with a limitation of subject imposed by the inspiration of the past. . . . And at last in our day men understood [a] canon, the idea of limitation at all, was the enemy. Men's eyes and hands were set free and men painted what they saw, and all those traditional themes—saints, angels, kings and queens, divinities, enchanted lands where Siren winds her dizzy horn—passed away from the paintings of all [who] would float on the crest of the wave." He concludes the section with a discussion of individualism in art. "Every painting was to be the perfect expression of a man, his good and bad, all that he was. . . . For the first time the arts have become a drama of character, and of that alone, in subject and in style."[8]

Some of this "philosophy" passes into the drafts of *The Player Queen,* try as Yeats might to keep it out. He is more interested, in the drafts than in the final version, in the players' repertoire, writing passages of script for the Noah play-within-a-play, and even passages from an "old play" written by the Poet, called "The Queen of Babylon." It is this play, on a "traditional" theme of kings, queens, and nobles, that the Player Queen wants acted. In Draft 8, "the Friend" (now "the Girl") shows the old play to the Prime Minister (now "Chancellor") and describes its plot (which is remarkably like the plot of *The Player Queen*). She tells the Chancellor: "There are very fine speeches in it, but Martin [the Poet] says there [is] no one now could play it or would like it if it could be played, because now it's real people, [who] would seem to gather up all the life of the land, who spring into the unknown like a dive into the sea—no mere maker of laws nor leader in battle—but the flavour of life, thirst for what exists, sheer flame, the flame that comes from us that are its fuel, people like themselves, pettish, troublesome, ordinary people like Noah's wife, they want to see" (*PQ,* pp. 82–83). Thirst for the "sheer flame" of "what exists" is also the force behind modern art as Yeats defines it in his "philosophic statement." Its qualities sound very Nietzschean in both places. Nietzsche's "Apollonic" joy in creation, his skepticism of metaphysical idealism, his embracing of "what exists," his bid to "live dangerously," as the "spring into the unknown like a dive into the sea"—all help create the new artistic canon and Yeats's interpretation of it—the change both in and around him.

Nietzsche also helps Yeats begin to see changes in aesthetic forms as part of a wider historical process based on antithesis. Nietzsche is not himself an advocate of individualism, though he advocates the strong individual's ability to create his or her own values in the modern world, where the old prescriptions have lost their strength. He advocates heroic individualism, and instinct and sensation, as valid ways of knowing—as the means out of a bog. But he is also, at the same time, a severe critic of "the modern." In *The Twilight of the Idols,* where he says so much about the importance and difficulty of attaining the beautiful and the "constraint" to transform life into perfection, he also discusses social issues. He takes up the decline of institutions, for instance:

> In order that there may be institutions, there must be a species of will, instinct, or imperative, anti-liberal even to malignity: a will for tradition, for authority, for responsibility throughout centuries. . . . The entire western world no longer possesses those instincts out of which institutions grow, out of which *futurity* grows; perhaps nothing is so much against the grain of its "modern spirit." We live for the present, we live very fast,—we live very irresponsibly: this is precisely what we call "freedom." That which *makes* institutions in reality is despised, hated, and repudiated: wherever the word "authority" even becomes audible, people believe themselves in danger of a new slavery. (*CW,* pp. 204–5)

A few pages on, Nietzsche reintroduces the subject of freedom and individualism: "At present one would have to make the individual possible in the first place, by *pruning* him—make him possible, that is to say, to make him an *entirety*. The very reverse happens: independence, free development. . . . This is true in politics, it is true in art" (*CW,* p. 208). "Entirety" is Zarathustra's aspiration; Nietzsche praises Goethe as a human representative of the type he admires. "What Goethe aspired to," says he, "was totality; he struggled against the severance of reason, sensuousness, emotion and will; . . . he disciplined himself to entirety, he *created* himself" (*CW,* p. 219). "Freedom" and creativity, Nietzsche says over and over again, require discipline, restriction, authority; expansion requires limitation; unity ("totality") requires multiplicity. Again and again, Nietzsche points to the only historical period since Christ when the balance of opposites was achieved, creating power: "Eras are to be measured by their *positive powers:* the period of the Renaissance accordingly, so profuse and fateful, presents itself as the last *great* period" (*CW,* pp. 200–210).

If Yeats finds, in his philosophical statement of 1908, strength and vitality in modern (i.e., impressionist) art, he also finds a disturbing lack of attention to formula: "the idea of limitation at all was the enemy." The direction of the essays shifts from an appreciation of the "athletic spirit" of Manet to that of Castiglione in *The Courtier*—the "Italian book" of the letter to his father. At the same time, *The Courtier's* insistence on the importance of "models" of behavior passes into Yeats's playwriting. The Player Queen stands for the representation of greatness, heroism, and nobility on the stage and as a model for life—qualities notably lacking, Yeats points out in his essays, in the art of the impressionist present. The emphasis on "character," he feels, is responsible for the decline of interest in beautiful form, and he repeats a conversation told him by a "very beautiful woman" in Paris whose friends are antimilitarist: "She said, 'my friends say that if a man is afraid to fight, he ought not to be ashamed to say so. I tell them that I think one cannot become brave without often, when one is very much afraid, pretending that one is quite calm. But they answer, "No, that sincerity is everything.' "[9] The dialogue reported by the very beautiful woman between herself and her friends is like the opposition Yeats establishes between the Player Queen and the Real Queen—the one upholding pretense, the other, sincerity. It is also like the opposition Yeats is working toward in the essays between Renaissance art and modern art. The pretense of the very beautiful woman and the Player Queen, and the beautiful forms of Renaissance art, are masks, or models of perfection—expressions of Nietzsche's self-overcoming through opposition, which is also self-becoming. The Player Queen says that, as Real Queen, she will "be herself."

Yeats finds this idea irresistible. It must have had resonance for him, when he found it in Nietzsche, for he had listened to Oscar Wilde read *The Decay of Lying* in 1888; the resonance continued as he read Castiglione's *The Courtier* in 1907. By means of the cultural grapevine, Castiglione, Nietzsche, and Wilde are connected; Nietzsche read Castiglione, Wilde read (or heard about) Nietzsche; and Yeats knew them all. Of the three, Nietzsche provides the most complex interpretation of the relationship between art and nature and the most compelling argument for art's importance; of the three, Yeats knew Nietzsche best. As he describes Castiglione's book in his final section he draws as much on *The Twilight of the Idols* as on *The Courtier* or *The Decay of Lying*. The nobles of Urbino, in the first years of the sixteenth century, Yeats recounts, were prescribed "a life of continual toil and continual schedule" until at last they attained "true beauty," which, in Yeats's version of Castiglione's definition, was "the spoil and monument of the victory of the soul."[10] Yeats then ponders the importance of the courtier's regimen in all things—conversation, dance, manners, and "a laborious training of the body"—and its effect upon art. His conclusion reads:

> The beauty of the men of the Renaissance as we see it [in] pictures and in chronicles, like that of the Greek men, whom Cicero found so much more handsome than the women, was, like all fine things, an artifice and a toil. A friend, who is very learned in pictures, reminds me that one does not find this in the first portraits of their generation, but only after some time. Their generation had something present to their minds which they copied. They would imitate Christ or Caesar in their lives, or with [their] bodies some classic statue. They sought at all times the realisation of something deliberately chosen, and they played a part always as if upon a stage and before an audience, and gave up their lives rather than their play.[11]

Yeats's ideas here owe something to Castiglione and something to Wilde, but his chief debt is to Nietzsche's passage in *The Twilight of the Idols* that had inspired him, I believe, to compose "Adam's Curse" some five years earlier: "*Beauty no accident*":

> Even the beauty of a race or family, the pleasantness and kindness of their whole demeanour, is acquired by effort. . . At Athens in the time of Cicero, who expresses his surprise with regard to it, men and youths were far superior to women in beauty: but what labour and effort in the service of beauty had the Athenian males required of themselves for centuries! . . . The strict maintenance of significant and select demeanour, an obligation to live only with those who do not "let themselves go," suffices perfectly for becoming significant and select; in two or three generations everything has become *inwardised.* It is decisive for the fortune of a people and of humanity, that civilisation begin at the *right place*—not at "soul." . . . The right place is body, demeanour, regimen, physiology; the *rest* follows therefrom. (*CW*, pp. 215–17)

In his conclusion to his statement about art, Yeats keeps Nietzsche's reference to Cicero intact, alludes to his idea that it takes some generations for the effects of the regimen to tell, and ends by a veiled acknowledgment (which Nietzsche makes openly) of the importance of the artifice to civilization: "They played a part always as if upon a stage and before an audience, and gave up their lives rather than their play."

The imitation of a model ("They would imitate Christ or Caesar in their lives") is an important consideration for Yeats; it opposes the modern distaste for models, "canons," or limits. As Richard Ellmann points out in *Eminent Domain,* Yeats kept in mind Wilde's phrase from *The Decay of Lying:* "Think of what we owe to the imitation of Christ, of what we owe to the imitation of Caesar." Ellmann quotes a passage from Yeats's *Per Amica Silentia Lunae* to illustrate Yeats's "complications" of Wilde's idea: "Some years ago I began to believe that our culture, with its doctrine of sincerity and self-realisation, made us gentle and passive, and that the Middle Ages and the Renaissance were right to found theirs upon the imitation of Christ or of some classic hero. Saint Francis and Caesar Borgia made themselves overmastering, creative persons by turning from the mirror to meditation upon a mask."[12] This passage implicitly refers to the "philosophical statement" of 1908 and amplifies it. In 1908, Yeats talks about the "sincerity" in vogue with the antimilitaristic friends of the beautiful woman in Paris and with contemporary artists, and about the importance of the imitation of Christ or Caesar. He does not, however, draw the explicit moral conclusion about either "sincerity" or "imitation" that he does in the *Per Amica* passage. The moral seems to be in the back of his mind in 1908, or on the tip of his tongue, when he talks about giving up life rather than "the play," but he only articulates it later. It is that "our culture" of self realization and sincerity has "made us gentle and passive" and that therefore the Middle Ages and the Renaissance "were right" in choosing models for imitation. He makes it clear that the "imitation" is far from passive, not life in a mirror, but meditation upon an opposite, a mask. This meditation helped St. Francis and Caesar Borgia "make themselves," and the selves so "made" were "overmastering," "creative." There is power in the mask and, in Nietzsche's word, *futurity*.

"Our culture's" gentleness and passivity, which he regards symptomatically, is terrifying to Nietzsche. His most extended analysis of its genesis and implications, *A Genealogy of Morals,* begins by questioning "the *value* of sympathy and the morality of sympathy": "More especially, the point in question was the value of "unselfishness," of the sympathizing, self-denying, self-sacrificing instincts. . . . Just here I saw the *great* danger threatening mankind; . . . just here I saw the beginning of the end, the stopping, the retrospective weariness, the will turning itself against life" (*GM,* pp. 7–8). In this book he praises Caesar Borgia as a superabundant type; in *The Twilight of the Idols* he defends his choice: "we modern men, with our thick wadded humanity, which will not by any means strike against a stone, would furnish a comedy to the contemporaries of Caesar Borgia to laugh themselves to death over. . . . The decline of hostile and distrust-awakening instincts—for that would be our "progress"—represents only one of the consequences in the general decline of *vitality*" (*CW,* p. 199). Yeats's passage from *Per Amica Silentia Lunae* carries out ideas he has been working on since he began reading Nietzsche. Specifically, it draws on the ideas he put into the essay in *Samhain,* 1904, when he distinquished between the "subjective" art of Keats, art of the "mirror," reflective of the poet's state of mind, and the "dramatic" art of Shakespeare and Villon, in which life itself makes one of its eternal gestures. Dramatic art externalizes emotion—or, as he comes to see, "imitation of Christ or of some classic hero" takes one outside oneself, and reconnects one with the social world.

A passage in the 1909 Journal enlarges on the social function of such "imitation," as Yeats sees it. He is discussing the etchings of Augustus John, who embodies, Yeats says, "the extreme revolt from academic form." His figures are ugly, by Renaissance canons and measurement:

> A gymnast set to train the body would find in all these some defect to overcome, and when he had overcome them he would have brought them in every case nearer to that ancient canon which comes down to us from the gymnasium of ancient Greece, and which when it is present marks, like any other literary element, a compact between the artist and society, a purpose held in common with his time to create emotions or forms which Nature also desires. John is interested not in the social need, in the perpetual thirst for ever more health and physical serviceableness, for bodies fitted for the labour of life, but in character, in the revolt of the individual from all that makes it like others. (*Mem,* p. 188)

The imitation of models for Yeats is, like ritual, a way of building and binding a community, bringing "fragments" into unity.

The philosophy Yeats derives from Nietzsche is beginning to focus on the idea of power, "the sun in his strength," which is released through opposition. As Nietzsche puts it in the passage defending Caesar Borgia, to "strike against a stone"—a metaphor Yeats must have appreciated for its esoteric as well as its literal resonance—makes sparks fly; the sparks are power or energy. Nietzsche always stresses the idea that it is necessary to create the energy, not for its own sake, but for life's. Yeats too, when he says in the Preface to *Poems, 1899–1905* that art's purpose is to "serve life," follows Nietzsche's lead, and when he writes Scenario 6 for *The Player Queen,* he reminds himself of the moral behind the mask. Near the end of the scenario, he says: "Some lines pointing the moral. It is not enough to be, but [stake] your life on your acting" (*PQ,* pp. 28–29). This thought echoes, or foreshadows, the ending of the "philosophical statement" in which Yeats says that the generations of the Renaissance "played a part always as if upon a stage and before an audience, and gave up their lives rather than their play."[13]

The Player Queen will stake her life upon her acting, imitation of an heroic model, because "it is not enough to be." Being is self-realization; it is static; it is sincere. Acting is self-overcoming, dynamic, and artificial. The very lineup of qualifiers under "being" and "acting" illustrates the way Yeats's mask theory works in practice. "Being" is both static and sincere; acting is both dynamic and artificial. Surely, logic says, static belongs with artificial, and dynamic with sincere. But that way, one achieves polar opposition without the possibility of contact or interchange, and it is *contact* of opposites that strikes the sparks. (For this reason Yeats, early and late, sees heterosexual intercourse as the metaphor for unity.) When a person acts, he or she embodies the conflict, or contact, of opposites, being "self," and representing the stage character or "mask." In *The Player Queen,* the Real Queen stands for the "being" or "sincere" half of the dichotomy. She refuses to act. She represents the self to the Player Queen's mask or anti-self. In his earlier terminology, the Real Queen is the "soul" to the Player Queen's "self." The self-soul dichotomy as Yeats represents it in the Common anthology's diagram depends on the interchangeability of the parts. In *The Player Queen* the parts are not interchangeable. Because the Real Queen can only be herself, she lacks the complexity of her counterpart, who can both "be" herself and "become" the Real Queen. Yeats gives more weight to the side of the Player Queen, so his equation does not balance, and dramatic sparks do not fly.

For Yeats, "passion and not thought makes tragedy." As he buries himself deeper in drafts of the play, the further into thought and away from tragedy he goes. The Journal he begins in December 1908 takes the place of the second series of *Discoveries* as his outlet for his philosophical tendency. Its form is more deliberately rambling than the earlier pieces on art, for, as he says in an early entry, "Every note must first have to come as a casual thought, then it will be my life. If Christ or Buddha or Socrates had written, they would have surrendered life for a logical process" (*Mem,* p. 139). However, the intractable fact remains that in the Journal, Yeats is "writing," and thus to some extent surrendering life for a logical process—as in *The Player Queen,* the Player Queen's "acting" is, and is known to be, a "play." Yeats is confronting head-on in both Journal and play the issue of the separation of life and art. Either explicitly or implicitly, this separation forms the theme of almost every Journal entry. He drafts the poem "Words" early in the Journal—

> I might have thrown poor words away
> And been content to live
>
> (*Mem,* p. 143)

—in which life with Maud Gonne is seen as a better alternative than the image or mask of life Yeats offers through "poor words."

Although he is expressing it more directly than before, this is not a new idea for Yeats, nor is it by any means original. The artist's separation from what he describes and longs for is a romantic theme; it forms a major strand of the cultural zeitgeist in the nineteenth century. Goethe, Byron ("The tree of Knowledge is not that of Life"), Flaubert, and Nietzsche—even Nietzsche—develop the concept of the artist's "alienation," which Henry James and Thomas Mann, among others, perpetuate in the early twentieth century. Nietzsche takes a strong and approving line on artists' alienation in an important passage in *A Genealogy of Morals:*

> We must guard against the error into which an artist is but too apt to fall from psychological contiguity (as the English call it) of supposing that he himself *is really* that which he is able to represent, to think out, to express in words. The fact is that, if he were such, he could under no circumstances represent it, nor think it out, nor express it in words. Homer would never have created an Achilles, Goethe would never have created a Faust, had Homer been Achilles, or Goethe Faust. A perfect and genuine artist is, for aye and

evermore, separated from that which is "real," actually existing. (*GM,* p. 131)

This separation constitutes what Nietzsche calls "a kind of intellectual perversity" (*GM,* p. 131), but it is necessary, for artists and thinkers. It is the way of power for "the most intelligent," justified by self-conquest and their fundamental optimism: " '*The world is perfect*' "—thus speaks the instinct of the most intelligent man, the affirmative instinct" (*CW,* p. 340). This is from the passage in *The Antichrist* in which Nietzsche advocates the most difficult task for the most intelligent: "With them asceticism becomes nature, requirement, and instinct" (*CW,* p. 340). The "perfection" that the artist finds is embodied in his work, not in his life. In *A Genealogy of Morals* Nietzsche speaks as a forerunner of aesthetic criticism: "it is certainly best to separate an artist so far from his work as not to take him as seriously as his work. All in all, he is but the condition of his work—the womb, soil, nay, at times even dung and manure upon which and out of which it grows, and hence, in most cases, something which must be forgotten if we would enjoy the work itself" (*GM,* p. 130).

An early draft of *The Player Queen* contains a detail that shows Yeats is interested in connecting "dung" and "art." He opens with a scene in which "the Friend" finds the script for Noah's wife, where the Player Queen has thrown it down on "the dung pit by the kitchen door . . . between the broken egg shells and an old shoe" (*PQ,* p. 36). On the surface, this detail illustrates the Player Queen's contempt for the part of Noah's wife, but the very juxtaposition of playscript and dung heap suggests another more causal connection; the artist is the womb or even "dung and manure" out of which his "perfected" life, his work, grows, as Nietzsche says. Yeats late in life again juxtaposes playscripts and scraps of "real life" in "The Circus Animals' Desertion," this time making the causal connection explicit:

> Those masterful images because complete
> Grew in pure mind, but out of what began?
> A mound of refuse or the sweepings of a street.
>
> (*VP,* p. 630)

An entry in his Journal of February 3, 1909, shows that he has taken his reading in Nietzsche to heart in many ways. The passage begins with the artist's defense of "unconsidered life": "Blake talking to

Crabb Robinson said once that he preferred to any man of intellect a happy thoughtless person, or some such phrase. It followed, I suppose, from his praise of life—'all that lives is holy'—and from his dislike of abstract things. . . . Nietzsche had it [the preference] doubtless at the moment when he imagined 'the superman' as a child." In *Thus Spake Zarathustra* Nietzsche never speaks of the superman as a child, but he does speak of the third metamorphosis of the spirit, the apotheosis of the struggle, as a child, representing creative innocence and affirmation (both characteristics of the superman). Yeats then takes up the distinction between artists and their work:

We artists suffer in our art if we do not love most of all *life* at peace with itself and doing without forethought what its humanity bids it and therefore happily. We are, as seen from life, an artifice, an emphasis, an uncompleted arc perhaps. Those whom it is our business to cherish and celebrate are complete arcs. Because the life we see is not the final end of things, the moment we attain to greatness of any kind by personal labour and will we become fragmentary, and find no task in active life which can use our highest faculties. We are compelled to think and express and not do. Faust in the end was only able to reclaim land like some officer of the Agricultural Board. It is right that Romeo should not be a man of intellect or learning, it is enough for us that there is nature in him. We see all his arc, for in literature we need completed things. (*Mem,* p. 158)

The emphasis on perspective in this passage, as well as the defense of the artist's separation from life, are Yeats's inheritance from Nietzsche. Nietzsche's moral imperative to the "most intelligent" to perform the "difficult task" becomes part of the difficult, fascinating relativity of all things for artist and philosopher. Yeats says that artists use their highest faculties to create "completed things," but are themselves fragmentary, complete only in the labor and will of creation. They are separated, by their imaginations, from the active people participating in life "without forethought"; they are the artifice, the unnatural ones, from those people's point of view. Yet the same "natural" people will become the Faust's and the Romeo's—"artifice" in their turn.

Nietzsche and Yeats justify the artists' separation from life by making it an essential and fruitful opposition. Art itself, complete, "perfect," is the mask for the artists' incompletion. To perfect the mask, artists need and use all life; the discipline they undergo in keeping to their "most difficult task" they then impose on their art. "There is a relation between discipline and the theatrical sense," says Yeats in his Journal: "If we cannot imagine ourselves as different from what we are and try to assume that second self, we cannot impose a discipline upon ourselves, though we may accept one from others. Active virtue as distinguished from the passive acceptance of a current code is therefore theatrical, consciously dramatic, the wearing of a mask. It is the condition of arduous full life" (*Mem,* p. 151). The distinction between "active virtue" and "passive acceptance of a current code" goes back to Yeats's sun-moon opposition of the Preface to *Gods and Fighting Men,* based on Nietzsche's distinction between master and slave morality, and looks forward to his statement in *A Vision,* that "the *primary* is that which serves, the *antithetical* that which creates" (*V,* p. 85). "Active virtue" is active, creative, and virtuous precisely because it is a struggle or conflict with the passive, the formless, and the incomplete in the world and in oneself.

Yeats engages in much introspection in his Journal; it reads on a personal level as a diary of self-deprecation and self-overcoming. He scolds himself for loss of temper, irritation, shyness. In a revealing note near the beginning of the Journal he suggests that perhaps he should seek out people he dislikes in order to conquer his "petulant self-combativeness." Then he writes: "It is always inexcusable to lose one's self-possession. It always comes from impatience, from a kind of spiritual fright at someone who is here and now more powerful, even if only from stupidity. I am never angry with those in my power" (*Mem,* p. 138). He finds the cure in the mask: "I escaped from it all as a writer through my sense of style. Is not one's art made out of the struggle in one's soul? Is not beauty a victory over oneself?" (*Mem,* p. 157). In another entry, he says that in order to oppose "the new ill-breeding of Ireland . . . I can only set up a secondary or interior personality created by me out of the tradition of myself, and this personality (alas, to me only possible in my writings) must be always gracious and simple. It must have that slight separation from immediate interests which makes charm possible, while remaining near enough for fire" (*Mem,* p. 142).

As in his "Tree of Life" piece in *Discoveries* (1906), Yeats again stresses the importance of distance, the right degree of separation, between his writing and his "immediate interests." His "secondary or interior personality" is possible to him only in his writings; it is that which he strives to become; it is his "active virtue"; it is his style, his mask. The "immediate interests" would then represent his self—his irritation, his shyness, his involvement in daily life when he is not striving to be "charming." "Charm" is the result, the end product, of self-overcoming or wearing the mask. It is the power, charisma, or mastery, that moves others, and it is born of the marriage of self and mask. The "slight separation" of self and mask parallels, on an individual level, the separation of life and art. The separation is essential for the creation of power, as long as the opposite poles remain "near enough for fire."

Another separation between opposites that is probably the most absorbing, and baffling, of all for Yeats, is the one between lovers. Both in drafts of *The Player Queen* and in the Journal, he theorizes about the nature of love, which is complicated by the fact, as he sees it, that each lover is composed of two parts, self and mask. His attempt to understand the "separation" between himself and Maud Gonne produces, as all agree, remarkably great love poetry. Its greatness depends on the complications he discerns involving self and mask. The first entry in the Journal is a draft of the poem "No Second Troy." Many of Yeats's interests and preoccupations come together in this poem: the heroic, as he expressed it especially in *Deirdre,* as something distinguished, solitary and proud; his new awareness of the difference between the "modern" and the "classical" (or Renaissance) styles of art, as he has expressed it in the "philosophical statement" of 1908; his newly whetted appreciation of the distinctions of social class; and encompassing all, his interest in the theory of the mask. As Yeats writes it in the Journal, the poem reads:

Why should I blame her that she filled my days
With misery, or that she would of late
Have taught to ignorant men most violent ways
Or hurled the little streets upon the great
Had they but courage to equal desire?
What could have made her peaceful with a mind
That nobleness made simple as a fire,
With / And beauty like a tightened bow, a kind

That is not natural in an age like this
Being high and solitary and most stern
Why what could she have done being what she is?
Was there another Troy for her to burn?

(*Mem,* p. 137)

Yeats is, as all agree, "mythologizing" Maude Gonne, in setting her up as Helen of Troy. For the purpose of this study, I shall only comment on the single most important opposition of the poem, the one between the "I" and the "she," the separation of lovers. In the first place, the speaker is tempted to blame "her" for filling his days with misery, reducing him to the state of hateful, impotent selfhood that other Journal entries show him trying to overcome. In the second place, he is tempted to blame her politics, teaching ignorant men violent ways and upsetting a social order he believes in (hurling "little streets upon the great"). But he "masters" his temptation to blame her by imagining her as someone or something else that is "not natural." There is much irony in the line, "Why what could she have done being what she is?" It is like the Player Queen's line to the Prime Minister, "I will have victory today by being myself." The Player Queen's "self" is her anti-self, the role or mask of Queen; the "what she is" of "No Second Troy" is similarly a mask, or image of an heroic prototype. Her beauty is "not natural in an age like this," where the cranky, the ugly, the sincere are considered fit matter for art. The striking point about what happens in "No Second Troy" is that the speaker of the poem is able to overcome himself—he is able not to "blame" the woman and not to remain powerless—by creating a mask for *her,* and thus for himself through his creation. If she becomes Helen, he becomes Homer.

The transformations of the poem help explain Yeats's prose interpretation in the Journal of the relationship between love and mask. He says: "It seems to me that love, if it is fine, is essentially a discipline, but it needs so much wisdom that the love of Solomon and Sheba must have lasted for all the silence of the Scriptures. In wise love each divines the high secret of self of the other and, refusing to believe in the mere daily self, creates a mirror where the lover or the beloved sees an image to copy in daily life. Love also creates the mask" (*Mem,* pp. 144–45). The speaker in "No Second Troy" divines the "high secret self of the other" as essentially heroic, and creates an image for his beloved to copy in daily life. Under this "regimen," the desired "self" is given a continual opportunity to shine. Yeats's insistance that love is a "discipline" full of wisdom is a far cry from the kind of passion, longing for changeless essences beyond nature, that he espouses at the turn of the century and even as late as 1904 in passages in the *Samhain* essays. Love as discipline? Love as wisdom? As in the oppositions he created in his plays, he is yoking opposites—now in the theoretical analysis of expository prose. He is understanding that what he conceives as "limitless," passion, demands limits for its expression in life as in art. It also demands action. If the "moral"—Yeats's own word—of *The Player Queen* is that "it is not enough to be," a related moral deriving from the Journal passage might be that it is not enough to love. For love to *move* and be helpful to the beloved, it must "act." "Action" for Yeats at this point is only possible as a kind of playacting, or a rising above one's uncertainty and confusion through concentration on a mask.

Drafts of *The Player Queen* written at about the same time as these Journal entries, in 1909, show him laboring to develop in the play the idea that "love also creates the mask." Draft 8 includes a dialogue between Yellow Martin (the Poet) and the Chancellor (the Prime Minister), in which the Chancellor demands that the players' play go on, and Yellow Martin explains that the leading lady (the Player Queen), his sweetheart, is missing. He has not searched for her, because to do so would be to show that he cared: "We that love passionate, proud women must keep the mask upon us though our heart is breaking, for if it slip off may be the happiness of a whole life is gone," he says. The Chancellor demands a search. Martin replies: "Very well, sir, I will tell my company to search by your orders, but I, sir, will go read a book in the garden, hoping that she will see me there and understand that I do not care" (*PQ*, p. 81). This seems a particularly negative use of the mask, and it does not pay off for Martin, who—lest he let the mask of uncaring slip—does not choose the Player Queen over "the Friend," and so loses her.

In a later draft, Yeats splits his character of "the Poet" into two poets, each other's opposites. One (Peter) presents the point of view of the mask; the other (Yellow Martin), the "sincerity" of the face. They represent rather transparently Yeats's own argument with himself, his own face and mask:

Peter. If you would only listen to me. Here I am with all my trifling, with my empty head, and I have won and tired of half a dozen women while you were losing one. Love is an art—a science if you will. You treat it as if it were the inspiration of Heaven. Why do you not give way to her a little, pretending to think she is right when you know she is wrong? . . .

Yellow Martin. But I wish her to be all the perfection I can imagine, and would be no less myself.

Peter. Seem a little, play a little. . . .

Y.M. But I love, and she would not think me worthy of her love if I did not show myself strong enough to be her master.

Peter. But only we who love lightly, keeping always our gaiety, are masters. Love masters you and so you are despised.

Y.M. But I love her; what else can I do?

(*PQ*, pp. 123–24)

Peter takes the point of view of Yeats in his 1909 Journal (sounding a good deal like Nietzsche, in his emphasis on seeming, and mastery through "gaiety") that love is a discipline—"an art—a science if you will." His advocacy of pretense sounds like an idea Yeats has expressed earlier, in his "Tree of Life" piece in *Discoveries,* 1906, when he speaks of deceiving "that exacting mistress," Life: "We must not give her all, we must deceive her a little at times. . . .Our deceit will give us style, mastery." The word *mastery* recurs in Peter's speeches; he rubs it in: "Love masters you and so you are despised." Martin does not deny it, but he protests that he is incapable of pretense. Like the poet in "Never Give All the Heart," he is "deaf and dumb and blind with love."

He is therefore doomed to unhappiness, for Yeats is coming to see happiness as synonymous with the ability to act. In a key passage in his Journal, he says:

I think all happiness depends on having the energy to assume the mask of some other self, that all joyous or creative life is a rebirth as something not oneself, something created in a moment and perpetually renewed in playing a game like that of a child where one loses the infinite pain of self-realization, a grotesque or solemn painted face put on that one may hide from the terrors of judgment, an imaginative Saturnalia that makes one forget reality. Perhaps all the sins and energies of the world are but the world's flight from an infinite blinding beam. (*Mem,* p. 191)

"Reality" in this passage, like "self-realization," is something to escape or forget. It must be overcome if one is to be happy. Nietzsche provides a definition of happiness in *The Antichrist* that may have some bearing on this passage. He writes in the form of a catechism:

What is good?—All that increases the feeling of power, will to power, power itself, in man.
What is bad?—All that proceeds from weakness.
What is happiness?—The feeling that power *increases,* that a resistance is overcome. (*CW,* p. 242)

For Nietzsche, too, reality is the most difficult, most painful thing there is; it is also what there is. It is what offers the "resistance" that is to be overcome by will, producing a feeling of increased power, or happiness. Will needs an object; for Nietzsche the object is life itself. Yeats in this Journal passage makes the object "the mask of some other self." He internalizes the struggle, necessarily. He knows that he must be "happy," or whole, before he can confront life, and sees the way to wholeness through conscious, willful self-division. He thus makes *himself* the resistance to be overcome as the means to increased power or happiness.

Another Nietzschean idea that feeds into Yeats's passage comes from the climactic section on beauty and art in *The Twilight of the Idols.* Nietzsche writes in praise of tragedy and of the tragic artist: "Bravery and self-possession in presence of a powerful enemy, an awful calamity, or a problem which awakens dread—it is this *triumphal* condition which the tragic artist selects and glorifies. In presence of tragedy the martial spirit in us celebrates its Saturnalia" (*CW,* p. 187).

Two entries before the "Saturnalia" passage in the Journal, Yeats describes one of his own painful memories, a "harm" he did to someone who died shortly after. He says, "Because of his death it has not been touched by the transforming hand—tolerant Nature has not rescued it from Justice" (*Mem,* p. 191). Within the space of a day or two, he writes of seeking a mask "that one may hide from the terrors of judgment." He implies that if one lacks the energy to assume the mask and to create an "imaginative Saturnalia," one simply drowns in fear and guilt. It is precisely fear and guilt from which Nietzsche feels the human spirit should be freed. When he writes the Journal passage, I think Yeats is also remembering Zarathustra's third and last metamorphosis of the spirit, the child: "The child is innocence and oblivion, a new starting, a play, a wheel rolling by itself, a prime motor, a holy asserting" (*Z,* p. 27). The transformation to "child" is anything but sentimental for Nietzsche. It must be won through to, following the second metamorphosis from camel to lion; it is emblematic of the most complete state of being humanly possible. Only the "child" is capable of "new creating." When Yeats, in "Against Unworthy Praise" (1910) imagines Maud Gonne as "half lion, half child" (*VP,* p. 260), he is giving her highest, most worthy, praise.

Nietzsche does not make the mechanics of the metamorphosis from lion to child explicit, but from all that he says about self-overcoming and the existence of antithesis in all things, Yeats deduces the way to make it happen for himself. In the words of the Saturnalia passage, the function of the mask is "rebirth," something "created in a moment and perpetually renewed," as "joyous and creative life," like the game of a child. The metamorphosis depends on "having the energy to assume the mask of some other self." It depends on the will to power confronting, as Nietzsche says in the passage on tragedy, "a powerful enemy, an awful calamity, or a problem which awakens dread." It is only when so confronted that the full power of the human spirit is called into "play." "In presence of tragedy the martial spirit in us celebrates its Saturnalia."

Although the central concern of Yeats's Saturnalia passage is the mask, the concept of tragedy runs through it as its antithesis. It is present in the "infinite blinding beam"—the flight from which creates, "perhaps," "the sins and energies of the world." It is present in "the terror of judgment," which forces on him the energy to "assume the mask." It is present in "the infinite pain of self-realization." Infinite pain, infinite beam, terror of judgment, all represent Nietzsche's "powerful enemy," or the "resistance" that must be "overcome" if one is to be happy and creative. The enemy seems to be for Yeats in this passage a kind of absolute knowledge of "reality"—better escaped from or forgotten. This kind of knowledge sounds a good deal like Silenus's "wisdom," which Nietzsche recounts in *The Birth of Tragedy:* "What is best of all is forever beyond your reach: not to be born, not to *be,* to be nothing. The second best for you, however, is soon to die" (*BT,* p. 34).

There is a good chance that when Yeats writes the Saturnalia passage, he finally has to hand *The Birth of Tragedy*. Oscar Levy, who was editing Nietzsche's *Complete Works* in English translation, brought out in 1909 *The Birth of Tragedy, Thoughts out of Season,* and volume one of *The Will to Power*. All three works are in Yeats's library today; the first two are numbered among the first 300 of the first edition's 1,000 copies published by T. N. Foulis. One can assume, therefore, that Yeats acquired them when the edition first appeared. All three volumes contain some uncut pages; of *The Birth of Tragedy's* 187 pages, 38 are uncut. The uncut pages occur randomly by two's and three's throughout the volume, which indicates to me that Yeats was reading fairly quickly—glancing through, rather than "chewing the cud." He was, after all, familiar with the argument, with the major concepts "Apollonian" and "Dionysian," and with the pieces exerpted by Ellis, Symons, and Common.

Even so, there is little doubt that the book interested him enormously. If "the shock of new material" galvanized him on reading Nietzsche in 1902–3, "the shock of recognition" would probably more accurately describe the effect of his reading in 1909. It is hard to believe that Yeats had not read the opening sentence of *The Birth of Tragedy* before 1909 (perhaps he had), so completely do the ideas accord with what he has said himself—generally, and specifically in the King's opening address in *The King's Threshold,* and in Cuchulain's definition of love in *On Baile's Strand*. The opening reads: "We shall have gained much for the science of aesthetics, when once we have perceived not only by logical inference, but by the immediate certainty of intuition, that the continuous development of art is bound up with the duplexity of the *Apollonian* and the *Dionysian:* in like manner as procreation is dependent on the duality of the sexes, involving perpetual conflict with only periodically intervening reconciliations" (*BT,* p. 21). Nietzsche argues that the moments of reconciliation between the Apollonian and the Dionysian produce the "child": the high Greek tragedy of Aeschylus and Sophocles. He defines the Apollonian as "the art of the shaper, Apollo" (*BT,* p. 21); as "the glorious divine image of the *principium individuationis,* from out of the gestures and the looks of which all the joy and wisdom of 'appearances,' together with its beauty, speak to us" (*BT,* p. 25). Apollo represents form, structure, limit. In contrast, the "Dionysian" breaks down the barriers. Nietzsche finds analogies for this state in "the non-plastic art of music" (*BT,* p. 21) and "drunkenness" (*BT,* p. 23). It is "the blissful ecstasy which rises from the innermost depths of man, ay, of nature, at this same collapse of the *principium individuationis.*" Under the "charm" of the Dionysian, "the covenant between man and man is again established," and also that between man and nature. Nietzsche calls it a condition of "Primordial Unity" and "equality of all peoples" (*BT,* pp. 25–26); a "mystic feeling of Oneness" (*BT,* p. 28).

After defining his principle terms, Nietzsche offers an account of the origin of Greek "Olympian" art—that of Homer and Phidias. It begins with the "folk wisdom" of Silenus, wisdom that demonstrates, Nietzsche says, the basic absurdity of existence. He continues: "The Greek knew and felt the terrors and horrors of existence: to be able to live at all, he had to interpose the shining dream-birth of the Olympian world between himself and them. . . .The same impulse which calls art into being, as the complement and consummation of existence, seducing to a continuation of life, caused also the Olympian world to arise, in which the Hellenic 'will' held up before itself a transfigurating mirror" (*BT,* pp. 34–35). It is hard not to see this passage, and others like it, as the foundation of Yeats's Saturnalia passage, where the mask is willed as an escape from pain and terror. Yet as I have shown, the ideas of the passage can also be traced to other works by Nietzsche.

More unmistakably the mark of *The Birth of Tragedy* are references Yeats makes at this time to appearance as "illusion." In a Journal passage that antedates the Saturnalia passage by about a month, Yeats discusses the difference between Eastern and Western philosophy, with emphasis on the West's insistence on "power and therefore body." "The historical truth of the Incarnation is indifferent," he says, "though belief in that truth was essential to the power of evocation." Then he says: "All civilization is held together by a series of suggestions made by an invisible hypnotist, artificially created illusions. The knowledge of reality is always by some means or other a secret knowledge. It is a kind of death" (*Mem,* p. 166). This thought emphasizes the dichotomy between "appearance" and "reality" that Nietzsche also stresses as a creative opposition in *The Birth of Tragedy.* Speaking of Sophocle's heroes who are "clear" and "precise," he says, "Those light-picture phenomena of the Sophoclean hero,—in short, the Apollonian of the mask,—are the necessary productions of a glance into the secret and terrible things of nature" (*BT,* p. 73). Further, he emphasizes the progenitive function of such "illusions": "The avidious will can always, by means of an illusion spread over things, detain its creatures in life and compel them to live on" (*BT,* p. 136). In Homer—"the inexpressibly sublime Homer"—he finds "the complete triumph of the Apollonian illusion" (*BT,* p. 37).

A letter Yeats writes his father in 1910 shows that his recent thoughts on "tragedy"—derived from *The Birth of Tragedy* almost certainly, and appearing in the essay "on 'tragic drama' " that he tells his father he has just finished—are influencing the direction of *The Player Queen* (now in its sixteenth draft). He says, "But of course really all my thoughts are on my long play, of which a great deal will be in rhyme. My theme is that the world being illusion, one must be deluded in some way if one is to triumph in it."[14] This thought about his play reveals a new low in his work on it. "Illusion" necessitating "delusion" spells disillusion in the author. One can see how Yeats arrived at his new theme. In the play, character after character either assumes or does not assume a mask; the mask begins to seem to him, after *The Birth of Tragedy,* a beautiful illusion hiding "secret and terrible things." Appearance itself is illusion, and "reality" is "a kind of death." In such a world, the only way to "triumph" is to be ignorant of the real nature of things, and thus to be deluded.

When Nietzsche repudiates *The Birth of Tragedy* in "An Attempt at Self-Criticism" (1886) and later in *Ecce Homo,* he calls it "romantic" and "pessimistic," and asks himself, "Can a deep hatred of the present, of 'reality' and 'modern ideas,' be more emphasized than it is in your artist-metaphysics?—which would rather believe in Nothing, or in the devil, than in the 'Now'?" He also calls it "intoxicating and stupefying" (*BT,* p. 13), and finds its only point of redemption in its recognition of the "Dionysian" as the moving force behind tragedy.[15] All the evidence suggests that in 1909 and 1910, Yeats is, if not intoxicated and stupefied by *The Birth of Tragedy,* temporarily incapacitated by the confusion into which it throws his thoughts.

The major dichotomy of *The Birth of Tragedy* resembles the "two movements of the soul" that Yeats tells Quinn back in 1903 he has "always felt"—the movement to transcend forms, and the movement to create forms. When he reads *The Birth of Tragedy,* Yeats seems to return to his old identification of the "Dionysiac" movement with tragedy itself. *The Birth of Tragedy* adds complexity and interest—further intoxication—to the Dionysian half of the orange as Yeats has "always felt" it, by making it mythopoeic, capable of reproducing "myth from itself" (*BT,* p. 131), and uncovering its historical link with primal ritual. The emotional state Nietzsche ascribes to the Dionysian is "ecstasy," to the Apollonian, "joy." It seems to me that, when Yeats reads *The Birth of Tragedy,* his old allegiance to the first half of the orange—involving as it does his allegiance to his studies of occult mysticism—is rekindled.

An entry in the Journal, on the nature of "Tragedy" and "Comedy," illustrates the divergence of his concepts of tragedy and mask. This entry becomes the basis of his essay on "The Tragic Theatre":

> Tragedy is passion alone and, instead of character, gets form from motives, the wandering of passion; while comedy is the clash of character. . . . Comedy is joyous because all assumption of a part, of a personal mask, whether the individualized face of comedy or the grotesque face of farce, is a display of energy, and all energy is joyous. A poet creates tragedy from his own soul, that soul which is alike in all men, and at moments it has no joy, as we understand that word, for the soul is an exile and without will. It attains to ecstasy, which is from the contemplation of things which are vaster than the individual and imperfectly seen, perhaps, by all that still live. The masks of tragedy contain neither character nor personal energy. They are allied to decoration and to the abstract figures of Egyptian temples. Before the mind can look out of their eyes the active will perishes, hence their sorrowful calm. Joy is of the will which does things, which overcomes obstacles, which is victorious. (*Mem,* p. 152)

Yeats organizes his oppositions tightly in this paragraph, and they seem to fall back on the old night-day, soul-self opposition. Comedy is day: self (individualized face), joyous energy, "active will," and mask or the "assumption of a part." It is clearly meant to represent the Apollonian half of the orange, the half of "appearance." Tragedy is night: universal soul ("alike in all men"), contemplation, "sorrowful calm." However, it is also the genre of "passion," and it attains to "ecstasy." "Passion" seems out of place in a catalog of chiefly passive virtues, and its placement indicates some confusion in Yeats's mind about tragedy itself. Yeats seems to want tragedy to embody the abstractions of his first half of the orange: transcendence, infinity. Certain of Nietzsche's attributions to the Dionysian help Yeats put tragedy on that half of the orange. The Dionysian is after all the deindividuating principle. Tragic figures on the Athenian stage represent the "universal," the "ideal"; they are connected with myth, which links all humanity to its root "terror" and sadness at the fact of individuation.

Yeats's 1910 essay "The Tragic Theatre" enlarges on the distinctions of the Journal entry. Yeats begins by explaining that, for him, Synge's *Deirdre of the Sorrows* reaches perfection with Deirdre's speech at the graveside, her "cry at the outset of a reverie of passion that mounts and mounts till grief itself has carried her beyond grief into pure contemplation." Then the player "ascended into that tragic ecstasy which is the best that art—perhaps that life—can give." At that moment, "we too were carried beyond time and persons to where passion living through its thousand purgatorial years, as in the wink of an eye, becomes wisdom; and it was as though we too had touched and felt and seen a disembodied thing" (*E&I,* p. 239). Tragedy at its best, in this view, achieves the mystics' goal by transporting one beyond "time and persons" to "pure contemplation," wisdom, the "disembodied." "Tragic ecstasy," as Yeats explains it, serves to reconnect one with the universal, the primordial, and in this respect to resemble Nietzsche's Dionysian state of *The Birth of Tragedy*.

The essay ends by describing "the face of old tragic paintings" that show "sadness and gravity, a certain emptiness even." Yeats hereby returns to the idea of the Journal entry that "the masks of tragedy contain neither character nor personal energy." He contrasts the tragic paintings with "modern art," where "vitality," or the energy of everyday matters, predominates. Then he connects the former to "the Tree of Life" and the latter to "that of the Knowledge of Good and Evil which is rooted in our interests." This seems a perverse kind of alignment, since the tragic faces are sad, grave, even "empty," and since tragedy itself as he has described it seeks the "disembodied." The Tree of Life has always represented the antithesis of material interest for Yeats, but it has not been so completely divorced from the energy of material life itself. The Tree of Life in this essay is now repository of the "tragic" knowledge of "reality," which is "a kind of death."

To join "life" and "death" under the rubric of "tragedy" is exactly what Nietzsche does in his formulation of the Eternal Return, where death is accepted and even rejoiced in as the necessity without which "life" could not go on. But never—not even in his first "pessimistic" work, *The Birth of Tragedy*—does he divorce "energy" from "tragedy." The Dionysian is the seat of energy, the condition that makes the Apollonian consciousness possible; the "marriage" of Apollonian and Dionysian creates tragedy; and never does Nietzsche separate "soul" and "body." In his Journal entry on tragedy, and in the essay, Yeats separates "self" and "soul" and aligns tragedy with soul. The Journal entry ends with this thought: "is not always the tragic ecstasy some realization or fulfillment of the soul in itself, some slow or sudden expansion of it like an overflowing well?" (*Mem,* p. 153). Here, tragic ecstasy belongs to the "soul in itself." The essay, written a year later, does not specify "the soul" as the agent of tragic ecstasy, but "the mind": "We feel our minds expand convulsively or spread out slowly like some moon-brightened image-crowded sea" (*E&I,* p. 245). Whether "soul" or "mind," the result is the same: either a "sudden" or convulsive expansion, or a slow one, like a moon-brightened sea. Yeats is following, almost word for word, Nietzsche's prescription in *Nietzsche contra Wagner* for the kind of art needed by those suffering from "impoverishment of life": they seek "repose, tranquility, smooth sea, or perhaps ecstatic convulsion and languor from art and philosophy."[16]

It seems improbable that Yeats wrote either Journal or essay with his volumes of Nietzsche open beside him. It is more likely that he read Nietzsche attentively and receptively; that some of Nietzsche's formulations, like this one, remained impressed on his impressionable mind; and that he "summoned" them when he needed them. That his recall is selective and partial is demonstrated by this example on "tragic ecstasy." He remembers "ecstatic convulsion" and "smooth sea," the sudden or slow response; he seems to forget that for Nietzsche, in the passage where these words occur, this reaction is created by decadent art for the impoverished, and that "tragedy" is its opposite. The "superabundant" are the ones who, because of their very strength, "want a Dionysian art and consequently a tragic insight and outlook."

Yeats does persist, always, in linking tragedy and passion. But his this-world / other-world dichotomy holds him in a vacillation that makes him direct the energy of passion now toward "this world" (as in *The King's Threshold, On Baile's Strand,* and *Deirdre*—where energy is rechanneled, at the end, back into "life"),—now towards "the other" (as in *The Shadowy Waters* and the essays on "the tragic"). Yeats is never content to stop the wheel, to leave passion either "here" or "there" for long, and so the vacillation continues, breeding new "life," new art. When he first published "The Tragic Theatre," in Gordon Craig's journal *The Mask* (thereby externally linking mask and tragedy), he appended some thoughts on his own plays that he deleted when he published the piece in *The Cutting of an Agate* (1919). He used them instead in his Preface to *Plays for an Irish Theatre* (1911). They are an important addition, for they bring two worlds, material and immaterial, together. He says: "It was only by watching my own plays upon the stage that I came to understand that this reverie, this twilight between sleeping and waking, this bout of fencing, alike on stage and in the mind, between men and phantoms, this perilous path as on the edge of a sword, is the condition of tragic pleasure, and to understand why it is so rare and so brief."[17] Yeats has never wanted to exclude the phantoms. Their inclusion in his "philosophy" is given a great boost by Nietzsche's belief, in *The Birth of Tragedy,* that "the presence of a god [Dionysus] behind all these masks is the one essential cause" of their "identity" (*BT,* p. 81). If figures on a stage "greaten till they are humanity itself," as Yeats says in "The Tragic Theatre," then the audience may experience the "tragic pleasure" that connects them with "a god," or phantoms, and the condition Yeats calls "sleep." He prefers to associate "sleep" with the supernatural, whereas Nietzsche's Dionysian state connects the individual with primordial nature itself. Perhaps, ultimately, there is not much difference; both Yeats and Nietzsche see this condition as one that dissolves consciousness of individuation. Yeats's impulse to set the two sides at war, as in "this bout of fencing," is Nietzsche's impulse as well. Tragedy is born from such a conflict of opposites, as Yeats implies in the passage deleted from "The Tragic Theatre." In such a conflict, both artist and audience walk "this perilous path as on the edge of a sword," balanced between "man" and "phantom," nature and the supernatural. They thus maintain "that slight separation" from either side that allows them to "know" both, while remaining "near enough for fire."

"Fire" is the result of the conflict, the passion or energy released when opposites meet, which in turn keeps the conflict going, the wheel in motion. This is what the Player Queen knows, in the wisdom of her "song" in the cider vat. The song becomes Yeats's poem "The Mask," published in 1910 as the first tangible evidence of his long struggle with that play. Yeats sketches it out in prose in one of his scenarios of the play, after telling himself that the Player Queen needs the "momentum" of love to act her part. Its earliest form reads:

> My beloved sang to me why do you wear that golden mask and eyes of emerald. I would know what you are, I would see your face. Put away that burning mask, I cannot see it without trouble. As I sang to my beloved, if I put away my mask your heart would no longer beat, beat violently. One has calm when one knows what people are.
>
> Ah, you would not sigh for me any longer; I wish for the praise of your sighs. That is why I will always wear my burning mask, with the eyes of emerald. Then my beloved sang to me, I do not even know if you are a friend or an enemy. (*PQ*, p. 30)

In 1910 the "song" reaches its almost final form, in the pages of the Journal. The entry is not dated, but it follows an entry dated August 10, 1910. On August 7, Yeats writes the letter to his father in which he describes the theme of his play as "the world being illusion." The poem thus reaches completion during his philosophical quandary about appearance and reality. It resolves the quandary, improving, as Nietzsche and Yeats believe art should, upon the uncertainties of life by outfacing, or outmasking, them. As it appears in the Journal, the poem reads:

> "Put off the mask of burning gold
> With emerald eyes."
> "O no my dear you make so bold
> To find if hearts be wild and wise
> And yet not cold."
> "I would but find what's there to find
> Love or deceit."
> "But 'twas the mask engaged your mind
> And after set your heart to beat
> Not what's behind."
>
> "But lest you are my enemy
> I must enquire."
> "O no my dear let all that be

What matter so there burn but fire
In thee and me."

(*Mem,* pp. 258–59)

The mask of this poem is not Yeats's tragic mask, which contains "neither character nor personal energy" (*Mem,* p. 152). It is Nietzsche's tragic mask, which contains both. It is gold, "burning gold." Nietzsche says, in *Thus Spake Zarathustra,* "Gold-lustre maketh peace between moon and sun." The golden mask of the masked speaker in the poem resolves antinomies in "the integrity of fire," making peace between moon and sun.

From the poem's context in *The Player Queen,* we know that the masked speaker is a woman, but one can read the poem without assigning a specific gender to either part; it is enough to know that the speakers are lovers. The unmasked speaker, call him "he," represents the "sincerity" Yeats has quarreled with in modern art. He represents the will to absolute truth that Nietzsche has quarreled with in *Nietzsche contra Wagner:* "No, this bad taste, this will, to 'truth at any price,' this madness of youths in love with truth—has become disagreeable to us: for we are too experienced, too serious, too jovial, too shrewd, too *profound.* . . . We no longer believe that truth remains truth when the veil is pulled off it" (*CW,* p. 92). "He" in the poem represents those advocates of "knowledge" who would separate love and deceit, friend and enemy, those "Socratic" thinkers who, for Nietzsche, have divorced instinct and reason.

"She" replies in the negative—"O no my dear," two times—but her position is the positive one; she represents affirmation of "life," of passion and of power. The passion and the power are achieved through the mask. "Oh those Greeks," says Nietzsche, "they knew how to *live!* For that end it is necessary to remain bravely at the surface, the fold, the skin, to worship appearance." Her mask of the poem is of course her appearance, which set his heart to beat, not "what's behind"—her "reality," whatever that may be. It really doesn't matter: "What matter!" "What matter" is an expression Yeats uses occasionally to mark a supreme moment. It seems forced, perhaps, in a poem like "The Gyres," where he rejoices in disintegration: "What matter though numb nightmare ride on top. . . . What matter?" (*VP,* p. 564).

Rejoicing in the face of the abyss in *Thus Spake Zarathustra* is a mask or appearance of courage. At the end of the book, there is a festival of Higher Men in Zarathustra's cave, which finishes in a Dionysian revel of sorts, where even the donkey, perhaps, dances: "And if in truth the ass did not dance that night, greater and stranger wonders happened, than the dancing of an ass would have been. In short, as Zarathustra's saying goeth, 'What matter!' " (*Z,* pp. 465–66). "What matter" is Zarathustra's heroic gesture of acceptance to life, his *amor fati*. The same sort of *amor fati* underlines the attitude of Yeats's "she" in "The Mask." She accepts that trial by "fire" may be painful—that love may be deceit and a friend may be an enemy. Her eyes are emerald—hard. She is a risk taker and a creator, and, says Zarathustra, "all creators are hard." It is hard to be hard, but it is the way not only to keep on, but to keep on with "wildness" or passion. She knows that only by refusing to "put off the mask" can hearts be both wild and wise without putting the fire out.

It is symptomatic that Yeats writes both his essay "The Tragic Theatre" and his poem "The Mask" at roughly the same time. Together they represent, and recapitulate, the ideas behind his two long-standing poles of opposition, night and day, or moon and sun, or soul and self. In the essay (representative of night), the soul seeks "ecstasy" through transcendence of the natural world; in the poem (representative of day), the soul creates a mask and so engenders the energy that sustains the "fire" of passion. Passion is present at both poles, but its end or goal is different at each. In the former ("tragic") manifestation, passion serves to direct player and audience beyond the world of conflict; in the latter, it serves to channel energy back into conflict, more conflict, more life.

Aesthetically, Yeats has been more successful working with the oppositions of the day-mask half of the dichotomy throughout the decade, the half inspired by Nietzsche. In drafts of *The Player Queen,* he labors to join the oppositions of the day with those of night, struggling to make a tragedy, or otherworld-directed drama, out of material whose energies are directed toward this world. He is trying to perform a synthesis of mask and tragedy in these early drafts, but because of a conflict between his own early tragic formula (reinforced by Nietzsche's *The Birth of Tragedy*), and his more recent notions about the mask (stimulated by Nietzsche's later thought that life itself is tragic and joyous), he is unsuccessful.

Yeats has in fact written the early drafts of *The Player Queen* as "comedy," as he uses the term in his 1909 Journal: "Comedy is joyous because all assumption of a part, of a personal mask . . . is a display of energy, and all energy is joyous." In all its drafts, the play's dominant mode is irony, and for irony to be tragic demands an abandonment (like Nietzsche's) of classical generic definitions of tragedy. Yeats's definition of comedy, in fact, is close to Nietzsche's late definition of Dionysian tragedy. Some four years later, Yeats rewrites *The Player Queen* specifically as comedy, possibly at the instigation of Ezra Pound,[18] and this time the redrafting goes "quickly and easily" (*VPl,* p. 761). Now free from what he has seen as the necessity of transcending appearances to reach an ultimate or absolute reality outside time, he can allow his ironies full play, and he almost manages, at the end of the version published in 1922, to turn his farce into tragicomedy. He allows Decima, the Player Queen, a moment of self-knowledge and disclosure that rises above—indeed, transcends—the multiple ironies the play has assembled. She does so, however, through the ironies; masked and masked again, divided twice, she is made whole, and is left to face the consequences of her choices and of her self-knowledge.

In the first decade of the twentieth century, the "thought" that prevents Yeats from completing *The Player Queen* as a tragedy is coming into his head. He sets it forth, in 1917, in *Per Amica Silentia Lunae,* where it bears its first mature harvest. But its seeds have been sown between 1902 and 1910, and it has put out shoots and blossoms during these years. The "thought" is the mask theory, and its "sower" is Nietzsche, who planted in Yeats's mind the concept of self-overcoming through antithesis. For Nietzsche, who preaches "the significance of earth," that concept embodies a tragic outlook, and it will come to do so also for Yeats.

Although unformulated as a theory, Yeats's ideas about the mask are multilayered and complex by 1910. His reading of Nietzsche supplied him with the basic "thought" of the mask, which on all levels involves the yoking of opposites to create power. In his 1909 Journal, Yeats says that the mask is a "second self" (*Mem,* p. 151); it is the product of self-division, of self-consciousness, and finally of self-overcoming. Yeats follows Nietzsche in bestowing profundity upon the "superficial"; appearance is not "merely" appearance, form not "merely" form. Nietzsche parts ways with Plato in declaring that appearance and reality, or outer and inner, or essence and substance, are one—equally true. In the "most intelligent," outer and inner are at war, but the conflict between what inner feels and outer shows creates energy, and that energy animates and unifies. It makes possible a synthesis that Richard Ellmann describes as "a paradox"—"Yeats's belief that the mask, a word which he chose deliberately because it was a creation of artifice, could be filled with instinct and passion."[19] Because the "second self" or the mask must be willed, and because it is achieved and maintained only with difficulty, the mask functions psychologically to increase the self's sense of power. For Nietzsche, the increase of power is "good"; it is also the prerequisite for creativity.

Aesthetically, the mask is art, the model and image of perfection; its opposite in this formulation is life. Yeats sees this clearly by 1910; he has seen it in "Adam's Curse," in which the poem itself perfects, or is the mask to, the experience of "one summer's end." Yeats says in "Poetry and Tradition" (1907), that as Artificers of the Great Moment, artists create through their "shaping joy" a "trysting-place of time and eternity." As artifice, or mask, art will "call up" its opposite, nature or real life, in the beholder, but life intensified, momentarily made "Great." All art is mask, but as a dialectical conflict of opposites, the "thought" of the mask also serves as a poetics, or a methodology, in the crafting of individual art works.

Real life as it runs its course through natural cycles is the object of the mask in its historical manifestation: as night masks (reverses but implies) day, as youth masks maturity, so one historical epoch masks and empowers another. Nietzsche's formula "Rome against Judea, Judea against Rome" is "a symbol" (*GM,* p. 53) for the conflict between historical periods that goes on continually, fueled by a people's collective will to power, or will to a mask. In *On Baile's Strand* and drafts of *The Player Queen,* in "No Second Troy," even in his 1903 letters speaking of the last century's desire to "transcend forms," followed by the new century's desire to "create forms," Yeats demonstrates his understanding of the "antithetical optics" of history as Nietzsche describes them.

In 1911, Yeats defines, as the condition of tragic pleasure, a state of mind that he likens to "a perilous path as on the edge of a sword." In this metaphor, and in the one that precedes it, where tragic pleasure is defined as "a bout of fencing," Yeats is saying explicitly for the first time that tragedy's effectiveness depends on a conflict, or balance, of opposites. The balance is precarious for Yeats, and perilous, but from now on his fascination with what's difficult will drive him to "mingle" the contraries of mask and tragedy, to make the peace between sun and moon that is also a victory.

7.

The Road to Zoagli

Toward *A Vision,* and Beyond

I have concentrated in this study on the years when Yeats first encounters Nietzsche's ideas—when, to use T. S. Eliot's thought, the ideas "quicken" him. At first, the quickening takes the form of a change of emphasis in his work, which is illustrated by the discussion of the properties of two of his central symbols, sun and moon. When he is in the throes of his first excitement with Nietzsche's ideas, Yeats thinks of the moon as passive, feminine, and reflective, and of the sun as active, masculine, and creative. The moon's poetic mode is the lyric; its metaphysical mode, the soul. The sun's poetic mode is the drama; its metaphysical mode, the anti-self, mask, or "created image." As I have shown, the impact of Nietzsche's thought provides what Yeats calls "the summons of the prouder Sun" in his work and thought—the swing in the balance between moon and sun to give more weight to the side of strength, will, and action.[1] The sun symbolizes the Apollonian desire to "create forms," in Yeats's early understanding of Nietzsche's terms.

The moon symbolizes cyclical change and nature itself in a mood, as Yeats says, "sad and desirous." His impulse of the nineties has been to leap out of time to the timeless—to seek a stone or elixir that will remove him or his heroes from their mortal bondage. He has understood tragedy as an expression of that ecstasy that frees the soul from the limitations of the natural world. After 1902, however, he begins to invest more and more of his own and his heroes' energy in "will," in combat not with supernatural forces but with themselves, or with other characters who represent contrary qualities. Their energy, force, pride, and determination to overcome are all Nietzschean qualities, and Yeats tends to identify these qualities with the sun in the first decade of this century.

The effect of Nietzsche's thought on Yeats's only begins to show in the years from 1902 to 1910. I shall not attempt an adequate coverage of Nietzsche's presence in Yeats's later work, but I want briefly to indicate that it is ubiquitous. In the five years after 1910, although Yeats gives much thought to the "moon's" half of the dichotomy in a renewed study of spiritualism, he continues to read books by and about Nietzsche. This reading keeps the ideas of conflict and heroic struggle alive in his mind. In 1910 he acquires the second volume of *The Will to Power.* In 1911, T. Fisher Unwin publishes Joseph Hone's translation of Daniel Halévy's *The Life of Friedrich Nietzsche.* Yeats acquires this book and reads it through; many pages are dog-eared in his copy, and there are marginal strokes beside a lyrical passage from Nietzsche's notebook.[2]

Halévy's *Life,* detailed and sympathetic, emphasizes the heroic Nietzsche. Halévy quotes at length from Nietzsche's notebooks and letters, as well as from his published works, to establish his sense of Nietzsche as "forerunner," at odds with his own historical period yet conscious, always, of his obligation to understand, describe, and "contradict" it. He sets Nietzsche up as the exemplar of an heroic ideal; he makes him the tragic hero of his own life and of his time. He shows Nietzsche teaching himself the value and meaning of the "tragic" for the present and the future. Commenting on Nietzsche's notes for *The Birth of Tragedy,* Halévy says: "We follow in his notes the movement of a mind which wishes to grasp the very idea of the tragic, athwart a vaguely-known Greece. Again and again we find this word *tragic* brought in as if it were a fundamental strain which the young thinker trains himself to repeat, like a child trying to learn a new word:—'Tragic Greece conquers the Persians. . . . Tragic man is nature itself in its highest strength of creation and knowledge: he trifles with sorrow. . . . The Tragic work of art—the tragic Man—the tragic State' "[3]

Halévy's book itself must have worked for Yeats like the power of a repeated lesson, drumming Nietzsche's morality of tragedy—already so deeply imbibed by Yeats—into his mind. Passages like this one on tragedy force the reader to identify "man" and "nature" and to recognize that identification as "tragic." Other passages reveal Nietzsche's connection of man and nature, and of man and history, as a process based on mutual reciprocity and mutual antagonism, from which the only "escape" is joy in the conditions of death and destruction as a necessary part of life and creation. These thoughts make their way into Yeats's mature philosophy, poetry, and plays.

In the Introduction to their *Critical Edition of Yeats's* A Vision *(1925),* George Mills Harper and Walter Kelly Hood supply some information that indicates Nietzsche was in Yeats's subconscious mind in 1914. Other details in their Introduction, which seeks to establish the genesis of *A Vision,* connect Nietzsche directly to that genesis. The earliest automatic-writing scripts of his wife, George, and Yeats's comments on them, make it clear that Nietzsche was well known to Yeats's "instructors," and that Nietzsche's thought stands directly behind Yeats's "symbolical system." As Harper and Hood note, Yeats himself suggests that *A Vision* is a development of the ideas of *Per Amica Silentia Lunae* (1916–17), and that in the months preceding *Per Amica*'s composition, Yeats was involved in "spiritualistic experiments," including experiments in automatic handwriting (*VA,* p. xii). Not only was Yeats directly involved in these experiments, but on at least one occasion he was consulted as an expert interpreter of automatic scripts. One such script, which Yeats was called on to interpret, contains the seed of "the system" of *A Vision.* We are given this piece of critical information by a spirit, the "Control" or speaker for whom George Yeats acted as a medium, or mouthpiece, in 1917. In one of the first pieces of automatic handwriting she produced after her marriage to Yeats, George took down the information about the origin of Yeats's "system." Yeats later recorded it, cryptically, in the notebook in which he kept his synopses of the scripts, as follows: "System said to develop from a script showed me in 1913 or 14. An image in that script used. (This refers to script of Mrs. Lyttelton, & a scrap of paper by Horton concerning chariot with black and white horses.) This told in almost earliest script of 1917" (*VA,* p. xii).

Harper and Hood tell the story of Mrs. Lyttelton's and W. T. Horton's "script" and "scrap" of which what is essential to this study are repeated references to Zoroaster and a double harness. Mrs. Lyttelton received a message from a "spirit" in 1914, advising her to seek "help" from Yeats: " 'Yeats . . . can help he has great gifts. Ask him about Zoroaster, perhaps he will understand.' " She received another message, about a month later, which said, "Yeats is a prince with an evil counsellor," and another:

> Zoroaster and the planets. If this is
> not understood tell him to think of
> the double harness—of Phaeton,
> the adverse principle
> the hard rings on the surf
> Despair is the child of folly
> If the invidious suggestion is not quelled
> there may be trouble.
>
> (*VA,* p. xii)

Yeats writes back to Mrs. Lyttelton that he is mystified—that he had "read with great excitement some years ago" *Thus Spake Zarathustra,* that the Controls "are harping on some duality, but what duality I do not know, nor do I know of an evil counsellor." He explains the interpretive difficulties: "The worst of this cross-correspondence work is that it seems to start the controller dreaming, and following associations of the mind, echoes of echoes. I wonder if they mean that my evil counsellor is a spirit and that he has come from reading Zarathustra—but no that is not it. . . . I cannot make it out" (*VA,* p. xiv). Yeats assumes that Mrs. Lyttelton's message about Zoroaster not only refers to him but comes, in some way, from his mind: "I wonder if they mean that my evil counsellor is a spirit and that he has come from reading Zarathustra." Yeats surely does not mean that the spirit has been reading Zarathustra, but that he (Yeats) has, and that the reading may have produced an "evil counsellor."

Yeats rejects that consequence of his reading ("no, that is not it"), but not the possibility that thoughts from his reading may be psychically transmitted to other minds. He identifies Zoroaster and Nietzsche's Zarathustra, but fails at the time to identify the "duality" upon which the Controls are "harping." The message speaks of the double harness of Phaeton; in Greek mythology, Phaeton is the charioteer who drives the horses of time, sun and moon.

Two days after receiving Mrs. Lyttelton's script, according to

Harper and Hood, Yeats received a "prophetic message" from his friend W. T. Horton. Written on two small sheets of paper, the message read:

> The fight is still raging around you while *you* are busy trying to increase the speed & usefulness of your chariot by means of a dark horse you have paired with the winged white one which for so long has served you faithfully and well. . . .
>
> Conquer & subordinate the dark horse to the white one or cut the dark horse away, from your chariot, & send it adrift. (*VA,* pp. xiv–xv)

Both Mrs. Lyttelton's and Horton's messages reveal a resistance to a powerful influence. Horton's is especially emphatic that a system based on antithesis, black and white, is inimical to Yeats. His message interprets Yeats's use of antithesis, the pairing of a "dark" horse with his faithful winged white one, as Yeats's attempt to "increase the speed and usefulness" of his chariot. If the chariot is Yeats's writing, the message is astute: Yeats has indeed increased the "speed" and "usefulness" of his writing through his deliberate search for "more of manful energy," his turn from lyric to dramatic forms, his development of the mask idea as a methodology. Yet these changes, which in effect employ the principle of opposition or doubleness (the double harness), are being resisted. Yeats himself suggests that his "evil counsellor" may have "come from reading Zarathustra," and it does not seem too farfetched to guess that in these "warning" messages, Yeats is still resisting Nietzschean thought, on the unconscious ("dreaming") level of his mind.

Consciously, however, he begins elaborating that thought in his work, where he depends increasingly on the double harness. In 1915, Yeats writes "Ego Dominus Tuus," the poem that introduces *Per Amica Silentia Lunae.* As is so often the case with Yeats, poetic practice precedes and embodies its theory; "Ego Dominus Tuus" sets forth ideas Yeats has been absorbing in his reading of Nietzsche since 1902, and adumbrates ideas of the prose essay. Like *Per Amica Silentia Lunae,* "Ego Dominus Tuus" is about the virtue, for the poet, in finding a mask, or as Yeats now calls it, an anti-self. Behind the poem and the essay lie the Nietzschean texts of self-overcoming and mastery; the necessity of the difficult task to arouse the will to creativity; the need for grace and ease, or *sprezzatura,* in art; and "antithetical optics," the perception of opposites and perspectivity in all things. Perhaps most important for "Ego Dominus Tuus," however, is Nietzsche's theory that artists often mistake or else deliberately mask their own inclinations in their work. In *Nietzsche contra Wagner,* Nietzsche describes Wagner as an artist who is a "master of minutiae," but who, because "he does not *wish* to be so," loves "the large walls and the audacious wall-painting" (*CW,* p. 66). Describing the sorts of disguises people will adopt to hide their pain and so to overcome themselves, Nietzsche says: "There are free, insolent minds which would fain conceal and deny that at the bottom they are disjointed and incurable souls—it is the case of Hamlet: and then folly itself may be the mask for an unhappy *over-assured* knowledge" (*CW,* p. 88).

Yeats builds these ideas into "Ego Dominus Tuus," a dialogue between "Hic" (this one) and "Ille" (that one). Both Hic and Ille are questers, but their objects differ. Ille declares that he seeks an "image," "my own opposite"; Hic replies: "And I would find myself and not an image." Hic is like "he" in "The Mask," a defender of sincerity, who "would but find what's there to find," and who believes that Ille's search is "delusion." Ille, like "she" in "The Mask," thinks the opposite: to believe you are a "self" and not an image is delusion. It is also "our modern hope"; the search for oneself, says Ille—sounding like Yeats in the 1908 "Discoveries" essays, and like Nietzsche in the Wagner tracts, inveighing against "the will to truth"—has diminished artists' power to create and has destroyed self-confidence. Without the discipline of the "image," or mask, which breeds "the old nonchalance of hand," we are "Timid, entangled, empty and abashed." Hic offers examples of artists who found themselves and loved the world, Dante and Keats respectively, and says that there must be artists who "have made their art / Out of no tragic war." Ille invents ingenious instances to prove that Dante and Keats were indeed antithetical questers, like himself, and "fashioned" in their work a vision opposite to themselves in their lives. Dante, says Ille, "set his chisel to the hardest stone"—echoing Nietzsche's espousal of the difficult task—and so, "driven out," he found masks:

> He found the unpersuadable justice, he found
> The most exalted lady ever loved by a man.
> (*Myth,* pp. 321–22)

It will be seven more years before Yeats writes his famous statement about tragedy: "We begin to live when we have conceived life as tragedy" (*AU,* p. 116). In this poem of 1915, however, he takes another step away from his commitment to the idea that in tragedy the soul seeks escape from the world of conflict and mortality. Art, Ille maintains, is made out of tragic war, and this time the war is fought entirely in the world, as a struggle between artists and their external circumstances. The struggle to find images that will satisfy artists' desires and allow them to overcome themselves is of course the idea of the mask. Yeats had, in his 1909 Journal, named this conflict as "joyous" and identified it as the condition of comedy. Now he calls this same conflict "tragic," and thereby moves decisively into Nietzsche's half of the orange.

His conversion to Nietzsche's concept of tragedy is not intellectually complete, or at any rate is not completely enunciated, until Yeats finishes the second book of his autobiography, *The Trembling of the Veil,* in 1922, and the first edition of *A Vision* in 1925. It is clearly underway, however, in "Ego Dominus Tuus." Events in Yeats's life, as Harold Bloom points out, "intervene" between the writing of the poem (winter 1915) and its sequel, *Per Amica Silentia Lunae* (spring 1917). They are the Easter Rising of 1916; a final marriage proposal to Maud Gonne; a new love: her daughter, Iseult; and withal, no marriage, though he is fifty-one. Bloom calls these years "the most important in Yeats's imaginative life."[4] Add to Bloom's catalog of events Yeats's composition of *At the Hawk's Well* (1915–16) and his essay on Noh drama (April 1916), and it is clear that these years were "chaotic" in Nietzsche's sense: full of creative turbulence.

Per Amica Silentia Lunae issues forth from the turbulence in the spring of 1917; in the fall, Yeats marries, and his wife begins to take down the first notes for *A Vision* in automatic handwriting. I shall focus on only one part of this story: that which follows Yeats's ideas of mask and tragedy to their sublunary convergence.

The major dichotomy of *Per Amica Silentia Lunae* resembles the one Yeats created in 1893 in his edition of Blake: that between the "personal" or "egoistic" "mood" on the one hand, and the "impersonal" or "universal" mood on the other. In this version, both poles are limits of the mind; both are subjective. Book 1 of *Per Amica Silentia Lunae, Anima Hominis,* describes conflict and its resolution at the "personal" pole; book 2, *Anima Mundi,* places that conflict at the "impersonal" pole, and elevates it to the spiritual realm, the "condition of fire." In *Anima Hominis,* man struggles with his anti-self; in *Anima Mundi,* with his Daemon, the spiritual form of the anti-self. Given my subject, I shall be content with *anima hominis,* the terrestrial pole, and leave to others the anima mundi. It is tempting to believe, with Harold Bloom, that Yeats's anima mundi is really the "general mind of Romantic poetic tradition, as Yeats has fused it together," and that "the dead . . . become metaphors for Romantic art, rather than principles who inform that art."[5] Nietzsche would believe that Yeats created anima mundi, and the books of the dead of *A Vision,* from a need or a will to power of his own; and Yeats admits, in *Anima Mundi,* that "all power is from the terrestrial condition, for there all opposites meet and there only is the extreme of choice possible, full freedom" (*Myth,* p. 356). Nietzsche chooses to place his faith in the earth; Yeats chooses to sing amid uncertainty, vacillating between beliefs. Yeats's commitment to the power of the terrestrial condition has been nourished by Nietzsche's belief, and his most central work embodies that commitment.

In *Anima Hominis,* Yeats clarifies his division (adumbrated in "Ego Dominus Tuus") between those who do not seek images or masks or anti-selves, and those who do. Those who do are masters of themselves and become the creators; those who do not—like Conchubar in *Deirdre*—are deluded. The creators will become his "antithetical" types in *A Vision;* the noncreative ones, his "primary" types. This division closely follows Nietzsche's distinction between "master" and "slave" morality. In *Anima Hominis,* Yeats says:

> [No] poet I have read of or heard of or met with [has] been a sentimentalist. The other self, the anti-self or the antithetical self, as one may choose to name it, comes but to those who are no longer deceived, whose passion is reality. The sentimentalists are practical men who believe in money, in position, in a marriage bell, and whose understanding of happiness is to be so busy whether at work or at play that all is forgotten but the momentary aim. They find their pleasure in a cup that is filled from Lethe's wharf, and for the awakening, for the vision, for the revelation of reality, tradition offers us a different word—ecstasy. (*Myth,* p. 331)

The poet's passion is now "reality"—reality as awakening vision, revelation. In his 1909 Journal, Yeats (under the influence of *The*

Birth of Tragedy) says, "The knowledge of reality is always by some means or other a secret knowledge. It is a kind of death" (*Mem,* p. 166). To "escape" that knowledge, Yeats's argument of 1909 runs, artists create beautiful, but illusory, forms to mask it. At that time, Yeats associated "escape," or flight from pain, with tragedy, and tragedy with ecstasy.

In the passage from *Anima Hominis,* he still connects "reality" and ecstasy, but now the vision of reality includes pain, and it is not escaped, but rather sought. The passage continues, " 'If I denied myself any of the pain I could not believe in my own ecstasy' " (*Myth,* p. 332). It appears that Nietzsche's insistence on the necessity of suffering has been borne in on Yeats. Perhaps, with Yeats as with Nietzsche, some real suffering in their own lives produced its effect. Zarathustra, who is Nietzsche's anti-self, or the voice of his own will to power and self-overcoming, says:

> Creating—that is the great salvation from suffering, and an alleviation of life. But for the existence of the creator pain and much transformation are necessary.
>
> Yea, much bitter death must be in your life, ye creators! Thus are ye advocates and justifiers of all perishableness. (*Z,* p. 117)

In *Anima Hominis,* Yeats's "great moment" arrives; he has his vision of reality: "I shall find the dark grow luminous, the void fruitful when I understand that I have nothing, that the ringers in the tower have appointed for the hymen of the soul a passing bell" (*Myth,* p. 332). Nietzsche's insistence on the fruitfulness of opposition, on the power generated by self-overcoming, on the passion of natural reality, and on the eternal joy of becoming leads Yeats to the synthesis of knowledge and power. He "understands" that he has "nothing." Only then, at this extremity of knowledge, does the will receive its greatest challenge, the greatest charge to its creative power. Nietzsche's tragic affirmation becomes possible, and Yeats's conception of life as tragedy, with the realization that life's highest moment, "the hymen of the soul"—the moment of synthesis—is also that moment's death. Conflict will continue, necessitating more suffering and continual fruitful loss. This vision of reality contains much compensation, but it also contains the possibility of a power, or "ecstasy," that transcends the original loss.

Having written *Anima Hominis,* in which he acknowledges and accepts loss—Zarathustra's "perishableness"—as the price of continuing his life as a creator, Yeats hardly needs the sudden surprising external verification of his ideas that he receives at the end of the year, through his new wife's experiments with automatic handwriting. On November 5, 1917, he begins to preserve the transcripts of their sessions, and discovers that "the system" is said to originate with the script and scraps of Mrs. Lyttelton and Thomas Horton. Harper and Hood take up the story: "On that day, in the second of two sessions, the Control offered the following information in answer to unrecorded questions by Yeats:

> Yes but with gradual growth
> Yes—one white one black both winged
> both winged both necessary to you
> one you have the other found
> the one you have by seeking is—
> you find by seeking it in the one you have.
>
> (*VA,* p. xvi)

It is clear that the "Control" has now accepted the dark horse as both winged and necessary. A further comment recorded the same day also seems to refer to the transactions with Mrs. Lyttelton and Horton: "That which was inimical was an evil spiritual influence that is now at an end" (*VA,* pp. xvi–xvii). Now Yeats is "authorized," as it were, to base his symbolic system on a structure wherein the conflict of opposites is central. Both horses are necessary.

Harper and Hood take the white and the dark horse to represent the sun and the moon, respectively. In their interpretation of the symbolism, "man comes into the world with one (white), but must find the other (black) 'by seeking it in the one you have' " (*VA,* p. xvi). They equate the white horse with the "outer, objective, and daily or 'primary self,' " and with the sun; the black horse, with the "inner, subjective, and 'antithetical self,' " and the moon (*VA,* p. xvii). They base their reading, in hindsight, on Yeats's equation of the sun with the "primary" and the moon with the "antithetical" cones of the 1925 version of *A Vision.* Since Yeats does make these equations in *A Vision,* it seems logical to associate the sun and moon with the script's horses, given the reference to Phaeton. The question is, how do sun and moon come to take on the values Yeats gives them in *A Vision*?

As we have seen, during the first decade of this century, after reading Nietzsche, Yeats began to equate the sun with the active, proud, masculine, creative half of the orange, the moon with the passive, feminine, and reflective. Sun or day represented "self" in the Common anthology dichotomy; moon or night represented "soul." In *A Vision* (1925), however, the symbol that he formerly called "the prouder Sun" becomes negatively defined as "the moonless night"; its time of greatest influence, Phase 1 of the Great Wheel, is the time when individuality is dissolved in "complete passivity, complete plasticity" (*VA,* p. 116). The moon dominates the Great Wheel, the principal symbol of *A Vision;* its phases represent "all possible human types" (*VA,* p. 12). Yeats has reversed his earlier valuation of sun and moon.

What happens between 1904 and 1917 to cause this reversal, I think, is that Yeats gradually becomes convinced of the creative power (if not the truth) of Nietzsche's ontological acceptance of nature. Yeats has always associated nature and the moon, but he comes to understand the purposes of nature in Nietzsche's sense, as the circumscription against which the human will must battle in order to create—in order, as Nietzsche says, to will at all. Furthermore, since 1904 Yeats has theorized continuously about self and mask. His self-soul dichotomy of the Common anthology becomes that of self and anti-self, and he begins to see that "we make poetry out of the quarrel with ourselves," as he says in *Per Amica Silentia Lunae* (*Myth,* p. 331). This new dichotomy is entirely subjective. In *A Vision,* Yeats identifies subjectivity and time, objectivity and space (*VA,* p. 129). The subjective side provides the basis for two creative quarrels. One is the quarrel (or conflict) of the will against time; the other is the conflict of the will against its opposite, the mask.

These two quarrels, with time and with oneself, are the most important sources of Yeats's creativity. When he sorts out the automatic scripts of 1917–22 and begins to write *A Vision,* he thinks that the anti-self or mask is the condition that "subjective" people impose on themselves as a task or discipline or object of desire, which arouses their will to greatest intensity and demands their creativity. Since their greatest creative challenge is posed by living itself, amidst the contradictions of "fate" and time, as Nietzsche has it, he comes to see that circumscription by the cycles of nature, symbolized by the moon, is both morally and aesthetically necessary. I think that Yeats is still resisting accepting the necessity of "lunar" circumscription in 1914 when he receives the scripts of Mrs. Lyttelton and Thomas Horton, but that the scripts themselves indicate a powerful "influence," as an "evil counsellor," at work in his mind. By 1917, when George Yeats's scripts begin to appear, he has accepted the conditions of conflict prescribed by Nietzsche, so that the "evil spiritual influence is now at an end." The moon then assumes its place as symbol of natural generation, within the limits and rhythm of which humans must perform their own regeneration.

The word *evil,* as in "evil spiritual influence," also appears to have been revalued by 1917. In describing the "terrestrial condition" in *Per Amica Silentia Lunae,* Yeats defines "evil" as "the strain one upon another of opposites" (*Myth,* p. 357). He defines "the vision of evil," in *A Vision,* as the conception "of the world as continual conflict"—a conception Shelley lacked, he notes (*VA,* p. 78). Earlier in *A Vision,* he describes Unity of Being:

> He who attains Unity of Being is some man, who while struggling with his fate and destiny until every energy of his being has been roused, is content that he should so struggle with no final conquest. For him fate and freedom are not to be distinguished; he is no longer bitter, he may even love tragedy like those "who love the gods and withstand them"; such men are able to bring all that happens, as well as all they desire, into an emotional or intellectual synthesis and so to possess not the Vision of Good only but that of Evil. (*VA,* pp. 28–29)

This account of the Unity of Being is a description of Nietzsche's *amor fati,* the supreme union of the state of Being and the state of Becoming, where fate and freedom are one. The "vision of evil" is necessary to Unity of Being, as the condition of perpetual conflict that makes it possible.

In an essay on *A Vision,* Northrop Frye takes exception to Yeats's "vision of evil" as evil; Yeats's "lack of a sense of evil," he says, "borders on the frivolous."[6] This criticism might equally be applied to Nietzsche, from whom Yeats derived his sense of evil and his concept of Unity of Being as the ability to form a synthesis of "all that happens" and "all they desire." "All that happens" for both Nietzsche and Yeats in their own personal lives contains much disappointment, but it is in the general life of their culture that, for them, the real evil lies. For Nietzsche, the evil is what he calls "nihilism," the will to nothing. War, tyranny, meanness, torture are evils preferable to the extinction of the will to live. In fact through their very horror—and this is one of Nietzsche's paradoxes—they foster the will to live. They stir us to our roots, shake our profound complacency. Surely there is evil in this idea; it seems to offer a choice of evils. Only Nietzsche prefers to call the conventional valuations of good and evil into question, to go "beyond" them for the purpose of revealing what to him is at stake, death of the instinct to live. Yeats is following the same road beyond good and evil by performing a transvaluation of values and insisting on the creative value of the "Vision of Evil" (*VA*, p. 29).

The means to synthesis, Unity of Being—which is Yeats's supreme good—is analysis, or the conflict of opposites, Yeats's "vision of evil." In *A Vision* Yeats performs an elaborate analysis of human nature, which has its counterpart in human history. The simple division of a whole into two parts—as sun-moon, or self-soul of the early mask theory—becomes a fourfold division, which Yeats calls the Four Faculties, with all parts in conflict. With this new analysis comes, simultaneously, his conception of life as tragedy.

He calls the Four Faculties Will, Mask, Creative Mind, and Body of Fate. The Mask is the Will's object and antithesis, the chosen image of desire; the Body of Fate is the Creative Mind's object and antithesis, the enforced image of perception of the external circumstances of life, given us by Fate. This four-part opposition is always operating in the individual human life, and in the collective life of the culture. The opposition takes the form Yeats calls "discord," which he defines as "the enforced understanding of the unlikeness of *Will* and *Mask* or of *Creative Mind* and *Body of Fate*" (*VA*, p. 24). Consciousness itself is discord, awareness of separation and division. This idea is close to Nietzsche's assertion in *A Genealogy of Morals* that human beings, seeking enemies, found themselves, and turned the force of their will to power against themselves, creating bad conscience and everything else besides; only a mind divided can know itself and can create. Yeats says: "Without this continual *discord* through *deception* there would be no conscience, no activity; and it will be seen later that *deception* is used as a technical term and may be substituted for 'desire.' Life is an endeavor, made vain by the Four Sails of its Mill, to come to a double contemplation, that of the chosen *Image,* that of the Fated *Image*" (*VA,* p. 25). This passage combines Nietzsche's idea that conscience derives from human consciousness of separation or individuation (Yeats's *discord*) and from Yeats's idea of 1906 that happiness, or success in love or in art, involves "deceit." *Deception* is positive; it is synonymous with "desire." It creates the Mask, the "chosen *Image.*" However, it also creates the knowledge of separation from the chosen Image and of circumscription by fate.

These ideas become clearer, and their connection with tragedy more obvious, in the light of a second passage, from *The Trembling of the Veil:* "Among subjective men (in all those, that is, who must spin a web out of their own bowels) the victory is an intellectual daily recreation of all that exterior fate snatches away, and so that fate's antithesis; while what I have called "the Mask" is an emotional antithesis to all that comes out of their internal nature. We begin to live when we have conceived life as tragedy" (*AU,* p. 116). In this version, tragedy is born, not of a "vain endeavor" at synthesis among the Four Sails of life's Mill, but out of the realization of that synthesis—out of the "victory" that is born of conflict every day. The most obvious thing that exterior fate snatches away, every day, is time, or life itself. The intellect, in compensation, must struggle to "clap its hands and sing, and louder sing / For every tatter in its mortal dress," as Yeats says in "Sailing to Byzantium" (*VP,* p. 407). It must replace, or recreate, values lost (youth, for instance), with values gained (wisdom or tragic knowledge, for instance). Meanwhile, the emotional will is kept from despair by *its* opposite, the Mask, which sets before it an image of desire so that it, too, lives on in joyful struggle. For Yeats, as for Nietzsche, this conception of life is tragic because it is, as Yeats says in the first passage, ultimately a vain endeavor. "At stroke of midnight [Nietzsche's twelfth hour] / God shall win" (*VP,* p. 561); man will die. This knowledge contains power, in Nietzsche's paradox, for it finds energy, and thus joy, in what is most difficult.

The moment when the most difficult knowledge becomes power, felt as a simultaneity of pain and joy—Yeats's "ecstasy"—justifies life. In *Thus Spake Zarathustra,* Nietzsche says:

> This moment hath my world become perfect. Midnight is noon also!

> Pain is a delight also! Curse is a blessing also! Night is a sun also. Go off! Otherwise ye will learn: A wise man is a fool also.
>
> Said ye ever Yea unto one delight? O my friends, if ye did, ye have also said Yea unto *all* woe. All things are chained, knotted, in love. (*Z*, pp. 472–73)

The doctrine of the Eternal Return, which Nietzsche in *Ecce Homo* calls the "fundamental conception" of *Thus Spake Zarathustra* and the "highest formula of affirmation that is at all attainable,"[7] requires the acceptance of life *exactly* as it is, with no hope of escape from circularity. "I myself," says Zarathustra, "pertain to the causes of the eternal return":

> I come back, with this sun, with this earth, with this eagle, with this serpent—*not* for a new life, or a better life, or an eternal life.
>
> I come eternally back unto this one and the same life, in the greatest things and in the smallest things, in order to teach once more the eternal recurrence of all things;
>
> In order to speak again the word of the great noon of earth and man; in order to proclaim again beyond-man unto man. (*Z*, pp. 321–22)

As this passage makes clear, the superman is not a messiah; he is ahistorical and mythological, and the Eternal Return as a concept acts as history's antithesis. When we can accept—and not only accept but embrace—the thought that joy means pain and, above all, that life means death, Zarathustra says, we have found a way to throw off guilt, to defeat time, to affirm the "innocence of becoming" or life's process itself as the highest good. This is the epitome, the hardest possible task, demanding, and worthy of, heroes. The acceptance of the return of "this identical and self-same life" is also, by antithesis, the way to accept (or create and embrace) change.

When Yeats is receiving "instruction" from the communicators who dictate his wife's automatic handwriting, he begins early in 1918 to cast about for typical examples to illustrate his twenty-six human Phases of the Moon in *A Vision*. Harper and Hood tell us that the first spots to be filled were Phases 12 and 18: "On 1 Jan. 1918, he [Yeats] was informed that Nietzsche belonged at 12 and Zarathustra at 18" (*VA*, p. xxxiii). In revision, Yeats removed Zarathustra, but kept Nietzsche as the sole exemplar of Phase 12, which is, Yeats writes in his description, "before all else the phase of the hero, of the man who overcomes himself, and so no longer needs, like Phase 10, the submission of others, or like Phase 11 conviction of others to prove his victory" (*VA,* p. 62). We recognize in Yeats's account of Phase 12 many of the characteristics he has given, and will give, his own heroes: solitariness, pride, moral strength. We also recognize how definitive for him has been Nietzsche's insistence on the need for opposition, and how deeply he has read Nietzsche as writer and as human—which is to say, as mask and as will. Phase 12 is, of all the "antithetical" phases, the one in which creation of a mask is a necessity of life, and Yeats says, clearly of Nietzsche, "one must always distinguish between the emotional Will—now approaching the greatest subtlety of sensitiveness, and more and more conscious of its frailty—and that which it would be, the lonely, imperturbable, proud Mask" (*VA,* p. 63). When one thinks of various of Yeats's self-disclosures, as for instance of "one that ruffled in a manly pose / For all his timid heart" (*VP,* p. 489), one thinks it likely that there is some self-disclosure written into the description of Phase 12, as well as some fine criticism of Nietzsche.

Perhaps Yeats's greatest tribute to Nietzsche, however, is to be found in his poem "A Dialogue of Self and Soul," written in 1928. The title refers us to the origin of the mask theory in the margins of the Common anthology in 1904, where "self" and "soul" are antagonistic seekers, one in day for power, the other at night for knowledge. The poem continues the argument, and recreates Yeats's preoccupation of 1904 with the thoughts of Nietzsche. "Self" in the poem expresses those thoughts; "Soul" knows it is confronting a Nietzschean, and advises Self to "scorn the earth"; to "think of ancestral night that can . . . / Deliver from the crime of death and birth." Nietzsche, as we know, willed the eradication of guilt; delivery from the crime of death and birth was his project. His means, however, was not contemplation of "ancestral night"—which Soul later explains is Heaven; but contemplation of the Eternal Return. In *The Twilight of the Idols,* Nietzsche says: "We immoralists especially endeavor with all our power to remove out of the world the notions of guilt and punishment. . . . it is only thereby that the innocence of becoming is restored" (*CW,* pp. 145–46). Self in Yeats's poem connects Nietzsche's Eternal Return with the idea of "the innocence of becoming"; the result is another "great moment," free from remorse and self-forgiven. Yeats also uses Zarathustra's expression "What matter!"—his gesture of acceptance. Soul becomes "dumb," and drops out of the debate, when he thinks that "Only the dead can be forgiven." But Self, fired by that thought, overcomes his own "frailty" (to use Yeats's Phase 12 word) by "imaging" it in the poem's final four stanzas. He does not seek to escape it, but to relive it and so to accept and finally rejoice in the thought of returning eternally "unto this one and the same life":

> A living man is blind and drinks his drop.
> What matter if the ditches are impure?
> What matter if I live it all once more?
> Endure that toil of growing up;
> The ignominy of boyhood; the distress
> Of boyhood changing into man;
> The unfinished man and his pain
> Brought face to face with his own clumsiness.

Finally, he is content to live it all again, to experience that moment that makes the whole worth reliving:

> When such as I cast out remorse
> So great a sweetness flows into the breast
> We must laugh and we must sing,
> We are blest by everything,
> Everything we look upon is blest.
>
> (*VP*, pp. 478–79)

"We immoralists," Nietzsche calls himself; yet he is, as Yeats knows, a moralist. When Yeats writes his Preface to *Letters to the New Island* in 1934, he talks about his own sense, as a young man, of isolation from "ordinary men and women." "Gradually," he says, "I overcame my shyness a little, though I am still struggling with it and cannot free myself from the belief that it comes from lack of courage, that the problem is not artistic but moral."[8] Of course, for Yeats, the problem is both artistic and moral. In an essay of 1924 he says: "new form comes from new subject matter, and new subject matter must flow from the human soul restored to all its courage, to all its audacity."[9] One of Nietzsche's greatest contributions to Yeats's life and work is his instilling of courage as a moral virtue. This courage, along with the "new subject matter" Nietzsche also provides, helps Yeats to find "the mask," to find fruitfulness in the void, and to understand historical cycles, and individual ones, as necessary parts of a whole, continuous design. The central characters of his plays endorse or give proof of the value of conflict, where the only remuneration is the conflict's perpetuation and knowledge, "tragic knowledge," of the value of that perpetuation. As he is dying, Cuchulain (in *The Death of Cuchulain,* 1939) sees the "shape" his soul will take after death, and it is "a soft feathery shape." His last words, as the Blind Man raises his knife to sever his head, are: "I say it is about to sing" (*VPl,* p. 1061). Cuchulain's statement is not intended to endorse a belief in an afterlife as absolute truth. Earlier, he has said emphatically, "I make the truth!" (*VPl,* p. 1056). It is intended to endorse a belief in the value of affirmation and continuity. Cuchulain does not say, "It is about to sing." He says, "I say it is about to sing." In "The Tower," Yeats says:

> Death and life were not
> Til man made up the whole,
> Made lock, stock and barrel
> Out of his bitter soul. (*VP,* p. 415)

Both Yeats and Nietzsche are clear that responsibility for making the truth rests on human shoulders.

The tradition that is Nietzsche's and Yeats's romantic heritage tends, as both foresaw, to become more and more fragmented in the twentieth century. They are both "last romantics" in their desire to create unity from fragment. They are also first moderns in their means to the end: fragmentation itself. Their "double vision," which finds value in both "black" and "white," acknowledges that fragmentation or division is now necessary in comprehending reality. Yeats's insistence on formal poetic structure, when he sees poetics dissolving around him into what he considers the chaos and monotony of free verse, is part of his adherence to the morality of the double vision, which sees form as the necessary counterpart to chaos and boredom—necessary if the poetry is to create the power that can regenerate the will.

Both Nietzsche and Yeats are at odds with their time, out of phase, in their insistence on the value of heroic individualism and social hierarchy, when the dominant movements have been in the opposite direction, toward democracy and communism. Both are aware of their untimely positions, and Yeats describes their dilemma in "Dove or

Swan" in *A Vision,* as he talks about the historical phases close to the present time. Blake and Nietzsche, he says, are among the few in this era who seek to establish, "in the midst of our ever more abundant *primary* information, antithetical wisdom": "They were begotten in the Sistine Chapel and still dream that all can be transformed if they but be emphatic; yet Nietzsche, when the doctrine of the Eternal Recurrence drifts before his eyes, knows for an instant that nothing can be so transformed" (*V,* p. 299). Nietzsche and Yeats both acknowledge that the absorption of the individual into the "primary" mass, and the fragmentation of thought into "specialization," is part of the changing historical spectacle whose overall design includes or contains within it the return of the opposite movement.

The intimacy of Yeats's connection with Nietzsche is indicated by two quotations, one from Nietzsche, one from Yeats. The one from Nietzsche is given in Halévy's *Life* on the page that also tells the name of his "albergo," or hotel, in Rapallo. We know Yeats read it because when Yeats was in Rapallo himself in 1929, he wrote Lady Gregory that he had found "the lodging, or rather tenement house, where Nietzsche lived for some months" (*L,* p. 773). Yeats could only have found Nietzsche's lodging in Rapallo because he had read Halévy's footnote on that page, which names the "little inn." Halévy quotes Nietzsche's description of the time and place in which he composed the first part of *Thus Spake Zarathustra:* "I was living on the charming little gulf of Rapallo. . . . In the morning I used to start out in a southerly direction up the glorious road to Zoagli . . . in the evening I would go round the bay of Santa Margherita as far as Portofino. . . . On these two roads came to me all the first part of Zarathustra."[10] The passage from Yeats is in the opening section of *A Vision* (1936), called "Rapallo." He celebrates, with gratitude, having finished that work, and he celebrates the place where it happened: "and the mountain road from Rapallo to Zoagli seems like something in my own mind, something that I have discovered" (*V,* p. 7). He is celebrating his own mind, drawing the mountain road to Zoagli up into himself. The two passages symbolize, and externalize, the Nietzsche-Yeats relationship. As Yeats makes himself responsible for the "discovery" of the road to Zoagli, appropriating Nietzsche's territory, so he takes Nietzsche's thought into his mind, draws it up into himself, and makes it his own. In so doing, he is acting as an originator. But as the road to Zoagli was not discovered by him, so his thoughts are not his own individual discovery either. The ideas of Nietzsche so useful to Yeats—the fragmentation of the self and at the same time the self's valorization through its overcoming—belong to his, and Nietzsche's, time. They become part of the conventions of modernism, whereby the notion of the creative self is both challenged and upheld.

Notes

1.

Introduction

1. Thomas Common, comp., *Nietzsche as Critic, Philosopher, Poet, and Prophet: Choice Selections from His Works.* The copy containing Yeats's marginalia is in the Deering Library at Northwestern University.

2. Richard Ellmann, *The Identity of Yeats,* pp. 91–97. On page 96, Ellmann says that Yeats read and annotated the anthology "in 1902," implying that the Common anthology was Yeats's introduction to Nietzsche. As I show in chapter 3, this was not the case.

3. Harold Bloom, *Yeats,* p. 33. The five are Blake, Shelley, Balzac, Pater, and Nietzsche.

4. Denis Donoghue, *Yeats,* p. 19.

5. See Introduction and passim to Patrick J. Keane, "Yeats and Nietzsche: The Antithetical Vision."

6. Michael Hamburger, *From Prophecy to Exorcism: The Premises of Modern German Literature,* p. 33. A more recent translation of the letters uses the same word, *anti-self,* with a note that the translator "adopted Michael Hamburger's (Yeatsian) translation of Nietzsche's word *Gegensatz*" (Christopher Middleton, ed. and trans., *Selected Letters of Friedrich Nietzsche,* p. 320).

7. G. Wilson Knight, *Christ and Nietzsche: An Essay in Poetic Wisdom,* p. 185.

8. Harold Bloom, *The Anxiety of Influence: A Theory of Poetry,* p. 95.

9. Ibid., p. 8.

10. Ibid., p. 50.

11. "John Eglinton," in *Uncollected Prose by W. B. Yeats,* ed. John P. Frayne and Colton Johnson, 2:257.

12. T. S. Eliot, "Reflections on Contemporary Poetry," p. 39.

13. " 'Is not style,' as Synge once said to me, 'born out of the shock of new material?' " *AU,* p. 323.

2.

"The Spirit of His Time"

1. Janko Lavrin, *Nietzsche and Modern Consciousness: A Psycho-Critical Study,* p. 4.

2. Erich Heller, "The Importance of Nietzsche," in *The Artist's Journey into the Interior and Other Essays*, p. 174.

3. J. P. Stern, *Friedrich Nietzsche*, pp. 17–18.

4. Daniel Halévy, *The Life of Friedrich Nietzsche*, p. 130.

5. Eric Bentley, *A Century of Hero-Worship: A Study of the Idea of Heroism in Carlyle and Nietzsche, with Notes on Wagner, Splengler, Stefan George, and D. H. Lawrence*, pp. 23, 34.

6. Heinrich Heine, *The History of Religion and Philosophy in Germany*, quoted in E. M. Butler, *The Tyranny of Greece over Germany: A Study of the Influence Exercised by Greek Art and Poetry over the Great German Writers of the Eighteenth, Nineteenth, and Twentieth Centuries*, p. 270.

7. Butler, *The Tyranny of Greece over Germany*, p. ix.

8. Michael Hamburger maintains that Pater's work shows "an unacknowledged debt" to Nietzsche in *From Prophecy to Exorcism: The Premises of Modern German Literature*, p. 29. I think the debt is more to Heine, but both are possibilities.

9. Christopher Middleton, ed. and trans., *Selected Letters of Friedrich Nietzsche*, p. 164.

10. Harold Bloom, *The Anxiety of Influence: A Theory of Poetry*, p. 131.

11. Percy Bysshe Shelley, "A Defence of Poetry," in Carl Woodring, ed., *Prose of the Romantic Period*, pp. 496, 497, 507.

12. Ibid., p. 510.

13. G. W. Knight, *Christ and Nietzsche: An Essay in Poetic Wisdom*, p. 23.

14. G. F. W. Hegel, *The Logic of Hegel*, pp. 144, 137–39.

15. Nietzsche, *Ecce Homo*, pp. 270–71.

16. G. F. W. Hegel, *The Phenomenology of the Mind*, pp. 2–3.

17. Halévy, *The Life of Friedrich Nietzsche*, p. 58.

18. Ursula Bridge, ed., *W. B. Yeats and Sturge Moore: Their Correspondence, 1901–1937*, p. 117.

19. Arthur Schopenhauer, *The World as Will and Idea*, 1:415.

20. Walter Pater, *The Renaissance: Studies in Art and Poetry*, p. 233.

21. Schopenhauer, *The World as Will and Idea*, 1:139.

22. Nietzsche, quoted in Stern, *Friedrich Nietzsche*, p. 28; Yeats, "A Prayer for Old Age," *VP*, p. 553; Yeats to Lady Elizabeth Pelham, January 4, 1939, *L*, p. 922.

23. Honoré de Balzac, "La peau de chagrin," in *"The Magic Skin," "The Quest of the Absolute," and Other Stories*, p. 101; Balzac, "Louis Lambert," in *About Catherine de Medici," "Seraphita," and Other Stories*, p. 185.

24. George Steiner, *In Bluebeard's Castle: Some Notes toward the Redefinition of Culture*, p. 18.

25. J-K. Huysmans, *Against Nature*, pp. 22, 33, 93, 220.

26. Paul Bourget, *Nouvaux Essais*, in Philip Stephan, *Paul Verlaine and the Decadence, 1882–1890*, p. 29.

27. Charles Ricketts, quoted in David S. Thatcher, *Nietzsche in England, 1890–1914: The Growth of a Reputation*, p. 123.

28. Hugo Kaatz, *Die Weltanschauung Friedrich Nietzsches*, quoted in Max Nordau, *Degeneration*, p. 453; Nordau, *Degeneration*, pp. 453–54.

29. Quoted in Thatcher, *Nietzsche in England*, p. 29.

30. Nordau, *Degeneration*, pp. 415–16.

31. Ibid., pp. 443–44.

32. Whistler, quoted by Hesketh Pearson in his Introduction to Oscar Wilde, De Profundis *and Other Writings*, p. 12; Wilde quoted ibid., p. 13.

33. Stephan, *Paul Verlaine and the Decadence,* p. 45.

34. Roger Shattuck, *The Banquet Years: The Arts in France, 1885–1918,* pp. 150, 185, 153.

35. Richard Ellmann, *Eminent Domain: Yeats among Wilde, Joyce, Pound, Eliot, and Auden,* p. 15.

36. Carroll V. Peterson, *John Davidson,* p. 39.

37. John Davidson, quoted in Patrick Bridgwater, *Nietzsche in Anglosaxony: A Study of Nietzsche's Impact on English and American Literature,* p. 49; Henri Mazel, quoted in Herbert W. Reichart and Karl Schlecta, eds., *International Nietzsche Bibliography,* p. 25; Davidson, quoted in Bridgwater, *Nietzsche in Anglosaxony,* p. 50.

38. Havelock Ellis, "Friedrich Nietzsche, I," p. 79.

39. For Elisabeth Forster-Nietzsche's misrepresentations, see Hamburger's *From Prophecy to Exorcism,* p. 39.

40. Ellis, "Friedrich Nietzsche, I," pp. 85–86.

41. Yeats, "William Blake and His Illustrations to *The Divine Comedy,* I," p. 41.

42. All quotations from the July installment of the Ellis article that follow in text are from pp. 70–81.

43. Nietzsche, *Ecce Homo,* p. 233.

44. Ellis, "Friedrich Nietzsche, III," p. 58.

45. Ellis, "Friedrich Nietzsche, II," p. 81.

46. Nietzsche, in Walter Kaufmann, *Nietzsche: Philosopher, Psychologist, Antichrist,* p. 215.

47. For a "suspicious" view of Nietzsche as liberator, see Conor Cruise O'Brien, *The Suspecting Glance,* p. 257 and passim.

48. Joseph Hone, *The Life of George Moore,* p. 257.

49. See Bridgwater, *Nietzsche in Anglosaxony,* pp. 44–45, for details of the plagiarism.

50. George Moore, *Hail and Farewell,* 1:49.

51. Harold Bloom, *Yeats,* p. 216.

52. *The Works of William Blake: Poetic, Symbolic, and Critical,* ed. Edwin John Ellis and William Butler Yeats, 1:242–43. Hereafter cited as Ellis and Yeats, *Blake.*

53. Yeats, "The Stone and the Elixir," in John P. Frayne, ed. *Uncollected Prose by W. B. Yeats,* 1:344–45.

54. Allan Grossman, *Yeats: A Study of* The Wind among the Reeds, p. xiv.

55. Yeats, "The Literary Movement in Ireland," in John P. Frayne and Colton Johnson, eds. *Uncollected Prose by W. B. Yeats,* 2:195.

56. Yeats, "The Irish Literary Theatre," ibid., 2:140.

57. Ibid., 2:141.

58. Yeats, "The Irish Literary Theatre, 1900," ibid., 2:200.

59. Yeats, "Mr. Yeats's New Play," ibid., 2:283–84.

60. Yeats, "The Literary Movement in Ireland," ibid., 2:194–95.

61. Ibid., 2:193–96.

62. Erich Heller, "Yeats and Nietzsche: Reflections on a Poet's Marginal Notes," *Encounter* 33, no. 6 (December 1969): 65.

63. Yeats, "A Symbolic Artist and the Coming of Symbolic Art," in Frayne and Johnson, *Uncollected Prose,* 2:133.

64. Yeats, "The Symbolism of Poetry" (1900), *E&I,* p. 162.

3.
"The Shock of New Material"

1. See especially George Moore's account of the edition's appearance in *Hail and Farewell,* 3:117–19.

2. Richard Ellmann, *Yeats: The Man and the Masks,* pp. 167–68. One lyric in six years is an underestimation, however, as Yeats wrote lyrics for the early version of *The Player Queen* in 1907, and certainly the lyric "Never Give All the Heart," whose composition in New York is verified by John Quinn in a letter to a friend (see B. L. Reid, *The Man from New York: John Quinn and His Friends,* p. 17), and "Old Memory," to which Yeats refers in a letter to Lady Gregory (Jan. 21, 1904) as having been written in a railway train coming from Canada, *L,* p. 427.

3. Ellis and Yeats, *Blake,* 1:22.

4. George Mills Harper, *Yeats's Golden Dawn,* pp. 115–16.

5. Terry Eagleton, *Criticism and Ideology: A Study in Marxist Literary Theory,* p. 152.

6. Yeats, "Ireland and the Arts, *E&I,* p. 203.

7. Yeats, Introduction to *The Oxford Book of Modern Verse, 1892–1935,* p. ix.

8. Lorna Reynolds, "Collective Intellect: Yeats, Synge, and Nietzsche," p. 87.

9. David Thatcher, "A Misdated Yeats Letter on Nietzsche," p. 286.

10. Richard Ellmann in *The Identity of Yeats,* p. 95; Peter Ure in *Yeats the Playwright: A Commentary on Character and Design in the Major Plays,* p. 132; Leonard Nathan in *The Tragic Drama of William Butler Yeats: Figures in a Dance,* pp. 91–93; Patrick Bridgwater in *Nietzsche in Anglosaxony: A Study of Nietzsche's Impact on English and American Literature,* p. 80; Lorna Reynolds in "Collective Intellect: Yeats, Synge, and Nietzsche," p. 89; Conor Cruise O'Brien in *The Suspecting Glance,* p. 72; Harold Bloom in *Yeats,* pp. 144–47; and Otto Bohlmann in *Yeats and Nietzsche: An Exploration of Major Nietzschean Echoes in the Writings of William Butler Yeats,* pp. 59–62.

11. Ellmann, *The Identity of Yeats,* p. 95.

12. J. B. Yeats in a letter to John Quinn, quoted in B. L. Reid, *The Man from New York,* p. 11.

13. See Joseph Hone, *The Life of George Moore,* p. 241.

14. Ibid.

15. Reid, *The Man from New York,* p. 10.

16. Ibid. The editions of Nietzsche—all but *Thus Spake Zarathustra* still in Yeats's library—are as follows: *Thus Spake Zarathustra: A Book for All and None,* trans. Alexander Tille (London: T. Fisher Unwin, 1899); *The Case of Wagner, Nietzsche contra Wagner, The Twilight of the Idols, The Antichrist* (in one volume), trans. Thomas Common (London: T. Fisher Unwin, 1899); *A Genealogy of Morals,* trans. William A. Haussmann and John Gray (London: T. Fisher Unwin, 1899).

17. I am grateful to Miss Anne Yeats for providing me with a list of books by and about Nietzsche in her father's library, including details of inscriptions, cuttings, markings, and annotations.

18. Richard J. Finneran, George Mills Harper, and William M. Murphy, eds., *Letters to W. B. Yeats,* 1:106–7.

19. Lady Gregory quoted by David S. Thatcher in *Nietzsche in England, 1890–1914: The Growth of a Reputation,* p. 140n.

20. Quinn, quoted in E. H. Mikhail, ed., *Lady Gregory: Interviews and Recollections,* p. 81.

21. Ibid., p. 80.

22. F. A. C. Wilson, *Yeats's Iconography,* p. 177.

23. Giorgio Melchiori, *The Whole Mystery of Art: Pattern into Poetry in the Work of W. B. Yeats,* p. 53.

24. Yeats, "The Stone and the Elixir," a review of Ibsen's *Brand,* in Frayne and Johnson, *Uncollected Prose,* 2:344. See chapter 2, above.

25. Ellis and Yeats, *Blake,* 2:59.

26. See Yeats's "The Theatre," *E&I,* p. 172.

27. Richard Ellmann, *James Joyce,* p. 104.

28. Yeats, quoted ibid., p. 108.

29. Ibid., p. 106.

30. Ibid., p. 105; and in Stanislaus Joyce, *My Brother's Keeper,* p. 196.

31. See *L.,* p. 382.

32. Ellmann, *Yeats: The Man and the Masks,* p. 155; Bloom, *Yeats,* pp. 165–66.

33. See Corinna Salvatori, *Yeats and Castiglione: Poet and Courtier,* p. 83, for a consideration of "Adam's Curse" and *sprezzatura.*

34. See Bloom, *Yeats,* p. 166.

4.
The Mask in the Making

1. Richard Ellmann, *Yeats: The Man and the Masks,* p. 175. See pages 174–79 for an excellent general discussion of Yeats's mask theory.

2. Arthur Symons, "*The Dawn of Day* by Friedrich Nietzsche," *The Athenaeum,* March 7, 1903, p. 298. The review is unsigned, the reviewer has been identified as Symons by David Thatcher in *Nietzsche in England, 1890–1914: The Growth of a Reputation,* p. 129.

3. Bernard Shaw, *Collected Plays with Their Prefaces,* 2:740, 776.

4. Arthur Symons, *Plays, Acting, and Music: A Book of Theory,* p. 18.

5. Ibid., pp. 19–20.

6. James Joyce, *A Portrait of the Artist as a Young Man,* p. 219.

7. Jane Ellen Harrison, *Prolegomena to the Study of Greek Religion,* p. 444.

8. Ibid., pp. 28–29.

9. Ibid., pp. 10, 445–46n.

10. Although the essay is dated 1900, only part I was published, in *The Dome,* in July 1900. Part II was first published in *Ideas of Good and Evil,* 1903.

11. See for instance Yeats's essay "What is Popular Poetry?" (1901), *E&I,* pp. 10–11.

12. Yeats, *John Sherman and Dhoya,* p. 40.

13. See chapter 2, above.

14. Yeats, "A Canonical Book," in John P. Frayne and Colton Johnson, eds., *Uncollected Prose by W. B. Yeats,* 2:300–301.

15. Ibid., 2:302.

16. For an exegesis of this "journey," see Yeats, *Mem,* pp. 103–4.

17. The "book upon his genius" is Henri Lichtenberg's *La Philosophie de Nietzsche* (Paris, 1898). The first acquisition of a book by Nietzsche was in July 1904, when the National Library of Ireland acquired *Works,* ed. Alexander Tille. I am grateful to Mr. Alf MacLochlainn, Director of the National Library of Ireland, for this information.

18. S. B. Bushrui, *Yeats's Verse Plays: The Revisions, 1900–1910,* passim. The changes are discussed in detail in chapter 5.

19. See B. L. Reid, *The Man from New York: John Quinn and His Friends,* pp. 17, 19.

20. Richard Ellmann, *The Identity of Yeats,* p. 96; Alex Zwerdling, *Yeats and the Heroic Ideal,* p. 20; Erich Heller, "Yeats and Nietzsche: Reflections on a Poet's Marginal Notes," p. 67; Patrick J. Keane, "Yeats and Nietzsche: The Antithetical Vision," p. 5; Conor Cruise O'Brien, *The Suspecting Glance,* p. 9; Patrick Bridgwater, *Nietzsche in Anglosaxony: A Study of Nietzsche's Impact on English and American Literature,* p. 75; Otto Bohlmann, *Yeats and Nietzsche: An Exploration of Major Nietzschean Echoes in the Writings of William Butler Yeats,* p. 1.

21. *The Library of John Quinn.*

22. Bohlmann, *Yeats and Nietzsche,* p. 2.

23. Attention is paid to the annotations in all the sources listed in note 20 above, and also in Thatcher, *Nietzsche in England, 1890–1914,* pp. 143–52. The most complete is by Thatcher. Criticism of the critics occurs in Thatcher, Keane, and Bohlmann.

24. Thomas Common, ed., *Nietzsche as Critic, Philosopher, Poet, and Prophet: Choice Selections from His Works,* p. 113. My version of the annotations has been supplied by Bohlmann in *Yeats and Nietzsche;* this one is found on page 8.

25. "The Sun's discipline is not of the kind the multitudes impose on us by their weight and pressure; but the expression of the individual soul . . . imposing its own pattern" (*Ex,* p. 26).

26. Common, *Nietzsche as Critic,* p. 114.

27. Ibid., p. 117; Bohlmann, *Yeats and Nietzsche,* p. 88.

28. Common, *Nietzsche as Critic,* p. 122; Bohlmann, *Yeats and Nietzsche,* p. 84.

29. Keane, "Yeats and Nietzsche," pp. 239–40.

30. Ibid., pp. 236, xxxix, and passim.

31. Ibid., p. 253.

32. Ellmann agrees in *The Identity of Yeats,* p. 93, that Yeats first uses the word *mask* in its complex sense in this marginal note, as do Thatcher in *Nietzsche in England,* p. 151, and Keane in "Yeats and Nietzsche," p. 64.

33. Common, *Nietzsche as Critic,* p. 3.

34. "Blake . . . was glad to be alive . . . but Shelley . . . hated life" (*E&I,* p. 94).

35. Common, *Nietzsche as Critic,* pp. 122–23.

36. Ibid., p. 124; Bohlmann, *Yeats and Nietzsche,* p. 29.

37. Heller, "Yeats and Nietzsche," p. 67.

38. Common, *Nietzsche as Critic,* p. 126.

39. Ellmann, *The Identity of Yeats,* p. 97.

40. Keane, "Yeats and Nietzsche," p. 236.

41. Bohlmann, *Yeats and Nietzsche,* p. 116.

42. Common, *Nietzsche as Critic,* p. 132.

43. Ibid., p. 109.

44. See Reid, *The Man from New York,* p. 17.

45. Joyce Carol Oates, *The Edge of Impossibility: Tragic Forms in Literature,* p. 143.

46. John Vickery, *The Literary Impact of* The Golden Bough, pp. 191–92.

47. "W. B. Yeats Delivers a Great Speech," in Frayne and Johnson, *Uncollected Prose by W. B. Yeats,* 2:311.

48. Ellmann, *Yeats: The Man and the Masks,* p. 114.

49. George Moore, *Hail and Farewell,* 3:115.

50. Ellmann, *Yeats: The Man and the Masks,* pp. 171, 179, 178.

51. Moore, *Hail and Farewell,* 3:113.

52. He pays one more debt to Nietzsche in this essay, possibly, when he calls John Eglinton "our one philosophical critic" (*Ex,* p. 160). Eglinton had just published his essay "A Way of Understanding Nietzsche," in which he compares Nietzsche to the ancients, and to Emerson, Thoreau, and Carlyle. The essay was reprinted in *Anglo-Irish Essays* (London: T. Fisher Unwin, 1917).

53. Quoted by Ellmann in *Yeats: The Man and the Masks,* p. 186.

5. *The Ceremony of Tragedy*

1. John P. Frayne and Colton Johnson, eds., *Uncollected Prose by W. B. Yeats,* 2:297–98.

2. See John P. Frayne, ed., *Uncollected Prose by W. B. Yeats,* 1:345.

3. Lionel Abel, in *Metatheatre: A New Dramatic Form,* follows Nietzsche's definition of the daemoniacal and its Shakespearean illustration. "Indifference to success or failure" is daemonic (p. 10); the tragic protagonist "acts as if he were invulnerable. This fiction leads him to destruction" (p. 3). "To go beyond the human is daemonic: Macbeth does it, and he forces Macduff to be daemonic too, by killing his wife and children" (p. 8).

4. Nietzsche, *Ecce Homo,* p. 273.

5. See Walter Kaufmann, ed., *The Portable Nietzsche,* p. 455.

6. Ibid., p. 459.

7. George Steiner, *The Death of Tragedy,* pp. 129, 193.

8. Harold Bloom, in *Yeats,* identifies this project as a "high Romantic desire, destructive of Christianity, 'to rid the world of penitence,' " p. 48.

9. Michel Haar, "Nietzsche and Metaphysical Language," in David B. Allison, ed., *The New Nietzsche: Contemporary Styles of Interpretation,* p. 29.

10. Gilbert Murray, *The Classical Tradition in Poetry,* p. 53.

11. Eric Bentley, *The Life of the Drama,* p. 17.

12. See especially "First Essay: 'Good and Evil,' 'Good and Bad.' "

13. Mircea Eliade, *Myths, Dreams, and Mysteries: The Encounter between Contemporary Faiths and Archaic Reality,* pp. 50–53.

14. Quoted by Richard Ellmann in *The Identity of Yeats,* p. 81.

15. S. B. Bushrui, *Yeats's Verse Plays: The Revisions, 1900–1910,* p. 15.

16. Ibid., p. 21.

17. Ibid., p. 25.

18. Roger McHugh, ed., *Ah, Sweet Dancer: W. B. Yeats—Margot Ruddock,* pp. 36, 39.

19. Peter Ure, *Yeats the Playwright: A Commentary on Character and Design in the Major Plays,* pp. 37, 41, 42; Bloom, *Yeats,* p. 151.

20. I am quoting from the 1906 version of the play, for as Yeats says in the Preface to *Poems, 1899–1905,* the rewritings did not alter its radical structure (*VP,* p. 850); as Ure says, "the revision [to 1906] simply brings to fuller life what was already there" (*Yeats the Playwright,* p. 35), and as Bushrui's book shows, virtually all revisions of these years worked like those of *The Shadowy Waters,* toward greater simplicity and forcefulness.

21. Quoted by Richard Ellmann in *Yeats: The Man and the Masks,* p. 114.

22. Bloom, *Yeats,* p. 151.

23. Other critics have pointed to a Nietzschean source for this speech: Joseph

Hone, *W. B. Yeats, 1865–1939,* p. 187; Denis Donoghue, *Yeats,* p. 57; David Thatcher, *Nietzsche in England, 1890–1914,* p. 156; Patrick Bridgwater, *Nietzsche in Anglosaxony: A Study of Nietzsche's Impact on English and American Literature,* p. 80; Otto Bohlmann, *Yeats and Nietzsche: An Exploration of Major Nietzschean Echoes in the Writings of William Butler Yeats,* p. 142.

24. Peter Ure identifies the "bursting pod" speech as illustrative of "Nietzschean joy," and quotes from the description of Dionysian ecstasy in *The Birth of Tragedy* to prove his point (*Yeats the Playwright,* pp. 39–40). The later works by Nietzsche, which we know Yeats had read when he wrote *The King's Threshold,* make the point better.

25. For Nietzsche on the moon, see chapter 4. Bloom identifies the leprous moon as a combination of Blake's leprous God, Urizen, and Shelley's sick moon, in *Yeats,* p. 151.

26. In John Vickery, *The Literary Impact of* The Golden Bough, p. 207.

27. Ure, *Yeats the Playwright,* p. 62.

28. S. B. Bushrui, *Yeats's Verse Plays,* p. 47.

29. Ibid., p. 70.

30. Ibid., p. 51.

31. A. Norman Jeffares, *W. B. Yeats: Man and Poet,* p. 152.

32. Patrick J. Keane, "Yeats and Nietzsche: The Antithetical Vision," p. 86; for Bohlmann, see *Yeats and Nietzsche,* p. 145.

33. Ellmann, *Yeats: The Man and the Masks,* pp. 166–67; Donoghue, *Yeats,* p. 122.

34. Joseph Hone, ed., *J. B. Yeats: Letters to His Son W. B. Yeats and Others, 1869–1922,* p. 97.

35. Quoted in Bridgwater, *Nietzsche in Anglosaxony,* p. 80.

36. A. R. Orage, *Friedrich Nietzsche: The Dionysian Spirit of the Age,* pp. 12, 83. Others are G. B. Shaw, W. H. Hudson, R. B. Cunningham Graham, H. G. Wells, and Edward A. Carpenter.

37. "The play" is identified as Russell's *Deirdre* by Joseph Hone in *W. B. Yeats,* p. 222.

38. All quotations from "The Tree of Life" that follow in the text are in *E&I,* pp. 270–72.

6.
The Perilous Path

1. Harold Bloom, *Yeats,* p. 157.

2. Thomas Common, ed., *Nietzsche as Critic, Philosopher, Poet, and Prophet: Choice Selections from His Works,* p. 134.

3. Allan Wade dates this letter "[?1909]," but Curtis B. Bradford establishes that it was written in 1908 (*PQ,* appendix 1).

4. He tells the story again in his Journal, identifying "the friend" as George Russell (*Mem,* p. 150).

5. Curtis B. Bradford, ed., "Discoveries: Second Series," p. 300.

6. Ibid., p. 301.

7. Ibid., p. 302.

8. Ibid., pp. 303–4.

9. Ibid., p. 304.

10. Ibid., p. 305.

11. Ibid., p. 306.
12. Richard Ellmann, *Eminent Domain: Yeats Among Wilde, Joyce, Pound, Eliot, and Auden,* p. 17.
13. Bradford, "Discoveries: Second Series," p. 306.
14. Wade dates this letter "August 7 [?1909]" (*L,* pp. 533–34), but Bradford establishes the year as 1910 (*PQ,* appendix 1).
15. Nietzsche, *Ecce Homo,* p. 271.
16. *CW,* p. 74. This passage also appears as the first selection in Common, *Nietzsche as Critic,* p. 3.
17. John P. Frayne and Colton Johnson, eds., *Uncollected Prose by W. B. Yeats,* 2:389.
18. Richard Ellmann, *Yeats: The Man and the Masks,* p. 215.
19. Ibid., p. 177.

7.
The Road to Zoagli

1. Yeats speaks of "the summons of the prouder Sun" in a note to his story "John Sherman," in *John Sherman and Dhoya,* ed., Richard J. Finneran, p. 40.
2. The dog-eared pages, in Daniel Halévy's *The Life of Friedrich Nietzsche* are 35, 58, 79, 207, 214, 261, and 263. The passage with marginal strokes is on page 213, beginning "*Et in Arcadia Ego.*"
3. Halévy, *The Life of Friedrich Nietzsche,* p. 94.
4. Harold Bloom, *Yeats,* p. 198.
5. Ibid., pp. 186–87.
6. Northrop Frye, "The Rising of the Moon: A Study of *A Vision,*" in Denis Donoghue and J. R. Mulrayne, eds., *An Honoured Guest: New Essays on W. B. Yeats,* p. 28.
7. Nietzsche, *Ecce Homo,* p. 295.
8. Yeats's Preface to *Letters to the New Island,* ed. Horace Reynolds, pp. xii–xiii.
9. Quoted by Richard Ellmann in *Yeats: The Man and the Masks,* p. 246.
10. Halévy, *The Life of Friedrich Nietzsche,* pp. 254–55.

Bibliography

Works by W. B. Yeats

The Autobiography of William Butler Yeats. New York: The Macmillan Company, 1953.

A Critical Edition of Yeats's A Vision *(1925)*. Ed. George Mills Harper and Walter Kelly Hood. London and Basingstoke: The Macmillan Press, 1978.

"Discoveries: Second Series." Ed. Curtis B. Bradford. *Massachusetts Review* 5, no. 2 (Winter 1964): 297–306.

Essays and Introductions. New York: The Macmillan Company, 1961.

Explorations. London: Macmillan and Company, 1962.

John Sherman and Dhoya. Ed. Richard J. Finneran. Detroit: Wayne State University Press, 1969.

The Letters of W. B. Yeats. Ed. Allan Wade. London: Rupert Hart-Davis, 1954.

Letters to the New Island. Ed. Horace Reynolds. London: Oxford University Press, 1934.

Mythologies. London: The Macmillan Press, 1959.

The Oxford Book of Modern Verse, 1892–1935. Ed. W. B. Yeats. New York: Oxford University Press, 1937.

Uncollected Prose by W. B. Yeats. Vol. 1. Ed. John P. Frayne. London: Macmillan and Company, 1970.

Uncollected Prose by W. B. Yeats. Vol. 2. Ed. John P. Frayne and Colton Johnson. London: The Macmillan Press, 1975.

The Variorum Edition of the Plays of W. B. Yeats. Ed. Russell K. Alspach. London: Macmillan and Company, 1966.

The Variorum Edition of the Poems of W. B. Yeats. Ed. Peter Allt and Russell K. Alspach. New York: The Macmillan Company, 1957.

A Vision. London and Basingstoke: The Macmillan Press, 1962.

W. B. Yeats: Memoirs; Autobiography—First Draft; Journal. Transcribed and edited by Denis Donoghue. London: Macmillan, 1972.

W. B. Yeats: The Writing of The Player Queen. Manuscripts of W. B. Yeats transcribed, edited, and with a commentary by Curtis Baker Bradford. Dekalb: Northern Illinois University Press, 1977.

"William Blake and His Illustrations to *The Divine Comedy,* I." *The Savoy* 2, no. 3 (July 1896):41–57.

The Works of William Blake: Poetic, Symbolic, and Critical. Edited with lithographs of the illustrated "prophetic books," and a Memoir and Interpretation by Edwin John Ellis and William Butler Yeats. 3 vols. London: B. Quaritch, 1893.

Works by Friedrich Nietzsche

The Birth of Tragedy: Or Hellenism and Pessimism. Trans. William A. Haussmann. Edinburgh and London: T. N. Foulis, 1909.

The Case of Wagner, Nietzsche contra Wagner, The Twilight of the Idols, The Antichrist. Trans. Thomas Common. London: H. Henry and Co., 1896.

The Dawn of Day. Trans. Johanna Voltz. London: T. Fisher Unwin, 1903.

Ecce Homo. Trans. Walter Kaufmann. New York: Vintage Books, 1967.

A Genealogy of Morals. Trans. William A. Haussmann and John Gray. London: T. Fisher Unwin, 1899.

Nietzsche as Critic, Philosopher, Poet, and Prophet: Choice Selections from His Works. Compiled by Thomas Common. London: Grant Richards, 1901.

The Portable Nietzsche. Ed. Walter Kaufmann. New York: Viking Press, 1954.

Selected Letters of Friedrich Nietzsche. Ed. and trans. Christopher Middleton. Chicago: University of Chicago Press, 1969.

Thus Spake Zarathustra: A Book for All and None. Trans. Alexander Tille. New York: The Macmillan Company, 1906.

Works about Yeats, Nietzsche, or Yeats and Nietzsche

Allison, David B., ed. *The New Nietzsche: Contemporary Styles of Interpretation.* New York: Delta, 1979.

Bentley, Eric. *A Century of Hero-Worship: A Study of the Idea of Heroism in Carlyle and Nietzsche, with Notes on Wagner, Spengler, Stefan George, and D. H. Lawrence.* Boston: Beacon Press, 1957.

Bloom, Harold. *Yeats.* London: Oxford University Press, 1970.

Bohlmann, Otto. *Yeats and Nietzsche: An Exploration of Major Nietzschean Echoes in the Writings of William Butler Yeats.* Totowa, N.J.: Barnes and Noble, 1982.

Bridge, Ursula, ed. *W. B. Yeats and T. Sturge Moore: Their Correspondence, 1901–1937*. London: Routledge and Kegan Paul, 1953.

Bridgwater, Patrick. *Nietzsche in Anglosaxony: A Study of Nietzsche's Impact on English and American Literature*. Leicester: Leicester University Press, 1972.

Bushrui, S. B. *Yeats's Verse Plays: The Revisions, 1900–1910*. Oxford: Clarendon Press, 1965.

Donoghue, Denis. *Yeats*. Glascow: Fontana/Collins, 1971.

Donoghue, Denis, and J. R. Mulrayne, eds. *An Honoured Guest: New Essays on W. B. Yeats*. London: Edward Arnold, 1965.

Ellis, Havelock. "Friedrich Nietzsche, I–III." *The Savoy* 1 and 2, nos. 2–4 (April, July, August 1896): 79–94, 68–81, 57–63.

Ellmann, Richard. *Yeats: The Man and the Masks*. New York: W. W. Norton & Company, 1948.

———. *The Identity of Yeats*. 2d ed. New York: Oxford University Press, 1964.

———. *Eminent Domain: Yeats among Wilde, Joyce, Pound, Eliot, and Auden*. New York: Oxford University Press, 1967.

Finneran, Richard J., George Mills Harper, and William M. Murphy, eds. *Letters to W. B. Yeats*. Vol. 1. London: The Macmillan Press, 1977.

Grossman, Allan. *Yeats: A Study of* The Wind among the Reeds. Charlottesville: University Press of Virginia, 1969.

Halévy, Daniel. *The Life of Friedrich Nietzsche*. Trans. J. M. Hone with an Introduction by T. M. Kettle, M. P. London: T. Fisher Unwin, 1911.

Harper, George Mills. *Yeats's Golden Dawn*. New York: Harper and Row, 1974.

Heller, Erich. "Yeats and Nietzsche: Reflections on a Poet's Marginal Notes." *Encounter* 33, no. 6 (December 1969): 64–72. This essay also appears in Heller, *The Disinherited Mind*. New ed. New York: Harcourt Brace Jovanovich, 1975, pp. 327–47.

Hollingdale, R. J. *Nietzsche*. London: Routledge and Kegan Paul, 1973.

Hone, Joseph. *W. B. Yeats, 1865–1939*. London: Macmillan & Co., 1962.

Hone, Joseph, ed. *J. B. Yeats: Letters to His Son W. B. Yeats and Others, 1869–1922*. London: Faber and Faber, 1944.

Jeffares, A. Norman. *W. B. Yeats: Man and Poet*. New Haven: Yale University Press, 1949.

Keane, Patrick J. "Yeats and Nietzsche: The Antithetical Vision." Ph.D. diss. New York University, 1971.

Kaufmann, Walter. *Nietzsche: Philosopher, Psychologist, Antichrist*. New York: Meridian Books, 1956.

Knight, G. Wilson. *Christ and Nietzsche: An Essay in Poetic Wisdom*. London and New York: Staples Press, 1948.

Lavrin, Janko. *Nietzsche and Modern Consciousness: A Psycho-Critical Study*. London: W. Collins Sons & Co., 1922.

McHugh, Roger, ed. *Ah, Sweet Dancer: W. B. Yeats—Margot Ruddock*. London and Basingstoke: Macmillan and Co., 1970.

Melchiori, Giorgio. *The Whole Mystery of Art: Pattern into Poetry in the Work of W. B. Yeats*. London: Routledge and Kegan Paul, 1960.

Nathan, Leonard. *The Tragic Drama of William Butler Yeats: Figures in a Dance*. New York and London: Columbia University Press, 1965.

O'Brien, Conor Cruise. *The Suspecting Glance*. London: Faber and Faber, 1972.

Orage, A. R. *Friedrich Nietzsche: The Dionysian Spirit of the Age*. London: T. N. Foulis, 1906.

Reichart, Herbert W., and Karl Schlecta, eds. *International Nietzsche Bibliography*. Chapel Hill: University of North Carolina Press, 1968.

Reynolds, Lorna. "Collective Intellect: Yeats, Synge, and Nietzsche." *Essays and Studies* 26 (1973): 83–98.

Salvatori, Corinna. *Yeats and Castiglione: Poet and Courtier*. Dublin: Allen Figgis, 1965.

Stern, J. P. *Friedrich Nietzsche*. Harmondsworth: Penguin, 1978.

Symons, Arthur. Review of *The Dawn of Day*, by Friedrich Nietzsche. *The Athenaeum*, March 7, 1903, pp. 297–300.

Thatcher, David S. "A Misdated Yeats Letter on Nietzsche." *Notes and Queries* 15 (1968): 286–87.

———. *Nietzsche in England, 1890–1914: The Growth of a Reputation*. Toronto: University of Toronto Press, 1970.

Ure, Peter. *Yeats the Playwright: A Commentary on Character and Design in the Major Plays*. London: Routledge and Kegan Paul, 1963.

Wade, Allan. *A Bibliography of the Writings of W. B. Yeats*. London: Rupert Hart-Davis, 1951.

Wilson, F. A. C. *Yeats's Iconography*. New York: The Macmillan Company, 1960.

Zwerdling, Alex. *Yeats and the Heroic Ideal*. New York: New York University Press, 1965.

Other Sources

Abel, Lionel. *Metatheatre: A New Dramatic Form*. New York: Hill and Wang, 1963.

Balzac, Honoré de. *"The Magic Skin," "The Quest of the Absolute," and Other Stories*. Ed. George Saintsbury. Philadelphia: Avil Publishing Co., 1901.

———. *"About Catherine de Medici," "Seraphita," and Other Stories*. Ed. George Saintsbury. Philadelphia: Avil Publishing Co., 1901.

Bentley, Eric. *The Life of the Drama*. London: Methuen & Co., 1965.

Bentley, Eric, ed. *The Theory of the Modern Stage: An Introduction to Modern Theatre and Drama*. Harmondsworth: Penguin, 1968.

Bloom, Harold. *The Anxiety of Influence: A Theory of Poetry.* New York: Oxford University Press, 1973.

Butler, E. M. *The Tyranny of Greece over Germany: A Study of the Influence Exercised by Greek Art and Poetry over the Great German Writers of the Eighteenth, Nineteenth, and Twentieth Centuries.* Boston: Beacon Press, 1958.

Eagleton, Terry. *Criticism and Ideology: A Study in Marxist Literary Theory.* London: Verso Edition, 1978.

Eliade, Mircea. *Myths, Dreams, and Mysteries: The Encounter Between Contemporary Faiths and Archaic Reality.* Trans. Philip Mairet. London: Fontana, 1968.

Eliot, T. S. "Reflections on Contemporary Poetry." *The Egoist* 6, no. 3 (July 1919): 39–40.

Ellmann, Richard. *James Joyce.* New York: Oxford University Press, 1959.

Gregory, Lady Isabella Augusta. *Gods and Fighting Men: The Story of the Tuatha de Danaan and of the Fianna of Ireland.* Arranged and put into English by Lady Gregory, with a Preface by W. B. Yeats. Gerrards Cross: Colin Smythe, 1970.

Hamburger, Michael. *From Prophecy to Exorcism: The Premises of Modern German Literature.* London: Longmans, 1965.

Harrison, Jane Ellen. *Prolegomena to the Study of Greek Religion.* 2d ed. Cambridge: Cambridge University Press, 1908.

Hegel, G. F. W. *The Logic of Hegel.* Translated from *The Encycolpedia of the Philosophical Sciences* by William Wallace. Oxford: The Clarendon Press, 1874.

———. *The Phenomenology of the Mind.* Trans. J. B. Baille. London: Swan Sonnenschein & Co., and New York: The Macmillan Company, 1910.

Heller, Erich. *The Artist's Journey into the Interior and Other Essays.* London: Secher & Warburg, 1966.

Hone, Joseph. *The Life of George Moore.* London: Victor Gollancz, 1936.

Huysmans, J.-K. *Against Nature.* A new translation of *À Rebours* by Robert Baldick. Harmondsworth: Penguin, 1959.

Joyce, James. *A Portrait of the Artist as a Young Man.* London: Jonathan Cape, 1956.

Joyce, Stanislaus. *My Brother's Keeper.* London: Faber and Faber, 1958.

The Library of John Quinn. New York: Anderson Galleries, 1923–24.

Mandelbaum, Maurice. *History, Man, and Reason: A Study in Nineteenth-Century Thought.* Baltimore and London: Johns Hopkins University Press, 1971.

Mikhail, E. H., ed. *Lady Gregory: Interviews and Recollections.* London and Basingstoke: The Macmillan Press, 1977.

Moore, George. *Hail and Farewell.* 3 vols. London: William Heinnemann, 1947.

Murray, Gilbert. *The Classical Tradition in Poetry.* London: Oxford University Press, 1927.

Nordau, Max. *Degeneration*. Translated from the second edition of the German work by George L. Mosse. New York: Howard Fertig, 1958.

Oates, Joyce Carol. *The Edge of Impossibility: Tragic Forms in Literature*. New York: Vanguard Press, 1972.

Pater, Walter. *The Renaissance: Studies in Art and Poetry*. London: Macmillan and Co., 1912.

Peterson, Carroll V. *John Davidson*. New York: Twayne Publishers, 1972.

Reid, B. L. *The Man from New York: John Quinn and His Friends*. New York: Oxford University Press, 1968.

Schopenhauer, Arthur. *The World as Will and Idea*. Vol. 1. Trans. R. D. Haldene and J. Kemp. London: Kegan Paul, Trench, Trubner & Co., 1883.

Shattuck, Roger. *The Banquet Years: The Arts in France, 1885–1918*. London: Faber and Faber, 1955.

Shaw, Bernard. *Collected Plays with Their Prefaces*. Vol. 2. London: The Bodley Head, 1971.

Steiner, George. *The Death of Tragedy*. London: Faber and Faber, 1961.

———. *In Bluebeard's Castle: Some Notes toward the Redefinition of Culture*. London: Faber and Faber, 1971.

Stephan, Philip. *Paul Verlaine and the Decadence, 1882–90*. Manchester: Manchester University Press, 1974.

Symons, Arthur. *Studies in Seven Arts*. London: Archibald Constable and Company, 1907.

———. *Plays, Acting, and Music: A Book of Theory*. London: Jonathan Cape, 1928.

Vickery, John. *The Literary Impact of* The Golden Bough. Princeton: Princeton University Press, 1973.

Wilde, Oscar. De Profundis *and Other Writings*. Introduction by Hesketh Pearson. Harmondsworth: Penguin, 1954.

Woodring, Carl R., ed. *Prose of the Romantic Period*. Cambridge, Mass.: Riverside Press, 1961.

Index